Memorial of the Descendants of the Hon. John Alden

A Family Genealogy

By Ebenezer Alden

PANTIANOS CLASSICS

Published by Pantianos Classics

ISBN-13: 978-1-78987-568-3

First published in 1867

Contents

Introduction

Genealogy is family history; to some a chaos of isolated facts; *very dry;* to others, facts revealing principles, laws, methods of the divine government.

Genealogy has its lessons for such as will study them; uses for such as can appreciate and interpret them. The family precedes the state. Love of kindred underlies true patriotism.

Hon. John Alden was one of the principal persons, and the last male survivor of the band of Pilgrims, who came to Plymouth in the May Flower in 1620. With few exceptions, and these mostly of recent date, all persons in this country bearing the name of Alden are his descendants. Of each of these who is at the head of a family, it is the plan of this work to give, as far as the facts are at hand, the name, residence, occupation of males over twenty-one years of age, date of birth, and, if deceased, of death, parentage and social position.

Descendants of the common ancestor bearing other names are noticed in connection with the families from which they originated. Families are usually numbered consecutively. In a few instances, individuals are so numbered. Numbers following the name of a *head* of a family, refer back to his or her parents. Numbers following the name of a *child* refer forward to his or her own family. Some abbreviations are used, which will be readily understood by the reader; such as, b. for born; d. for died: s. son; dau. daughter &c.

Errors in a first edition of a work like this are unavoidable. Persons discovering mistakes, or omissions, particularly, in relation to their own families, will confer a favor, by correcting the one and supplying the other; and by making a memorandum of the same, and enclosing it by mail to the author of this Memorial at Randolph, Mass., by whom it will be carefully preserved, so that the next edition, when called for, may be more worthy of patronage than the present. Should sufficient materials be collected, they will be issued in the form of a supplement.

Correspondents and all others who have kindly contributed facts to this work, or have intimated their wish to obtain copies of it when printed, will please accept the thanks of the author; also custodians of public records, through whose courtesy he has had free access to their archives.

Two hundred and forty-six years have passed since the Pilgrims, driven from their homes in the old world, found a refuge in the new. They came not for conquest, nor for fame; but to secure for themselves and for their posterity civil and religious freedom. In the hour of peril they trusted in God, and He sustained them. "A little one has become a thousand, and small one a strong nation." They *"still live"* in their principles; may I not add, in their posterity? What we have received at so great cost, let us transmit to others as a sacred trust. It will be a power in the future, as it has been in the past. Doing this, we shall not have lived in vain. E. A.

Randolph, Mass., Dec. 22, 1866.

Memorial – First Generation

1. I. Hon. John Alden, ancestor of most persons bearing the name of Alden in this country, was one of the Plymouth Pilgrims, and the last male survivor of those who came in the May Flower, and signed the compact in her cabin in 1620.

He was not of the Leyden Church,, but, as Bradford in his "History of Plymouth Plantation" informs us, "was hired for a cooper at Southampton, where the ship victuled; and being a hopful yong man was much desired, but left to his own liking to go or stay when he came here; but he stayed and maryed here."

He was distinguished for practical wisdom, integrity and decision, and early acquired and retained during his long life a commanding influence over his associates. He was much employed in public business, was an assistant to the Governor for many years: and in every position he occupied fulfilled his duties promptly and to the satisfaction of his employers.

His ancestors in England have not been traced, so far as is known to the writer.

He was born in 1599, and died at Duxbury 12th September 1687, "in a good old age, an old man, and full of years; and was gathered to his people, — and his sons buried him."

He m. probably in 1621, Priscilla, dau. of Mr. William Molines, or Mullens, who, with his wife came also in the May Flower, and both died in the February succeeding their landing.

Tradition represents Priscilla to have been very beautiful in her youth; and John also was a comely person; and considering his other accomplishments, it is not surprising, that when he "was sent by Captain Standish, after the death of his wife, to solicit her hand in marriage, she preferred the messenger to the message,

> "As he warmed and glowed, in his simple and eloquent language,
> Quite forgetful of self, and full of the praise of his rival,
> Archly the maiden smiled, and, with eyes overrunning with laughter
> Said, in a tremulous voice, 'Why don't you speak for yourself, John?'"

Their residence after a few years was in Duxbury, on the north side of the village, on a farm which is still in possession of their descendants of the seventh generation, having never been alienated.

He made no will, having distributed the greater part of his estate among his children during his life time. Jonathan, his third son with whom he resided on the old homestead, administered on his estate, and made a final settlement with the heirs June 13, 1688,

The settlement is as follows; "We whose names are subscribed, personally interested in the estate of John Alden senior of Duxbury, Esquire, lately deceased, do hereby acknowledge ourselves to have received, each of us our full personal proportion thereof from Jonathan Alden, Administrator thereof, do by these presents for ourselves, our heirs and executors acquit, discharge fully the said Jonathan Alden, his heirs forever of and from all rights, dues, demands whatsover, relating to the aforesaid estate.

In witness wheref we have hereunto subscribed and sealed this 13 day of June Anno Domini 1688,

John Alden, (*Seal.*)
Joseph Alden, (*Seal.*)
Pavid Alden, (*Seal.*)
Priscilla Alden, (*Seal.*)
William Paybody, (*Seal.*)
Alexander Standish, (*Seal.*) in the right of Sarah, my wife, deceased,
John Bass, (*Seal.*) in the right of my wife Ruth, deceased,
Mauv Alden, (*Seal.*)
Thomas Dillano, (*Seal.*)

As only eight children are named in this instrument, it was supposed until recently that he had no more. Bradford, however, states in his history, that at the time of his writing, John Alden and his wife Priscilla were both living, and had eleven children; and that their eldest daughter was living, and had five children. In the document copied above, her name is writ, ten Priscilla,

CHILDREN

1. John b. abt. 1622 (2)
2. Joseph b. 1624 (3)
3. Elizabeth b, 1625 (4)
4. Jonathan (5)
5. Sarah (6)
6. Ruth (7)
7. Mary (8)
8. David (9)
9, 10, 11, *names unknown.*

Second Generation

2. II. Capt. John Alden of Boston, eldest son of John (1.) was b. in Plymouth in 1622, was admitted freeman in 1648; was a mariner, and about 1659 removed from Duxbury to Boston. He was an original member of the Old South Church in Boston at its organization May 12th and 16th, 1669. His residence was in Alden Lane, now Alden Street. He was a man of sound judgment, active business habits and unexceptionable moral character, and acquired considerable property.

During the witchcraft delusion in 1692, he was accused and taken to Salem for examination, where he acquitted himself admirably, yet was imprisoned in Boston for several weeks, when he escaped and went to Duxbury, but soon returned and gave himself up, and was under bonds until the delusion had passed away, and he with all others similarly accused was legally discharged.

He d. 14 March, 1702, a. 80. His will was dated 17th of Feb. 1701-2.

His estate was divided into five parts. 1. To John Alden, his eldest son. 2. William Alden. 3. Zachariah Alden. 4. dau. Elizabeth Walley. 5. Unto the chil-

dren of my son Nathaniel Alden deceased, equally; — lives with his dau. Walley, to whom he gives his house after his decease. His sons John and William
are named executors.

For eleven years after he was admitted freeman in 1648, we have no account of his residence or pursuits. Probably he was then as afterwards a
mariner.

Dec. 17, 1659 a dau. Mary was born to Mm by his wife Elizabeth _____.

"April 1, 1660 John Aldine was married to Elizabeth Everell widow, the
Relict of Abiell Everell deceased by Jno. Endicott, Gov." She was the dau. of
Wm. Phillips of Watertown and Saco.

"The Inventory of the goods of Abiell Everell deceased were appraised by
John Sunderland and John Sanford, being chosen thereunto by Mr. John
Alden and Elizabeth his wife, she being formerly the wife and later the widow of Abiell Everell, beforesaid. Taken 15, 12. 1660, amt. £119. Jno. Alden
deposed 22 Feb. 1660. Gen. Reg. vol. 10, p. 268.

CHILDREN

2. John 20 Nov. 1660, died young without issue.	8.* Zechariah, 8 Mar. 1667
3.* Elizabeth 9 May 1662, d. 14 July 1662.	9. William. 10 Sept. 1609, (12)
	10. Nathaniel, 1670. (13)
4. John 12 Mar. 1662-3. (10)	11. Zachariah. 18 Feb. 1673. (14)
5 * William, 10 March, 1663-4.	12. Nathan. 17 Oct. 1677.
6. Elizabeth, 9 April, 1665. (11)	13. Sarah, 27 Sept. 1681.
7.* William, 5 Mar. 1665-6.	14. Henry (15)

8. III. Joseph Alden, Bridgewater, Farmer, son of John, (1) b. 1624, d. 8 Feb.
1697, a. 73.

He was admitted freeman in 1650: had his father's proprietary share in
Bridgewater, where he settled in that part of the town, now West Bridge-
water. His will was dated 14 Dec. 1696, and proved 10 March 1697; widow
Mary and son John executors.

He m. Mary dau. of Moses Simmons Jun.

CHILDREN

1. Isaac. (16)	and, as Mitchell conjectures
2. Joseph, b. 1667. (17)	4. Elizabeth. (19)
3. John. (18)	5. Mary. (20)

If this conjecture is correct, it seems passing strange that neither they nor
their families were noticed in his will.

4. II. Elizabeth Alden, dau. of John (1.) was b. abt. 1625, and died at Little
Compton, R. I. 31 May, 1717, a. 93.

The following notice is copied from the Boston News Letter, 17 June 1717.
"Little Compton, 31 May, 1717. This morning died here Mrs. Elizabeth Paybody, in the 93d year of her age. She was a daughter of John Alden Esquire

and Priscilla his wife, daughter of Mr. William Mullens. This John Alden and Priscilla Mullens were married at Plymouth, where their dau. Elizabeth was born. She was exemplary, virtuous and pious, and her memory is blessed. She has left a numerous posterity, her grand dau. Bradford is a grandmother."

She m. "William Pavbody of Duxbury and afterwards of Littie Compton, "who was a man of great respectability, and d. lo Dec. 1707, a. 87.

CHILDREN

1. John. I Oct. 1645, d. 17 Nov. 1669. 2. Elizabeth. 24 April, 1647, m. 1666, John Rogers. 3. Mary, 7 Aug, 1648, m. 1669, Edward Southworth. 4. Mercy, 2 Jan. 1649-50. m. 1671, John Simmons. 5. Martha, 24 Feb. 1650-51. m. 1677, John Seabury. 6.* Priscilla, 16 Nov. 1652, d. 2 Mar. 1652-3. 7. Priscilla. 15 Jan. 1653-4. m. Rev. Ichabod Wiswell. 8. Sarah, 7 Aug, 1656, m. 1680, John Coe. 9. Ruth, 22 June. 1658, m. 1672, Benjamin Bartlett, Jr. 10, Rebecca, 16 Oct. 1660. m. William Southworth. 11. Hannah, 10 Oct. 1662, m. 1683, Samuel Bartlett. 12. William, went to Little Compton. 13. Lydia, 3 Oct. 1667.

5. II. Captain Jonathan Alden, Duxbury, son of John, (1.) inherited and occupied the home of his father, and was the administrator of his estate. He died Feb. 1697, and was buried underarms on the 17th day of that month, on which occasion an address was delivered at his grave by Rev. Ichabod Wiswell; a copy of which has been preserved, and copious extracts therefrom may be found in the Collection of American Epitaphs by Rev. Timothy Alden Jun. D. D. vol. 3, Art. 622.

He m. 10 Dec. 1672, Abigail, dau. of Benjamin Hallett Esquire, of Barnstable. She d. Aug. 17 1725, a. 81, and was buried in the Old Burying Ground.

CHILDREN

1. Andrew (21)	3. John (23)
2. Jonathan (22)	4. Benjamin (24)

6. II. Sarah Alden, dau. of John (1.) m. Alexander Standish, son of Capt. Miles Standish.

CHILDREN

1. Miles, who d. 15 Sept. 1739, leaving a family. 2, Ebenezer, who d. 1734, leaving six children. 3. Lorah, who m. Abraham Sampson. 4. Lydia, who m. Isaac Sampson. 5. Mary, who m. Caleb Sampson. 6. Sarah, who m. Benjamin Soule. 7. Elizabeth, who m. Samuel Delano.

7. II. Ruth Alden, dau. of John, (1.) d. 12 Oct. 1674. m.
8 Feb. 1057, John Bass, of Braintree, son of Dea. Samuel Bass, sen. He d. 12 Sept. 1716, a. 84.

CHILDREN

1, John, 20 Nov 1608: who m. Abigail Adams. 2. Samuel, 25 Mar. 1660. 3. Ruth, 28 Jan. 1602, 4. Joseph, 10 Dec. 1665: who m. Mary Belcher, 1688. 5. Hannah 22 June 1667: m. Joseph Adams. 6. Mary, 12 Feb. 1669 m. Christopher Webb. 7. Sarah, 29 Mar. 1672: m. 7 Jan. 1692 Ephraim Thayer, d. 19 Aug, 1751, a. 79, 5 m.

A very full account of her descendants may be found in Thayer's Family Memorial, Part 2.

8. II. Mary Alden, dau. of John Alden (1.) was living in 1688, and d. before 1690, when her husband m. a 2 wife. She m. before 1667 Thomas Delano of Duxbury.

They had one child: — 1. Thomas.

9. II. David Alden, of Duxbury, son of John Alden (1.) was a prominent member of the church; a man of great respectability, and much employed in public business.

He died in 1719: apart of his estate in Middleborough, having been appraised 20 May, 1719. He m. Mercy, dau, of Constant Southworth.

CHILDREN

1. Ruth, b. 1674, (25)	3. Benjamin, (27)
2. Alice, abt. 1682, (26)	4. Samuel. 1689. (28)

Note. — *Rebecca* is mentioned in the Col. Rec. as of marriageable age in 1661, Anna Alden m. Josiah Snell Dec. 2 1699. Mitchell says she was dau. of Zachariah. Who was he? Priscilla m. Samuel Cheesbrook in 1699.

Third Generation

10. III. Capt. John Alden, Boston, Mariner, s. of John, (2) was b. 12 Mar. 1663: d. Boston 1 Feb. 1729-30 a. 67. *Grave Stone, Chapel Burying Ground.* He left a will, of which his widow Susanna and son Nathaniel were executors. He m. in 1684 Elizabeth, dau. of William Phelps, senior – *Rec. of Old Norfolk.* She d. 1 Feb, 1719, a, 50. *Grave Stone.*

CHILDREN

1. Elizabeth, 7 Nov. 1687,	7, Ann, 7 July 1699 (34)
2. Hannah, 20 Nov. 1688, (30)	8. Nathaniel, b. 6 July, 1700, (35)
2. John. 20 Sept. 1690, (31)	9.* Thomas, 13 Aug. 1701, d. same day.
4. Mary, 15 Dec. 1691, (32)	10. Catherine, 17 Sept. 1704.
5.* Catherine. 19 Aug. 1697, d, 31 Oct. 1702,	11. Thomas 1 Mar. 1707, (36)
6. Gillam, 7 July 1699 (33)	12.* William, 9 May. 1710, d. 27 Dec. 1714.

He m. 2 Susanna Winslow, 22 Nov. 1122. - *Bost. Rec.*

11. III. Elizabeth Alden", dau, as is supposed of John (2.) b. 9 Apr, 1665, m. John Seabury of Duxbury, 9 Doc, 1697.

12. III. Capt. William Alden, Boston, mariner, s. of John (2.) b, 10 Sept. 1669, d. 9 Feb. 1729, a. 60. *Grave Stone*. His will was presented for probate, 26 June, 1732, by his wid. Mary Alden. Inventory £1139.16.

He m. 21 May, 1691, Mary Drury, b. 10 July 1672.

CHILDREN

1.* Mary, 10 Feb. 1693, d. Oct. 2, 1702.	5. Mary, 12 June 1706.
2. Elizabeth, 10 Mar. 1695, (37)	6. Drury, 12 May 1708.
3. William, 23 July, 1697.	7. John, 22 Jan. 1711.
4. Lydia, 22 Dec, 1701, (38)	

13. III. Nathaniel Alden, Boston, mariner, son of John (2.) h. 1670, d, prob. 1701, but before 17 Feb, 1702,

A letter of Administration on his estate, which was rendered insolvent, was granted to James Gooch Esq., principal creditor, 4 July, 1702, Benjamin Gallup was appointed guardian to his junior children, Mary, Nathaniel, Hepzibah and Phillips.

He m. 1 Oct, 1691, Hepzibah Mountjoy, who, after his death, m. 8 June, 1703, John Mortimer.

CHILDREN

1. Mary, 20 Aug, 1692.	4. Hepzibah, (40)
2. Nathaniel. 6 Aug. 1694, (39)	5. Phillips, 31 Dec, 1698.
3.* Elizabeth, 1696, d.bef. her father.	

14. III. Zachariah Alden, Boston, mariner, s. of John (2.) b, 1673, gr. Harvard College, 1692; d, 1709, a 36. Administration on his estate was granted 18 Aug. 1709. to his widow Mary Alden. Inventory £22.16.

He m. 1700, Mary Viall, and they had a son,

1. Zachariah, 11 Oct. 1701, (41)

A Mary Alden d. in Boston 11 Feb. 1727, a. 56.

15. III, Henry Alden, Dedham. Dr. Wight informs me that Henry Alden went to Dedham after 1700. His name first appears 30 Aug. 1704. Eight acres of land were granted to him between the years 1700 and 1706. The ride was, married men had 12 a: unm. men 8 acres. His name not on the list of marriages."

Henry Alden m. Deborah — , and they had one child,

William b. 11 Aug. 1700. (42)

Henry Alden d. Feb. 18, 1730.

Thayer says that he was probably son of John Alden Sen. of Boston. It may be so, but neither is his baptism found in Boston, nor is he or his son mentioned in the Will.

16. III. Isaac Alden, Bridgewater, farmer, son of Joseph (3.) m. 2 Dec 1685, Mehitabel, dau. of Samuel Allen, b. 1660.

CHILDREN

1. Mehitabel, 7 Mar. 1687, (43)
2. Sarah, 22 Sept. 1688, (44)
3. Mary, 20 July, 1691, (45)
4. Isaac, 10 Mar. 1692, (46)
5. Ebenezer, 15 June, 1693, (47)

6. John, 1694, (48)
7. Mercy, 30 Oct. 1606, (49)
8. Abigail, 128. July 1699.
9. Jemima, 7 Jan. 1702, (50)

17. III. Deacon Joseph Alden, Bridgewater, farmer: son of Joseph (2,) was b. 1667; lived in what is now South B.; was a deacon in the church there and much esteemed.

His will is dated, 12 Nov. 1743, having not his signature, but his mark, shewing that at that time he was from infirmity unable to write. He died 22 Dec. 1747, a. 80.

He m. 1690, Hannah, dau. of Daniel Dunham of Plymouth: She d. 13 Jan. 1748, a. 78.

CHILDREN

1. Daniel. 29 Jan. 1691, (51)
2.* Joseph, 26 Aug. 1693, d. 9 Dec. 1695.
3. Eleazer, 27 Sept. 1694, (52)
4. Hannah, Feb. 1696, (53)
5. Mary, 10 Apr. 1699, (54)

6.* Joseph, 5 Sept. 1700: d. 5 Oct. 1700.
7.* Jonathan, 3 Dec, 1703: d. 10 Nov. 1704.
8. Samuel, 20 Aug. 1705, (55)
9. Mehetabel, 18 Oct. 1707, (56)
10. Seth, 6 July, 1710, (57)

18. III. John Alden, Bridgewater and Middleborough, farmer, son of Joseph (3.) had his father's homestead in West Bridgewater, which, 20 June 1700, he conveyed to Isaac Johnson, and removed to Middleboro', where he d. 29 Sept., 1730 a. 56.

He m. Hannah, dau. of Capt. Ebenezer White of Weymouth, who was b. 12 May, 1681, and d. 5 Oct. 1732.

CHILDREN

1. David, 18 May, 1702, (58)
2. Priscilla, 2 Mar, 1704, (59)
3. Thankful, 3 May, 1709, (60)
4. Hannah, 24 Mar. 1708, (61)
5. Lydia, 18 Dec. 1710, (62)
6. Mary, 18 Nov. 1712, (63)
7. Abigail, 8 Sept. 1714, (64)

8. Joseph, 11 Sept. 1716, (65)
9. John, 8 Oct. 1718, (66)
10. Ebenezer, 8 Oct. 1720, (67)
11. * Samuel d. young.
12. *Nathan, 12 June, 1723 d, young.
13. Noah, 31 May, 1725. (68)

19. III. Elizabeth Alden, dau. Mitchell thinks, of Joseph Alderi (Fam. 3.) m. 1691, Benjamin Snow, and d. 1705.

CHILDREN

1. Rebeckah. 1694, m. a Campbell. 2. Benjamin, 1696. 3. Solomon, 1698. i. Ebenezer, 1702. 6. Elizabeth, 1705, m. Joseph Carver.

20. III. Mary Alden, of Bridgewater, dau. of Joseph Alden (3.) as Mitchell says, m. 1700, Samuel Allen of B.

CHILDREN

1. Joseph, 1701. 2. Benjamin, 1702. 3. Mary, 1704, m. H. Kingman. 4. Rebeckah, 1706, m. John Kingman., 5. Matthew, 1708. 6. Seth, 1710. 7. Abigail, m. Shubael Welsh, 1730.

21. Andrew Alden, Lebanon, Ct., s. Jonathan (5.) m. at Duxbury, 4 Feb. 1714, Lydia Stamford.

CHILDREN

1. Jabin, 19 Nov. 1714.	5. Walter, (72)
2. John, 23 July, 1716, (69)	6. Lydia, (73)
3. Prince, 28 Oct. 1718, (70)	7. William, (74)
4. Andrew, 20 June, 1721, (71)	

22. III. Jonathan Alden of Duxbury, Marshfield, and Lebanon, Ct., son of Jonathan (5.) m. 17 Jan. 1717-18, Elizabeth Arnold, widow of Anthony Waterman of Marshfield, and lived to a great age.

CHILDREN

1. Josiah.	3. Seth, 1721, (75)
2. Anthony, 1720.	4. Austin, 1729, (76)

23. III. Col. John Alden, of Duxbury, s. Jonathan (5.) was b. 1680; inherited the old homestead, and d. 24 July, 1739, a. 59.

He was affable in his manners, highly respected, and much employed in public business. Like his father he had a taste for military pursuits; was early an officer in the militia, and Colonel in 1732.

Involuntary servitude in those days had not been abolished in Massachusetts, and he owned one slave by the name of Hampshire, probably "a military necessity."

He m. 1709, Hannah, dau. of Capt. John Briggs.

CHILDREN

1. *John, 7 Oct, 1710, d. 15 Oct. 1712.	5. *Deborah, 16 May, 1721, d. 2 Oct.
2. Samuel, 7 Nov. 1712, (77)	1730.
3. Judah, 10 Aug. 1714, (78)	6. Briggs, 8 June, 1723, (80)
4. Anna, 14 June, 1716, (79)	7. Abigail, 27 Feb. 1727, (81)

24. m. Dea. Benjamin Alden, of Duxbury, son of Jonathan (5.) carpenter, was drowned near the Gurnet, 14 April, 1741.

He had a wife Hannah who d. 8 Jan. 1763. If there is no mistake in the record, it is somewhat singular that bearing the same name she should have died on the same day as Hannah wife of Benjamin, Fam. 25.

25. III. Ruth Alden, dau. of David Alden, (9.) b. 1674, m. 29 Nov. 1694, Samuel Sprague of Duxbury and afterwards of Rochester, Mass.

"He was son of John Sprague and Ruth (Bassett) Sprague of Duxbury, and d. 25 July, 1740, in the 75th year of his age. She d. 2 July, 1758 in her 84th year, as on grave stone in Rochester, Mass., or aged 84 as in Town Records of Rochester." For these facts I am indebted to Mr. F, B. Dexter.

CHILDREN

1. Noah, 18 Jan. 1606-7. 2. Elizabeth, 4 July, 1699. 3. Nathaniel, 10 Jan. 1702-3, d. 1739. 4.* Samuel, 23 June, 1704. d. Jamaica, 1727. 5 * Mary 20 Dec. 1706, d. 19 Apr. 1708. 6. Priscilla, 18 Mar. 1709, d. 23 Oct. 1779 m. B. Hammond and afterwards Rev. Thomas West of Rochester. 7. Ruth, 30 Aug. 1714, d. unm. 9 Apr. 1733.

26. III. Alice Alden, dau. of David (9.) m. 5 Dec. 1706, Judah Paddock of Yarmouth. She d. a. 93. Her name was sometimes written Alithea.

CHILDREN

1. Reuben, 1707. 2. Judah, 1711. 3. Samuel, 1711. 4. Mary, 1714. 5. Grace, 1716. 6. Rebecca, 1718, who m. Thomas Spooner 10 June, 1742. 7. Nathaniel, 1724.

27. III. Benjamin Alden of Duxbury, son of David, (9.) m. Hannah, who d. 8 Jan. 1763, a. 74.

CHILDREN

1. Mary, 1 Jan. 1710 (82)	5. Ichabod, 4 Oct. 1719.
2. Sarah, 5 Apr. 1712.	6. Bezaleel, 15 May, 1722. (84)
3. Elizabeth, 12 Sept. 1714; and d. of	7. Wrestling, 11 Oct. 1724, (85)
Apoplexy, 9 July, 1771.	8. Abiather, 19 July, 1731, (86)
4. David, 14 Feb. 1717. (83)	

28. III. Capt. Samuel Alden, of Duxbury, son of David (9.) b. 1689, d. 24 Feb. 1781, a. 92 years, 2 mo. 3 d. was a farmer, much respected for the soundness of his judgment and consistent christian character.

He. m. 26 Feb. 1728, Sarah Sprague, who d. 28 Mar. 1773. a. 70.

CHILDREN

1. Rebeckah, 4 Jan. 1730, (87)	5. Samuel, 13 Aug. 1737, (91)
2. Sarah, 2 Dec, 1731, (88)	6. Ichabod, 11 Aug. 1739, (92)
3. John, 30 March, 1734, (89)	7. Abigail, (93)
4. Alice, 5 Sept. 1735, (90)	

29. III. Anna Alden of Duxbury, dau. of Zachariah Alden. Mitchell says, but on what authority I know not, was m. 21 Dec. 1699, to Josiah Snell. She d. 1705. He d. 1753.

1. Josiah, 1701. 2. Abigail, 1702, m. 1734, Israel Sylvester. 3. Zachariah, 1704.

Note. — "Priscilla Alden called gr-dau. of May Flower John, but who was her father I see not, m. Samuel Cheesborough 4 Jan. 1699 and had children."

Savage.

Fourth Generation

30. IV. Hannah Alden dau. of Capt. John Alden (10.) b. 20 Nov. 1688, m. John Jones of Hopkinton: prob. had ch.

31. IV. John Alden, Boston mariner, son of John (10.) was b. 20 Sept. 1690; was a shipmaster, and d. prob. 1727: m. 1 May 1718, Anna Braine.

CHILDREN

1. Anna, 29 June, 1722, Boston Rec. 2. Benjamin, 18 Sept. 1724. Boston Rec.

His widow Anna was appointed administrator of his estate, 12 June, 1727: returned an Inventory £123.12, 3 July, 1727, and an account of commissioners with her adm. account, 30 Nov. 1727. One item is, funeral charges of the deceased in Jamaica: making it certain that Thayer's conjecture that he settled in Needham is incorrect. See (94).

32. IV. Mary Alden of Boston dau. John Alden (10.) was b. 15 Dec. 1691: m Joseph Brightman of Boston.

33. IV. Gilam Alden, Boston, s. John (10.) was b. 7 July, 1699, d. 25 Dec. 1726, in the 28th year of his age. *Grave Stone.*

34. IV. Anna Alden, of Boston dau. John (10.) was b. 16 July, 1699, m. Dr. Henry Burchsted of Lynn.

35. IV. Nathaniel Alden of Boston, son of John. (10) Uncertain whether he had a family.

36. IV. Thomas Alden, Boston, s. John, (10) was b. 1707. m. Jane ____.

CHILDREN

1. Thomas, 26 June, 1725.   3. John, 30 Oct. 1729.
2. William, 26 Oct. 1727.

This family is put down from Boston Records, and the father is supposed to have been the 11th child of John 3, fam. 10.

37. IV. Elizabeth Alden, of Boston, dau. of William Alden (12) b. 10 Mar. 1695, m. 26 July, 1720, Thomas Batterly, of Boston.

38. IV. Lydia Alden, of Boston, dau. William (12) b. 22 Dec. 1701, m. Peter Britton 12 Nov. 1722.

39. IV. Nathaniel Alden, of Boston, s. of Nathaniel, (13) was b, 6 Aug. 1694: m. Mary ____.

1. Elizabeth, 1730, (95)
2. Nathaniel, 1731.

3. Hannah, 1735, perhaps others.

40. IV. Hepzibah Alden of Boston, dau. of Nathaniel Alden (13) m. Nathaniel Hayward 28 April, 1718.

41. IV. Zachariah Alden, of Boston, son of Zachariah Alden, (14) was b. 11 Oct. 1701, m. Jemima ____.

CHILDREN

1. Mary, Barton, 8 March 1725. m. 2 Lydia Crane 1728 had ch. in Milton.

2. Lydia, 3 June, 1730.
3. *Zachariah, 1731; d. 1733.

42. IV. William Alden, Needham, (?) s. Henry Alden, (15) b. 14 Aug. 1709, m. Ruth ____, who d. 17 Dec. 1766: had 1 ch. Mary— who d. 20 May 1740.

Is this William of Needham, who made his will 3 Feb. 1779, calls himself old, whose wife Mary was appointed sole executor, approved 26 May, 1780? He names son William, a minor, also a dau. Sarah, wife of Thomas Newhall, also a dau. Mary Alden, a minor.

43. IV. Mehetabel Alden, of Bridgewater, dau. of Isaac, (16) b. 7 Mar. 1687, and d. between 1720 and 1723, m. Benjamin Richards 1711.

CHILDREN

1. Mehitable, 1712, who m. David Packard, 1737. 2. Joseph, 1714, went to Stoughton, whose son Joseph was a Colonel in the Rev. War. 3. Daniel, 1716, m. 1740, David Packard. 4. James, 1718, m. Susan Pratt. 5. Sarah, 1720, m. Wm. Packard.

44. IV. Sarah Alden, Bridgewater, dau. Isaac Alden, (16) was b. 1688, m. 1712 Seth Brett of Bridgewater.

CHILDREN

1. Samuel, 1714. 2. Silas, 1716. 3. Sarah, 1713. 4. Simeon, 1718. 5. Seth, 1722, who was b. after his father's death, became a minister and was ordained in 1747 as pastor of a congregational church in Freetown, organized the same year. He was dismissed in 1775 and the church became extinct. After he husband's death, she m. Dea. Recompense Cary in 1727, and had a dau. Abigail, b. 1729.

45. Mary Alden, of Bridgewater, dau. Isaac, (16) b. 1691, d. 1782, a. 82, m. John Webb, of Braintree.

46. IV. Isaac Alden, of E. Bridgewater, s. Isaac, (16) was b. 10 Mar. 1692, d. unm: left a large real estate. There is extant a copy of the Bay Psalm Book long used in the churches of Bridgewater in conducting public worship, in which his name is written.

47. IV. Capt. Ebenezer Alden, East Bridgewater, farmer, s. Isaac, (16) was b. 1693, d. 1776, a. 83, was the last surviving member of the Founders of the First Church in E. Bridgewater, which was gathered in 1724. He was a surveyor, and much employed in public business. He m. 1707, Anna dau. of Joseph Keith and gr. dau. of Rev. James Keith the first minister in Bridgewater, who was ord. in 1664 and d. 23 July 1719 a. 76.

His "Bridgewater Monitor preached on 14 d. VI m. 1717 to a new assembly of Christians at their entering into the New Edifice for the worship of God among them" is worthy of being reprinted and circulated anew, as a valuable tract on Temperance and good morals.

CHILDREN

1. Anna, 19 Feb. 1718, (96)
2. Susanna, 29 Apr. 1719, (97)
3. Abigail, 27 Dec. 1721, (98)
4. Nathan, 10 Aug. 1727. (99)
5. Ezra, 9 March, 1732, (100)

The three dau. were all married 22 Nov. 1738.

48. IV. John Alden of Bridgewater, s. Isaac (16) b. 1694, d. 1762, a. 67, m. 1727, Hannah Kingman, dau. of Henry Kingman. She d. 1744, a. 39.

CHILDREN

1. John, 1729.
2. James, 1729.
3. Isaac, 1731. (101)
4. Jonathan, 1733, (102)
5. Hannah, 1736.
6. *Adam, 1738.
7. * A son, d. soon.
8. Abigail, 1712, d. young.
9. Keziah, 1743.

He m. 2 Rebecca Nightingale in 1745, and had
10. Rebecca, 1745.
11. John, 1747, (103)
12. *Esther, 1749.
13. James, 1751, (104)
14. Adam, 1754.
15. Joseph, 1755.
16. Benjamin, 1757, (105)

49. IV. Mercy Alden of Bridgewater, dau. of Isaac Alden, (16) was b. 1696, m. 1725 Zaccheus Packard of Bridgewater, who d. 1775.

CHILDREN

1. Eleazer, 1727, m. Mary Richards. 2. Seth, 1733, m. 1761, Mary Perkins. 3. Simeon, 1736. 4. Mercy, m. Ezra Warren, 1757.

50. IV. Jemima Alden, Bridgewater, dau. Isaac Alden, (16) m. Dea. Thomas Whitman, East Bridgewater.

CHILDREN

1. Simon, 1728. 2. Peter, 1730. 3. Benjamin. 1732. 4. Jemina, 1734, m. 1750, David Keith, 5. Nathan, 1736. 6. Amos, 1738. 7. William, 1740. 8. Isaac, 1745. Descendants from this family very numerous.

51. IV. Daniel Alden, Esquire, of Bridgewater and Stafford Ct., farmer, s. Joseph, (17) was b. in Bridgewater in 1691, d. in Stafford, 3 May, 1767, was a magistrate: m. 1717, Abigail Shaw, dau. of Joseph Shaw. She d. 12 July, 1755, a. 61. She was a sister of Rev. John Shaw, first pastor of the Cong. Church in S. Bridgewater, b. 1729, who was ord. 1731, and gr. fa. of Hon. Lemuel Shaw, C. J. Sup. Crt. of Mass.

CHILDREN

1. Joseph. 20 Nov. 1718. (106)
2. Daniel, 5 Sept. 1720. (107)
3. Abigail, 3 Dec. 1722. (108)
4. Zephaniah, 13 Sept. 1724. (109)
5. *Hannah, 23 May, 17.26; d. 2 July, 1726.
6. Hannah, 17 Dec. 1727. (110)
7. *Mehetabel, 23 May, 1729, d. 13 July 1729.
8. Barnabas, 10 Sept. 1732. (Ill)
9. Ebenezer. 11 Aug. 1734; d. July July, 1755.
10. *Mary, 12 May, 1737; d. 6 Mar. 1738.
11. Mary.

Note. — March 2, 1765, d. at Stafford, Ct. Rebeccah, wife of Daniel Alden Esq., aged 66, probably second wife of Daniel above named.

Epitaph on the tomb stone of Ebenezer Alden (51-9) written by Rev. John Shaw of Bridgewater: —

"Look here, gay youth, behold in me,
The place where you must shortly be,
Perhaps in youth must fall as I,
In early youth to Jesus fly."

52. IV. Eleazer Alden, Bridgewater, s. Joseph, (17) b., 1694; d. 30 Jan. 1773, a. 79, m. 1720, Martha Shaw, dau. of Joseph Shaw. She d. 1769 a. 69.

CHILDREN

1. Jonathan, 1721, (112)
2. Eleazer, 1723. (113)
3. *Absalom, 1725, d. 1727.
4. David, 1727. (114)
5. Joshua, 1729. (115)
6. *Caleb, 1731, d. 1733.
7. Ezra, 1734. (116)
8. Timothy, 1736. (117)

53. IV. Hannah Alden of Bridgewater, dau. of Joseph Alden, (17) was b. 1696, d. 1777, a. 81; m. 1722, Mark Lothrop of Easton.

CHILDREN

1. John. 2. Seth, who m. 1758, Thomas Conant. 3. Jonathan, who 1747, m. Susanna Johnson. 4. Joseph.

54. IV. Mary Alden, Bridgewater, dau. of Joseph Alden, (17) was b. 1699; d. 14 Feb. 1782, m. 1719, Timothy Edson of Bridgewater, who afterwards removed to Stafford, Ct.

CHILDREN

1. Hannah, 1720. 2. Timothy, 1722. 3. Anna. 4. Abijah, 1725, who m. Susanna Snow, dau. of James Snow. 5. Jonathan, 1728, who was in Ashfield in 1776. 6. Mary, 1730, who m. 1758, James Snow Jr.

55. IV. Samuel Alden, Titicut, s. Joseph, (17) was b. 1705; d. 1785, a. 80, m. 1728, Abiah, dau. of Capt. Joseph Edson.

CHILDREN

1. Abiah, 1729. (118)
2. Mehetabel, 1732. (119)
3. Sarah, 1734. (120)
4. Samuel, 1736. (121)
5. Josiah, 1738. (122)
6. Simeon, 1740. (123)

7. *Silas, d. a. '21.
8. Mary.
9. *Hosea, killed by the kick of a horse. He m. 1752, 2 wife, dau. of Josiah Washburn.

56. IV. Mehetabel Alden, dau. Joseph, (17) was b. 1707; d. 11 Apr. 1737, a. 37. Mid. Rec. 1730.

57. IV. Capt. Seth Alden, Bridgewater, s. Joseph, (17) was b. 1720, d. 6 Sept. 1784, a. 75; m. 1741, Mehetabel, dau. of Eleazer Carver. She d. 14 Feb. 1757.

CHILDREN

1. Oliver, 1740. (124)
2. Seth, 1741. (125)

3. *Caleb, 1744.
4. Joseph, 1747. (126)

58. IV. David Alden of Middleborough, s. John, (18) was b. 18 May 1702, d. 24 Aug. 1763, a. 61; m. Judah Paddleford, who d. 1802, a. 94.

CHILDREN

1. Solomon, 21 Nov. 1728. (127)
2. David, 14 Jan. 1730. (128)
3. Rufus. 19 Nov. 1731. (129)
4. Huldah, 8 Oct. 1733. (130)

5. Job. 24 Sept. 1737. (131)
6. Silas, 10 Oct. 1739. (132)
7. Abigail, 19 May. 1744. (133)
8. Peter, 17 Feb. 1747. (134)

59. IV. Priscilla Alden, dau. of John, (18) was b. 1764, m. Abraham Borden. Mid. Rcc.

60. IV. Thankful Alden, dau. of John Alden, (18) who was b. 1709, d. 29 Oct. 1732, a. 26; m. 14 Dec. 1727, Francis Eaton of Kingston.

61. IV. Hannah Alden, dau. of John, (18) b. 1708, m. Thomas Wood.

62. IV. Lydia Alden, dau. John, (18) was b. 1710, adm. to Mid. chh. 1735, m. Samuel Eddy of Mid. who d. 1746, a. 36. She m. 2. John Fuller, who d. at Halifax, Mass, 1766, a. 74.

CHILDREN

1. Samuel. 2. Nathan, who had numerous descendants.

63. IV. Mary Alden, dau. John, (18) was b. 1712: d. 1 Aug. 1787, a. 75, m. 1735 Noah Thomas.

64. IV. Abigail Alden, dau. John, (18) b. 1714: adm. to Mid., chh. 1739: d. Jan. 1744, a. 30, m. 1735, Nathan Thomas, who was b. 1707.

65. IV. Joseph Alden of Middleborough, farmer, s. of John, (18) b. 1716, m. 1 Apr. 1742, Hannah Hall.

CHILDREN

1. Ebenezer. (135)	7. Fear. (141)
2. Amariah. (136)	8. Eunice. (142)
3. Moses. (137)	9. Lois. (143)
4. Phebe. (138)	10. Abner. (144)
5. Hannah. (130)	11. Eliab. (145)
6. Joseph. (140)	

m. 2 "Wid. Deborah "Williamson: no issue.

66. IV. John Alden, Middleborough, farmer, s. of John, (18) was b. 8 Oct. 1718; d. 27 March, 1821, a. 102 years 5 mos. 19 days. He was adm. to Mid. chh. 19 Aug. 1742, was a member nearly seventy-eight years. A good portrait of him is in Pilgrim Hall, Plymouth. On the day he completed his hundredth year a century sermon was preached at his house by Rev. Isaac Tompkins, pastor of a church in Haverhill, which was printed Text, 2 Tim. 4, 6-8. In a note to the sermon it is said that "He married young: that his. first wife, by whom he had five, children, died at the age of 27. By his second and last wife, he had fourteen children. She has been dead eleven years. The whole number of his descendants is 219: viz, 19 children, 62 gr. children: 134 gr. gr. children; and 4 of the fifth generation. Of these, deceased 43, living 173." The discourse was delivered 10 Sept. 1818. He m. Lydia Lazell, dau. of Simon Lazell.

CHILDREN

1. John, 7 Feb. 1740. (146)	4. Susanna, 29 Aug. 1715. (149)
2. Mary, 22 Not. 1741. (147)	5. Lydia, 11 Dec. 1747, (150)
3. Nathan, 22 Aug. 1743. (148)	

He m. 12 July, 1750, Rebecca, dau. of Zechariah Weston, who d. 1810.

CHILDREN

6. *Priscilla, 15 May, 1751; d. 22 Oct. 1751.	12. Lucy. 12 Aug, 1762. (162)
7. *Ruth, 15 Oct. 1752; d. 25 Aug. 1753.	13. Joel, 27 June 1764. (153)
	14. *Son.
8. Elijah, 13 June, 1754. (158)	15. * Daughter.
9. Rebecca, 18 Apr. 1756.	16. Ruth, 13 Mar. 1769. (154)
10. Hannah, 18 Apr. 1758,	17. Seth. 7 Feb. 1770. (155)
11. Sarah, 9 Feb. 1760.	18. Betsey, 13 Apr. 1773. (156)
	19. Elihu, 20 Aug. 1775. (157)

67. IV. Ebenezer Alden of Middleborough and Ashfield, son of John, (18) was b. 1720. At the age of twenty he went to Cuba with many others from New England, where he was taken prisoner and suffered great hardships, not being released for ten years. After his return he settled in Ashfield. Hem. 1, Ann Whitaker, 2, Rebecca Smith: but I am not aware that he had issue by either.

68. IV. Rev. Noah Alden of Stafford, Ct., and Bellingham, Mass., the son of John Alden, (18) was b. May 30, 1725-; and 4. at Bellingham, 5May, 1797, a. 72.

He was received to Mid. Cong, church, 7 March, 1742; dis. to the Cong. chh. in Stafford, Ct. 1749, and continued a member there until 1753, when he changed his religious views; became a Baptist minister, and was ordained at Stafford, Ct. June 5, 1755, and in Bellingham, 12 Nov. 1766 He was a member of the Convention for adopting the Constitution of Massachusetts, and Vas a very pious and worthy man. He was one of four ministers who formed the Warren Association in 1767. See a further notice of him in the annals of the American Pulpit, by Rev. Dr. Spragde. He m. Mary Vaughn.

CHILDREN

1. Joanna, (158)	4. Elisha. (158a)
2. Lucy, who m. a Marshall.	5. Israel. (158b)
3. Ruth, who m. Benj. Thayer.	6. Noah. W (158c)

69. IV. John Alden, Lebanon, Ct. son of Andrew, (21) "was b. 1716, m. Elizabeth Ripley.

CHILDREN

1. Parthinia, (159)	5. Roger, 1748. (163)
2. Violetta, (160)	6. Elizabeth.
3. John, (161)	7. Son. - d. soon.
4. Judah, (162)	8. Son. - d. soon.

70. IV. Major Prince Alden, son of Andrew, (21) b. 1718; d. 1804, a. 86. He went from Litchfield Co. Ct. to Wyoming Co. Pa. in 1773, or 1774; purchased a large tract of land, lying in Hanover and Newport Townships; owned, also, several other tracts, the whole being anthracite coal land, now very valuable. He d. at Meshoppin, Pa. He m. Mary Fitch, who d. in Newport Township, Pa. in 1801. Their children were all born in New England.

CHILDREN

1. Mason Fitch. (164)	6. Andrew. (169)
2. Mary. (165)	7. Prince. (170)
3. Abigail. (166)	8. John. (171)
4. Sarah. (167)	9. Daniel. (172)
5. Lydia. (168)	

71. IV. Andrew Alden, son of Andrew, (21) was b. 1721; d. ___; m. ___ Rebecca Stamford.

CHILDREN
1. Fear. (173)

72. IV. Walter Alden, son of Andrew, (21) b. __; m. __, Wid. Jane Blackman.
73. IV. Lydia Alden, dau. of Andrew, (21) b. __, m. __ Seth Alden. (75.)
74. IV. William Alden, son of Andrew, (21) m. _, ___ Metcalf.

CHILDREN

1. Eunice.	4. Sarah.
2. William.	5. Lydia.
3. Jabin.	6. Andrew.

75. IV. Seth Alden, Lebanon, Ct. son of Jonathan, (22.3) was b. 1721, d.; m. , Lydia Alden, (73.)

CHILDREN

1. Seth.	5. Felix.
2. Sybil.	6. Joab.
3. Jonathan.	7. Melissa.
4. Lydia, m. perhaps Paul Spooner. (174)	8. Sarah.
	9. Christian.

76. IV. Dea. Austin Alden, Gorham, Me. son of Jonathan, (22) b. 25 Mar. 1729, at Marshfield; d. Gorham, Me. 23 Mar. 1804, a. 75. He was Town Clerk of Gorham from 1778 to 1804. His homestead in Gorham has never been out of the family. It was first occupied by Austin Alden, then by his son Josiah, then by his son Gardner, then by his son Henry, who now, 1859, owns and occupies the same.

He m. 25 Nov. 1756, Salome Lombard of Barnstable, who was b. 10 June, 1736, and d. before 1781.

CHILDREN

1. Elizabeth, 3 Oct. 1757. (175)	5. *Hezekiah, 15 July, 1767: d. 27 Nov. 1768.
2. Josiah, 31 Mar. 1760. (176)	
3. Humphrey, 21 Jan. 1763. (177)	
4. Anner, 14 Apr. 1765. (178)	

77. IV. Samuel Alden, Duxbury, son of Col. John, (23) was b. 1713, settled in England: d. 1744, a. 32: was master of a merchant ship. He bequeathed the homestead which he had inherited, to his brother Briggs. He left also about £10,000 to his sisters, much of which was lost through the unfaithfulness of the Trustees.

He m. Edith ___, but had no children.

78. IV. Capt. Judah Alden of Duxbury, son of Col. John (23) was b. 1714: d. ___, while in command of a merchant vessel, on his passage to Scotland, having shortly before m. ___ Rowe of Boston.

79. IV. Anna Alden, dau. of John, (23) was b. 14 June, 1716, d. 1 July, 1801, a. 89; m. 8 Feb. 1739, Benjamin Loring.

"They were both very exemplary and devoted christians."

CHILDREN

1. Mary, 1739. 2. *Benjamin, 1742, d. 174.5. 3. *Sarah, 1744, d. 1745. 4. Benjamin, 1745, d. 1752. 5. Samuel, 1747. 6. Judah, 1749. 7. Daniel, 1751. 8. John, 1752. 9. Seth, 1755. 10. Lucy, 1758, d. 1847, a. 89, m. Dr. Jabez Fuller.

80. IV. Col. Briggs Alden, Duxbury, son of John, (23) was b. 1723; d. 4 Oct. 1796, a. 73. He occupied the ancestral estate. He was early elected an officer in the militia; a Major in 1762, and Colonel in 1776. He was a magistrate, an active man in business affairs, and after the British Parliament asserted their right to tax the Colonies without their consent, untiring in his efforts to sustain the Continental Congress, and the liberties of his country.

He m. 19 Nov. 1741, Mary Wadsworth, who d. 20 May, 1812, a. 88.

CHILDREN

1. Hannah, 24 Oct. 1743. (179)	6. Edith, 3 Jan. 1754, d. unm. 7 Jan. 1815, a. 61.
2. John, 24 Jan. 1745: drowned 1766.	
3. Deborah, 7 Aug. 1748. (180)	7. Abigail, 7 July, 1755. (183)
4. Judah, 3 Oct. 1750. (181)	8. Samuel, 1 July. 1757. (184)
5. Nathaniel, 30 Mar. 1752. (182)	9. Amherst, 22 July, 1759; d. unm. 1804, a. 45.

81. IV. Abigail Alden, dau. of John, (23) b. 1727, m. ____, Col. Anthony Thomas of Marshfield.

CHILDREN

1. Briggs. 2. Waterman. 3. Judah.

82. IV. Mary Alden of Duxbury, dau. of Benjamin, (25) was b. 1710, d. 1789, a. 78; m. 31 Dec. 1734, Dr. John Wadsworth, who d. 26 Mar. 1799, a. 92.

He had served in the Canada war; was a very eccentric character, but a man of energy, and an able physician. His son John, (82) gr. at Harvard College in 1762, and was Tutor there from 1770 until his death in 1777.

CHILDREN

1. Mercy, 28 Dec. 1736, who m. 1763, Joshua Cushman. 2. John, Nov. 1739, who d. as stated above. 3. Salumith, 10 Mar. 1742, who m. 1770, Ezra Weston. 4. Sarah, 23 Dec. 1744, who m. 1774, John Neal.

83. IV. David Alden, Cape Elizabeth, Me. son of Benjamin, (25) was b. 1717, and d., was published 10 Nov. 1750, m. Elizabeth Thorndike of Portland, Me.

CHILDREN

1. David. (185)	3. Benjamin. (187)
2. James. (186)	4. John. (188)

84. IV. Bezaleel Alden, Duxbury, son of Benjamin, (25) was b. 1722, d. 9 Feb. 1799, a. 77. m. 22 Dec. 1749, Lydia Bartlett, who d. 24 Mar. 1810, a. 84.

CHILDREN

1. Benjamin. (189)	3. Isaiah, 26 Nov. 1758. (190)
2. Lydia. 1755, d. unm. 12 Nov. 1812, a. 68.	

85. IV. Wrestling Alden, Duxbury, son of Benjamin, (27) was b. 1724; d. 4 Sept. 1813, a. 89, m. ___, Elizabeth ___; who d. 24 Mar. 1807, a. 81.

CHILDREN

1. Michal, Feb. 1748-9, d. unm. at Marshfield, Nov. 1, 1841 a. 91.	7. Patmos, 1759, d. unm. 14 Apr. 1836, a. 77.
2. Bartlett, 22 Mar. 1749-50. (191)	8. Abiathar, 1763.
3. Wrestling, 14 June, 1751.	9. Sabra, 1764, d. unm. 1 Jan. 1842, a. 77.
4. *Son, 24 June, 1753.	
5. Priscilla, 1756, d. unm;	10. Mary, 1767, d. ___, unm.
6. Sarah, 1758.	11. Rebecca Partridge, 1769. (192)

86. IV. Dr. Abiathar Alden, Scarborough, Me. son of Benjamin, (27) was b. 19 July, 1731, was by profession a physician, and it is said possessed uncommon metaphysical talents.

He probably commenced business in his native town, but, if so, soon removed to Saco Me. where he resided until the commencement of the Revolutionary War. Being a tory he on one occasion gave offence to some of his whig neighbors who armed themselves, and placing him on his knees upon a hogshead, required him to recant and make confession, or suffer instant death. He signed the confession and was released. Pie then removed to Scarborough, where he resided until his death.

87. IV. Rebecca Alden, dau. of Samuel, (26) was b. 1730; d. 21 July, 1818, a. 88, m. 27 Nov. 1760, Capt. Thomas Frazier, who d. 1782.

CHILDREN

I. Samuel Alden, 1763. 2. *Rebecca, bap. 1767. 3 Rebecca, 1769, who d. 7 Nov. 1840, a. 71. In her last will she left $500 to the Pilgrim Society. "The tears of the poor are her eulogy." Hist. Dux.

88. IV. Sarah Alden, dau, of Samuel, (26) was b. 1731, m. 10 Mar. 1757, Col. Gamaliel Bradford, who d. 9 Jan. 1807.

CHILDREN

1. Perez, Nov. 14, 1758. 2. Sophia, 1761. 3. Gamaliel. 4 Nov. 1763, father of Dr. Gamaliel, b. 1795, gr. H. U. 1825, Sup. Mass. Gen. Hos. 1833, d. Oct. 22, 1839. 4. Alden, 19 Nov. 1705, long Sec. of State of Mass., gr. H. C. 1786 d. 1843. 5. Daniel, 1771. 6. Sarah, 1768, who m. William Hinkley. 7. Jerusha, 1770, who m. Ezra Weston, 8. Gershom, 1774.

89. IV. John Alden, Duxbury, son of Samuel, (28) who. was b. 1734; d. at Crown Point, 1761, a. 27.

90. IV. Alithea Alden, dau. of Samuel; (28) was b. 1735, and d. Apr. 1820, a. 76, m. 8 Jan. 1767, William Loring, Esquire, of Duxbury, who d. 18 Oct. 1815.

CHILDREN

1. William, 1768. 2. George, 1770. 3. Ichabod, 1774. 4. Joshua, 1774, 5. Samuel, 1775. 6. Alden, 1780. 7. Sophia, 1783. 8. Clarissa, 1785. 9. Bailey, 1786, who gr. Brown U. 1807, ord. Pastor, N. Andover, 19 Sept. 1810. resigned, 1 Mar. 1849, on account of ill health.

91. IV. Samuel Alden of Duxbury, son of Samuel, (28), was b. 1737; d. 29 Feb. 1799, 63; m. 21 July, Abigail Sylvester.

CHILDREN

1. * Samuel 12 June, 1778, d. young.	3. Lucy. (194).
2. Abigail. (193)	4. Nancy, d. unm.

92. IV. Col. Ichabod Alden, Duxbury, son of Samuel, (28), was b. 1739, was killed at Cherry Valley, N. Y. 11 Nov. 1778, a. 39. He was Lt. Colonel in 1775, in the eight months service in the 25th regiment. He m. Mary Wakefield.

CHILDREN

1. John, 25 Nov. 1774. (195)	2. Rebecca Partridge, 7 Aug. 1777. (196)

93. IV. Abigail Alden, dau. of Samuel, (28) m. 27 Oct. 1768, Rev. Francis Winter, who, gr. H. C. 1765 and d. 1826..

Allen says he was a patriot of the Revolution and chaplain, and that he d. at Bath, Me.

94 IV. John Alden, Needham, son of ? (see F. 3.)

His will is dated 26 June, 1782, names a wife, sons John, Henry, Samuel, Thomas, dau. Jemima Pratt, Alice Capron, Mary Paine, and gr. dau. Lydia Smith. Silas was executor. *Bos. Rec.* 82, 378. He m. 26 Nov. 1728, Thankful Parker.

CHILDREN

1. * Jemima, 9 Mar. 1730, d. in infancy,
2. John, 9 Oct. 1731. (197)
3. Alice, 12 July, 1733. (198)
4. Henry, 27 Nov. 1734. (199)
5. Silas, 1736. (200)
6. Samuel, 1743. (201)
7. Moses.
8. Moses.
9. Thomas. (202)
10. Thankful. (203)
11. Mary. (204)

Note. — Mary Alden, Boston, m. 8 Feb. 1721, Samuel Kneeland of Boston. Boston Records.

Fifth Generation

95. V. Elizabeth Alden of Boston, dau. of Capt. Nathaniel, (39) m. abt 1750, Capt. John Homans of Dorchester, his 2 wife. He was b. 1703; m. 1, Hannah Osborne, who d. 1747. Hed. in 1778, a. 75.

The children of John and Elizabeth Homans were, 1. John. 2. Thomas. 3. Samuel. 4. Stephen. 5. Rebecca. 6. Lucy. Dr. John Homans d. in 1800, a. 47, m. Sarah Dalton, was the father of John Homans, M. D. of Boston, late President of the Mass. Med. Society, who m. 1816, Caroline, dau, of Dudley Walker Esq., and they have had eleven children.

96. V. Anna Alden, dau. of Ebenezer, (47) b. 1718, d. 1788, a. 70, m. ___, Eleazer Washburn, 'E. Bridgewater.

They had children, 1. Susanna, 1740, who m. Jeptha Byram. 1772. 2. *Zenas, 1741. 3. *Anne, 1742. 4. Anne, 1743, who m. Amos Whitman, 1764. 5. Eleazer, 1746. 6. Asa, 1749, who went to New York. 7. Levi, 1752. 8. Oliver, who m. Hannah Gannet, 1781. 9. Alden, 1753, who m. Sarah Harding. , 10. Isaac, 1760.

97. V. Susanna Alden, dau. of Ebenezer, (47) b. 1719, d. 1783, a. 64., m. 1738, Ephraim Casey, Bridgewater, who d. 1791, a. 70.

They had children, 1. Anna, 1739, d. unm. 1804. 2. Azubah, 1741, m. Josiah Johnson. 3. Phebe, 174-2, m. 1761, Ezra Allen. 4. Ephraim, 1748. 5. Susanna, 1750, m. 1774, Asa Keith. 6. Huldah, 1762, m. 1785, Simeon Allen. 7. Daniel, 1754.

98. V. Abigail Alden, dau. of Ebenezer, (47) m. Ebenezer Byram, Jim. Esq., Bridgewater, who removed to Wiadham, Morris Co. N. J., and d. 1765.

CHILDREN

1. Huldah, 1739. 2. Huldah. 1710, who m. and was the gr. mother of Rev. Philip Lindley, v. Pres. of N.J. Collegs. 3. Edward. 1742. 4. Ebenezer, 1744. 6. Napthah 6. Joseph 7. Abigail. 8. Anne, who m. and was the gr. mother of Lewis Condit, M. D. Mem. Congress. 9. Mary. 10. Phebe.

99. V. Dea. Nathan Alden, E. Bridgewater, son of Ebenezer, (47) b. 1727, d. 1807, a. 80; m. 1750, Mary Hudson, dau. of Daniel Hudson, who d. 1755.

CHILDREN

1. Nathan, 2 July, 1751. (205) m. 2, 1757, Lydia Richards, dau. of Benjamin Richards; had 2. *Isaac, 1758.

100. V. Ezra Alden, E. Bridgewater, son of Ebenezer, (47) b. 1732, and d. before 1771, m. Rebecca, dau. of Josiah Keith of Easton; d. 1777.

CHILDREN

1. *A son, 1757. 2. *Abbe, 1759, d. young. 3 Abigail, 1761, who m. Geo. Vining. 4. Isaac, 1763. (206) 5. Susanna, 1766, who m. George Allen and went to Cummington, Mass.

101. V. Isaac Alden, Bridgewater, farmer, son of John, (48) b. 1731; d. before 1760; m. Martha, dau. of Solomon Packard, who m. 2, 1760 Israel Bailey.

CHILDREN

1. Abigail, 1757. (207)	2. Isaac, 1753.

102. V. Jonathan Alden, Bridgewater, son of John, (48) was b. 1732; d. 18 Feb. 1825, a. 93; m. 1766, Experience, dau. of Cornelius Washburn.

CHILDREN

1. Mehetabel, 1767. (208)	4. Daniel, 3 Mar. 1773.
2. Isaac, 19 Oct. 1771. (209)	5. Ezra. (211)
3. *Joanna. (210)	6. John. (212)

He m. 2, Hannah, dau. of Thomas Greene, and wid. of Thomas White, and had ch.

7. Samuel Greene. (213)	10. Mary. (215)
8. * Joseph, d. young.	11. Jonathan, who went to New York
9. Cyrus, 30 May, 1783. (214;	State. (2.6)

103. V. John Alden, Warwick, son of Jonathan, (48) b. 1747; blacksmith, m. Charity Cook of Sterling, who d. 1781.

CHILDREN

1. Levi. (217)	4. Mary. (220)
2. John. (218)	5. Beriah, 1780, d. unm. Claremont, N.
3. Charity, (219)	H.

He m. 2, Elizabeth, dau. of Richard Gleason; m. 3, Patience Gleason, sister of the preceding. The three wives all died in child birth.

He m. 4, Keziah More in 1786, had ch.

6. Patience Gleason.	9. Jonathan Phinney. (222)
7. George Frederic, who d. Troy, N. Y.	10. Isaac.
8. Elizabeth. (221)	

104. V. James Alden, son of John, (48) m. ____.

CHILDREN

1. Chester. (223)
2. York, unm. went to Indiana.
3. Samuel. (224)
4. Joseph. (224a)

105. V. Benjamin Alden, son of John, (48) m. ____.

CHILDREN

1. Adam. (225)
2. Amos.
3. Harry.
4. *Ch. d. young.

106. V. Joseph Alden, Stafford, Ct. son of Daniel, (51) b. 1718, d. 2 Jan. 1768, of fever at Worcester, Mass. while on a journey, m. 1742, Susanna, dau. of Solomon Packard.

CHILDREN

1. * Zenas, 1745.
2. * Martha, 1747, d. young.
3. Zenas. (226)
4. Eliah, 1750; living unm. 1813.
6. Joseph. (227)
6. Benjamin. (228)
7. Zephaniah.
8. Abashai. (229)
9. Patty. (230).

107. V. Dea. Daniel Alden, Stafford, Ct. Cornish and Lebanon, N. H. farmer, son of Daniel, (51) was b. in Bridgewater, Mass. 1720; d. at Lebanon, N. H. 18 May, 1790, a. 70. He first settled in Bridgewater, whence he early removed to Stafford, Ct; was a deacon in the church, a magistrate, much engaged in public business, often in the Legislature, and universally respected. About L782, he sold his farm at Stafford and removed to Cornish, N. H. where he resided eight years; when becoming infirm, he went to live with his eldest son at Lebanon, N. H. where he died as above stated.

He m. 1747, Jane, dau, of Seth Turner of Weymouth, Mass. A descendant of Humphrey Turner of Scituate, Mass. She was b. 30 Mar. 1725, and d. at Lebanon, N. H. 6 May, 1817, a. 92. She retained her memory, and other mental faculties to the last; was a devoted christian, had a great respect for her Puritan ancestors, and never grew weary of answering inquiries relating to their character and condition. To her, my venerable grandmother, I am indebted for many facts relating to her husband's ancestry as well as her own. She has been long dead; but her memory is very precious.

CHILDREN

1. Sarah. (231)
2. Hannah, 1750. (232)
3. Abigail, Oct. 1750, (233)
4. Daniel. (234)
5. Ebenezer, 4 July, 1755 (235)
6. Mehitabel, d. unra.
7. *Mary, d. young.
8. An inf. 8 Apl. 1761, d. 9 Apl. 1761.
9. Jesse, 30 May, 1763. (236)
10. Samuel, 1768. (23 7)

11. Isaac, 11 Feb. 1770. (238) | 12. *Inf. d. soon.

108. V. Abigail Alden, dau. of Daniel, (51) was b. 1722, m. 1742, Eleazer Whitman of E. Bridgewater.

They had children, 1. *Mary. 1743. 2. *Eliah, 1745. 3. * Abigail, 1747* 4. *Hannah, 1747. 5. *Jepthah, 1748. 6. Mary, 1751. 7. Joshua, 1753. 8. Eleazer, 1755, d. 1646, a. 91. Deacon in the E. Bridgewater church, eminent for his piety, and charitable benefactions. 9. Ephraim. 1757, Abington, whose son Jared Whitman Esq. gr. Br. Un. 1805. and is still living (1866) in S. Abington. 10. *Asa, 1761. 11. Abigail. 1763.

109. V. Zephaniah Alden, Stafford, Ct. son of Daniel, (51) b. 1724, was celebrated for his wit; was twice married, but left no issue.

110. V. Hannah Alden, dau. of Daniel, (51) b, 1727, m. Joshua Blodgett of Stafford, Ct.

They had children, 1. Joseph, 1757, gr. Dart. Coll. 1783, ord. pastor of the Cong. Chh. in Greenwich, Mass. 8 Nov. 1786, d. 20 Nov. 1833, a. 76. Ha was an able and faithful minister. 2. Benjamin. 3. Alden. 4. Eli. 5. Ezra. 6. Abigail. 7. Hannah. 8. Eleanor, who m. a Thresher. 9. Olive, who m. an Abbott.

111. V. Barnabas Alden, Ashfield, son of Eleazer, (52) b. 1732, was twice m. had two sons and several daughters.

112. V. Jonathan Alden, Ashfield, son of Eleazer, (52) b. 1721, d. 1801, or perhaps 1805. See Thayer Mem. and also Hist. Br. m. 1743, Experience, dau. of Nathaniel Hayward of Bridgewater, who d. 1809, a. 90.

CHILDREN

1. Amos, (239)	6. Huldah, (243)
2. Jonathan. (240)	7. *Seth, d. a. 14.
3. Mary. (241)	8. Howard. (244)
4. *Caleb, d. a. 21.	9. Experience. (245)
5. Azubah. (242)	

113. V. Eleazer Alden, Bridgewater, son of Eleazer, (52) b. 1723, d. 1803, a. 80, m. Sarah Whitman, dau. of Nicolas Whitman, who was b. 1726, d. 18 Apr. 1818, a. 92.

CHILDREN

1. Martha. 1752. (246)	4. Sarah, 1759, d. 1778, a. 19.
2. Mary, 1754, d. unm.	5. Hannah, 1762. (248)
3. Abigail, 1756. (247)	6. Eleazer, 1767. (249)

114. V. David Alden, Ashfield, son of Eleazer, (52) b. 1727, d. 1807, a. 80, m. his cousin Lucy Thomas.

CHILDREN

1. Isaac. (250)
2. David. (251)
3. John. (252)

4. Lydia. (253)
5. Enoch, a physician. (254)

115. V. Lt. Joshua Alden, Bridgewater, son of Eleazer (52) b. 1729, d. 21 Mar. 1809; was a farmer: had a competence. From 1756 to 1809, he kept an accurate bill of mortality in South Bridgewater. In his last will he left a legacy to the South Parish, and in gratitude they erected a monument to his memory.

He m. 1786, Mary Carver, dau. of Eleazer Carver, who was the widow of Seth Alden. (125) She d. 1811, a. 63. They had no children.

116. V. Deacon Ezra Alden, Greenwich, Mass. son of Eleazer, (52) was b. 1754, d. 1818, a. 84. In early life he united with the church in Stafford, Ct. where he resided until 1770, when he removed to Greenwich, Mass. where he was received into the Congregational church, Sept. 20th, was elected deacon in 1775, and continued to officiate in that office until prevented by the infirmities of age. He m. Miriam, dau. of Uriah Richardson of Stafford Ct. and gr. dau. of Rev. Jacob Greene of Hanover, N. J.

CHILDREN

1. Sarah. (255)
2. Judith. (256)

3. Eunice. (257)
4. Ezra. (268)

M. 2, Sarah, dau. of Capt. Benjamin Ruggles of Hardwick and wid. of Abiel Harwood. She united with the chh. in Greenwich 28 June, 1778.

5. *Miriam, d. 28 Oct. 1784.
6. Dorothy. (259)
7. Anna, (260)

8. *Abel, d. 11 Nov. 1784.
9. Alice. (261)
10. Milium. (262)

117. V. Rev. Timothy Aluen, of Yarmouth, Mass. son of Eleazer, (52) was b. in Bridgewater, 24 Nov. O. S. 1736; graduated at Harv. Coll. in 1762; was ordained pastor of the Congregational Church in Yarmouth, 13 Dec. 1769, and d. 13 Nov. 1828, a. 92, having nearly completed the fifty-ninth year, of his ministry to one people. "lie was a" faithful and devoted pastor," and eminently "a man of prayer."

He m. Sarah, dau. of Rev. Habijah Weld of Attleborough, Mass. She d. suddenly of apoplexy, 28 Oct, 1796, in the fifty-ninth year of her age, while her husband was absent on a journey. A funeral sermon was preached on the occasion by Rev. John Mellen, which was afterwards published. The following epitaph was written by the surviving consort:

"Ye friends, that weep around my grave,
　Compose your minds to rest,
Prepare, with me, for sudden death,
　And live forever bless'd."　　　　　　　　　　　Alden's Epitaphs, 1. 60.

1. Timothy, 1771. (263)
2. Isaiah, 1772, (264)
3. Martin, 1773. (265)

4. Oliver, 1775. (266)
5. Sarah Weld, 1776. (267)
6. Martha Shaw, 1778. (268)

118. V. Abiah Alden, dau. of Samuel, (55) b. 1729, m. Seth Harris of Middle-borough; dis. to chh. in North Bridgewater, 1759, d. 1797, a. 73.

Their children were, 1. Seth. 2. Abiel. 3. Oliver, 4, John. 6. Rebecca

119. V. Mehetabel Alden, dau. of Samuel, (55) b. 1732; m. Joshua Packard and removed to Maine.

Their children were, 1, Caleb, 1758. 2, Joshua, 1759. 3. Ralph. 4. Libbeus. 5. Mehitabel.

120. V. Sarah Alden, dau. of Samuel, (55) b. 1734; m. Timothy Packard who d. 1780, a. 48.

Their children were, 1. Calvin, 1762, who settled in Easton. 2. Luther, 1764 3. Sarah, 1767. 4. Timothy, 1769. 5, Perez, 1771. 6. Josiah Edson, 1776.

121. V. Samuel Alden, Abington, carpenter, son of Samuel, (50) b. 1736, d. 1816, a. 81. He was a very worthy man; mem. of the Bap. chh. in Randolph, now East Stoughton. He m. Hannah Williams of Raynham.

CHILDREN

1. Daniel. (269)
2. Silas, 1765. (270)
3. Joseph. (271)
4. Samuel. (272)
5. Williams, 1772. (273)

6. *Hosea. (274)
7. Hannah. (275)
8. Seth, 1777. (276)
9. Hosea.

122. V. Josiah Alden, Ludlow, farmer, son of Samuel, (55) b. 1738; first settled in Bridgewater, then removed to Wales; m. 1761, Bathsheba Jones of Raynham.

CHILDREN

1. Elijah. (277)
2. Azel. (278)
3. Abiah. (279)
4. Bathsheba.
5. Charity. (280)

6. Josiah. (281)
7. Lucy. (282)
8. Rebecca. (283)
9. Benjamin. (284)

123. V. Simeon Alden of Titicut and Bridgewater, son of Samuel, (55) b. 1740, m. 1763, Mary, dau. of Seth Packard.

CHILDREN

1. Simeon, 1764. (285)
2. Alpheus, 1665. (286)
3. Silas, 1766. (287)
4. Solomon, 1767. (288)

5. Mary, 1769. (289)
6. David. 1771. (290)
7. Jonathan. 1775. (291)
8. Isaac, 1777. (292)

9. Lot, 1781. (293)

124. V. Oliver Alden, Bridgewater, son of Cap. Seth, (57) b. 1740; d. 29 Sept. 1825, a. 85, m. 1765, Experience, dau. of Solomon Leonard; she d. 14 Oct. 1818, a. 75.

CHILDREN

1. Caleb, 1766. (294)
2. Experience, 1769. (295)

3. *Oliver, 1770. d. 12 Nov. 1775.
4. *Cromwell, 1773, d. 31 Oct. 1775.

125. V. Seth Alden, Bridgewater, son of Seth, (57) b. 1742; d. 29 Aug. 1775, m. 1767, Mary, dau. of Eleazer Carver, who d. 1811.

CHILDREN

1. Seth, 1769. (296) 2. Mehetabel, 1771. and three others, who d. in 1775.

After her husband's death the widow m. Lt. Joshua Alden. (115)

126. V. Capt. Joseph Alden, Bridgewater. son of Seth, (57) b. 1747, d. 8 Apr. 1803, a. 55; m. 1774, Bethiah, dau. of Eleazer Carver, who d. 1821, a. 06.

CHILDREN

1. Mehetabel. 1775. (297)
2. Joseph, 1777. (298)
3. David, 1780. (299)
4. Thomas, 1782. (300)
6. Cyrus, 1785. (301)

5. Eunice, 1788. (302)
7. Bethiah, 14 June, 1790. (303)
8. Seth, 21 May, 1793. (304)
9. Betsey, 13 Oct, 1796. (305)

127. V. Solomon Alden, Bridgewater, farmer, son of David, (58) b. 1728; m. 1755, Sarah Hall.

CHILDREN

1. Sarah, 1756. (306)
2. Solomon, 1757. (307)
3. Noah. (308)
4. Alexander. (309)

5. Amasa. (310)
6. Hannah. (311)
7. A dau. m. Eliphalet White. (312)
8. Mary, m. Elijah Alden. (313)

128. V. Dea. David Alden, Middleborough, son of David, (58) b. 1730, d. abt 1813; m. Rhoda Leach.

CHILDREN

1. Caleb. (314)
2. Rufus. (315)

3. David. (316)
4. Andrew. (317)

5. Huldah. (318)
6. Rhoda. (319)

129. V. Rufus Alden of Middleborough, son of David, (58).
130. V. Huldah Alden, dau. of David, (58) b. 1733.
131. V. Job Alden, Middleborough, son of David, (58) b. 1757, m. Lucy ___.

CHILDREN

1. Lucy, 17 Dec. 1765.
2. Phebe, 31 May, 1767.
3. Job, 29 Nov. 1768. (320)
4. Spooner, 2 Sept. 1770.

5. Peter Oliver, 20 Aug. 1772. (321)
6. Ebenezer, 20 Sept. 1774. (322)
7. Spooner, 18 Sept. 1779. (323)
8. Augustus, 16 June, 1781. (324)

Mid. Rec.

132. V. Silas Alden, son of David, (58).

133. V. Abigail Alden, dau. of David, (58) b. 19 May, 1744; d. 25 Jan. 1845, a. nearly 101, m. Zephaniah Leonard of Raynham and Taunton, Mass. who was b. in 1736; was sheriff of Bristol County, in which office he was succeeded by his son Horatio, Esq. that office having been filled by the two upwards of seventy years.

They had two children, 1. Abigail. 10 July, 1769. 2. Horatio. Abigail m. 8 Mar. 1795, David West, and after his death, 2, Andrew Cunningham.

For an obituary notice of Mrs. Leonard, see Ch. Register, 25 Mar. 1845. See also Gen. Reg. vol. 5, p. 414, and vol. 14, 83-4.

134. V. Peter Alden, son of David, (58). No account.

135. V. Ebenezer Alden, Middleboro', son Joseph, (65) m. 1 Apr. 1742, Hannah Hall. Mid. Bee.

136. V. Amariah Alden, Middleboro', son of Joseph, (65).

137. V. Moses Alden, Middleboro', son of Joseph, (65).

138. V. Phebe Alden, Middleborough, dau. of Joseph, (65).

139. V. Hannah Alden, dau. Joseph, (65).

140. V. Joseph Alden, Middleborough, son Joseph, (65).

141. V. Fear Alden, dau. Joseph, (65) m. ___ Hall, Raynham.

142. V. Eunice Alden, Middleborough, dau. Joseph, (65). No account.

143. V. Lois Alden, dau. Joseph, (65) m. Hall, Raynham.

144. V. Abner Alden, Bristol, R. I. b. 1764: gr. Bro. U. R. I. 1787; was eminent as a teacher; published several school books; never married.

145. V. Eliab Alden, Cairo, N.Y. son of Joseph, (65) was b. abt 1762, m. Mary Hathaway.

CHILDREN

1. Eliab. (325)
2. Abner, 1790. (326)
3. Levi. (327)

4. Charles Henry. (328)
5. Mary. (329)
6. Joseph, 4 Jan. 1807. (330)

146. V. John Alden, New Bedford, son of John, (66) was b. 1740; m. Lois, dau. of Gideon Southworth.

CHILDREN

1. Mary. (331)
2. *Sarah, d. young.
3. John. (332)

4. Lydia. (333)
5. Sally.
6. Lois.

7. Gideon.
8. Seth.
9. Nathan.

147. V. Mary Alden, dau. of John, (66) was b. 1741; d. 8 Sep. , m. Calvin Delano, Dartmouth.

They had children, 1. Lydia. 2. Alden. 3. Deborah.

148. V. Nathan Alden, son of John, (66) b. 1743, m. Priscilla, dau. of John Miller, Mid.

CHILDREN

1. John, 6 Dec. 1767. (333a)	4. *Lydia, 14 Nov. 1771; d. 6 Dec. 1775.
2. *Priscilla, 7 Oct. 1769, d. 16 Oct. 1773.	5. Polly, 11 Dec. 1776.
	6. Earl, 3 Nov. 1779. (335)
3. Otis, 11 Oct. 1773. (334)	7. Nathan. 20 June, 1788. (336)

149. V. Susanna Alden, dau. of John, (66) m. Joseph Tripp, New Bedford.

They had children, 1. ___, d. young. 2. Joseph, m. 2 Samuel Proctor, had 3. Sukey. 4. William. 5. Charles.

150. V. Lydia Alden, dau. John, (66) who d. 19 June, 1775; m. John Spooner, New Bedford, who d. 1773.

They had 2 ch. 1. John. 2. Thomas, who died 31 May, 1799.

151. V. Elijah Alden, Mid. son of John, (66) was b. 1754; d. 26 June, 1820, m. 1779, Mary Alden, dau. Solomon, (127). She d. 22 Sept. 1839, a. 84.

CHILDREN

1. Israel, 11 May, 1780. (337)	6. Elijah, 10 June, 1790. (338)
2. Lucinda, 17 Aug. 1781; d. 12 May, 1849.	7. *Mary, 17 Dec. 1792, d. 1793.
	8. Mary, 27 Apr. 1794.
3. Vienna, 25 Dec. 1783.	9. Daniel, 12 Sep. 1795. (339)
4. Serena, 29 Jan. 1783. (337a)	10. *Olive, 12 July, 1796, d. 22 June 1821.
5. Jared, 9 Apr. 1788.	

152. V. Lucy Alden, dau. John, m. 1794, Eleazer Cary, Bridgewater. She d. 1795.

153. V. Jael Alden, dau. John, (66) b. 1764, m. Isaac Jones, Raynham. They went to New Bedford.

They had 4 ch. 1. Alden. 2. Philander. 3. 4. names unknown.

154. V. Ruth Alden, dau. John, (66) m. Walter Howard, Bridgewater.

They had 2 ch. 1. Alden. 2. Ruth,

155. V. Seth Alden, Middleboro'; son of John, (66) b. 1770; d. 22 Feb. 1855, a. 85, unm.

156. V. Betsey Alden, dau. John, (66) m. Daniel Thomas. Middleborough.

They had 8 children. 1. Daniel, 1794. 2. Hercules, 1796. 3. Lewis, who d, in Ohio. 4. Eliza, 1799, who m. Eliab Caswell. 5. Rebecca, 1801. 6. *Edward, 1803; drowned 1814. 7. John Alden, 1804. 8. Jane, 1807.

157. V. Elihu Alden, Dixmont, Me. son of John, (66) b. 1775, m. Lydia Mitchell of Readville, Me.

CHILDREN

1. Lucy. 2. Milbury. 3, Weston. 4. ____.

158. V. Joanna Alden of Bellingham, dau. of Rev. Noah Alden,. (68) m. 1783, Rev. Aaron Leland of Chester, Vt. who was Lieut. Gov. of the State.

158a. V. Lieut. Elisha Alden, Stafford, Ct. son of Rev. Noah, (68) was b. 1745; d. 3 Mar. 1826; m. Irene Markham of Enfield, Ct. who was b. 1742, d. 13 Dec. 1830.

CHILDREN

1. Elisha. (382)	4. Samuel. (385)	7. Serena. (388)
2. Nathan, 1768. (383)	5. Darius. (386)	8. Fear. (389)
3. Simeon. (384)	6. Spencer. (387)	9. Joanna. (390)

159. V. Parthenia Alden, dau. of John, (69) m. Woodbridge Little, Esq.

160. V. Violetta Alden, dau. of John, (69) m. Isaac Fitch.

161. V. John Alden, son of John, (69). No particulars received.

162. V. Judah Alden, Lebanon, Ct. son of John, (69) was a Captain in the Revolutionary war.

163. V. Major Roger Alden, Meadville, Pa. and "West Point, New York, son of John, (69) was b. in Lebanon, Ct. in 1748; gr. Yale Coll. 1773; Mr. at Columb, Col. was an officer in the Revolutionary war, settled soon after at Meadville. Pa.; was appointed Ordinance Storekeeper at West Point, 20 Jan. 1825, and continued to hold the office to the time of his death 5th Nov. 1836.

Major Alden m. and left two children, viz; a daughter who was m. to Captain Henry Swartwout, who graduated at the Military Academy in 1827; d. at Fort Meade, Florida, 1802. after twenty-five years faithful and meritorious service. His widow is still (1866) living. The son, Bradford R. Alden, entered the Military Academy July 1st, 1827; grad. 1831, as second Lieutenant; promoted First Lieutenant' 1836, Captain, 1842; resigned 1853. He served at the Academy as Teacher of French, Assistant Professor of Mathematics, Instructor of Infantry Tactics, and from 1840 to 1852 as Commandant of the Corps of Cadets. He served also as Aid de Camp of General Scott. His subsequent history, as far as I know, is, 'Failing to obtain a commission to serve against the Rebellion, in consequence of his disability from his wound received in Oregon, he embarked extensively in boring for Petroleum in Western Penn., and devised improved methods of relining and burning coal oil, 1861—1865.' He was eight and a half years under my supervision and his father during the same time. Two worthier persons I have never known," *General S. Thayer.*

This is high commendation from one so well able to discriminate character, and to whom the country is so much indebted for the military ability and prowess of the brave men who trained our soldiers and led them on to victory during the late fearful struggle.

Other facts were promised, but have failed to reach me. Should they be received in time they will be inserted in the Supplement.

164. V. Mason Fitch Alden, Meshoppin, Pa. son of Prince, (70) was b. ___, d. ___. "He with his brother John erected the first forge for manufacturing bar iron and bloomers at Nanticoke Creek on the Susquehannah River in 1776. This old work was carried on until 1830 by Stewart and Sons, when the forge was abandoned.

In 1778 he was a soldier in Captain Ransom's company. He m. Mary Thompson.

CHILDREN

1. William. (340) | 2. Sarah. (341) | 3. Abigail. (342)

165. V. Mary Alden, dau. of Prince, (70) "m. Abraham Pike and had three children now 1859, deceased. One or two grandchildren are supposed to be living at the West."

166. V. Abigail Alden, dau. of Prince, (70) m. John Lawson;

Had 3 ch. 1. Samuel. 2. Mary. 3. Hannah, b. Sept. 1782, who m. Rev. Stewart Pearce, to whose son Stewart Pearce, Esq. of Wilkesbarre, Pa., I am indebted for an account of the descendants of Maj. Prince Alden.

After the death of her husband who was fired upon, and killed, and scalped by Indians, as he was passing along the road from Hanover to Wilkesbarre, Pa., 8 July, 1782, she m. in 1787, Shubael Bidlock, brother of Rev. Benjamin Bidlock.

They had 3 ch. 1. John. 2. Lydia.* 3. Shubael: the last two d. young.

167. V. Sarah Alden, dau. of Prince, (70) m. Nathaniel Cook; had ch. and removed West.

168. V. Lydia Alden, dau of Prince, (70) m. Rev. Benjamin Bidlock;

Had 3 ch. 1. Benjamin Alden. 2. Mary. 3. Mehetabel. All m. and had families. Benjamin was a lawyer and a Rep. to Congress from Pa. four years; was two years in the Pa. Assembly; was appointed minister to New Granada, and d. at Bogota in 1849.

169. V. Andrew Alden, son of Prince, (70) m. Elizabeth Atherton; lived near Owego, N. Y.; had several children, and removed "West.

170. V. Prince Alden, son of Prince, (70) m. Sally Nesbitt from Ct.; had several ch. all in the "West.

171. V. John Alden, son of Prince, (70) m. Nancy Jameson; had ch.; all in the West.

John Alden was taxed in Hanover Township in 1796; was a volunteer soldier in the suppression of the whiskey insurrection, sergeant in Capt. Bowman's company.

S. Pearce's Annals, p. 538.

172. V. Daniel Alden, son of Prince, (70) m. Anne Brooks; all in the West. He was a volunteer soldier in 1794.

173. V. Fear Alden, dau. of Andrew, (71) m. probably Andrew Beaumont.

174. V. Lydia Alden, dau. probably of Seth Alden, (75) d. 19 June, 1775; m. 25 Mar. 1769, John Spooner of Dartmouth, son of Thomas Spooner and Re-

35

becca Paddock, dau. of Judah Paddock and Alice Alden, (26). John Spooner was b. 23 April 1745, d. 20 Feb. 1773.

Their children were, 1. John. 2. Thomas.

175. V. Elizabeth Alden, dau. of Dea. Austin, (76) was b. 3 Oct. 1757, m. 27 Mar. 1777, Jesse Harding of Gorham, Me.

176. V. Josiah Alden, Gorham, Me. son of Austin, (76) was b. 1760, d. 8 Nov. 1834, a. 74; was Town Clerk of Gorham from 1804 to 1815; m. Oct. 1782, Mary Robinson of Cape Elizabeth.

CHILDREN

1. Austin, 3 Nov. 1784. (343)
2. Salome, 12 Nov. 1786. (344)
3. Charles, 20 Jan. 1789. (345)
4. Hannah, 20 Jan. 1791.
5. Nancy, 13 Feb. 1793. (34(5)
6. Gardner, 13 Jan. 1795. (347)
7. Lucy, 9 Apr. 1797.

177. V. Humphrey Alden, Gorham, Mc. son of Austin, (76) was living in 1839.

178. V, Anner Alden, dau. of Austin, (76) was b. 1765; m. 1785; Warren Nickerson; had 8 ch. b. in Orrington, Mc.

179. V. Hannah Alden, dau. of Briggs Alden, (80) was b. 1743, d. 1790; a. 47; m. 1767, Capt. John Gray of Boston.

180. V. Deborah Alden, dau. of Briggs, (80) was b. 1748, d. 1792, at Newburg, N. Y.: m. 1767, Caleb Coffin of Nantucket:

They had children, 1. Caleb. 2. Hannah 3. Fanny; m. 2, Major Isaac Belknap, a Revolutionary officer of Newburg, N. Y. They had ch. 4. Amelia, 27 June, 1779, who m. Charles Birdsall, and d. Newburg, 13 Jan. 1859, a. 80. 5. Alden, 14 Mar. 1781. 6. Judah, 5 Oct. 1785. who m. Betsey, wid. of Seth Winsor. 7. Lydia, Feb. 1788, d. unm. 8. Deborah, 14 Dec. 1792, who m. Seth Brooks of East Boston.

181. V. Maj. Judah Alden, Duxbury, son of Briggs, (80) was b. 1750, and d. 12 Mar. 1845, a. 94: was an officer in the Revolutionary war; highly respected as a soldier and citizen; President of the Society of the Cincinnati; m. — Welthea Wadsworth, b. 1758, d. 3 Mar. 1841, a. 81.

CHILDREN

1. Lucinda, 5 Dec. 1780. (348)
2. John, 2 Nov. 1784. (349)
3. Briggs, 6 Oct. 1786. (350)
4. Mercy, 1788. (351)
5. Welthea, 1792. (352)
6. *Judah.
7. *Hannah, 1795, d. 1804.
8. *Judah, 1797, d. 1806.
9. Mary Ann, 1801.
10. Samuel. 1805. (353)

182. V. Nathaniel Alden, Freeport, Me, son of Briggs, (80) was b. 1752, m. 28 Jan. 1783, Rebecca Ripley, dau. of William N. Ripley of Duxbury. She was b. 11 Sep. 1760; d. 14 Jan. 1843.

CHILDREN

1. *John, 1784, d. 1784, a. 3 d.
2. Samuel, 19 July, 1785. (354)

3. Welthea, 27 Dec. 1788.
4. *Joanna, 1792, d. 1797.

5. William, 1797, d. Canton, China. 9 Oct. 1825, a. 28.

183. V. Abigail Alden, dau. of Briggs, (80) was b. 1755, d. 1800, a. 45; m. Nov. 1784, Hon. Bezaleel Howard of Bridgewater, who d. 1830, a. 78.
They had children, 1. John Alden. 2. Beza.

184. V. Samuel Alden, Duxbury, son of Briggs, (80) b. 1 July, 1751, d. Nov. 1778, a 27, in consequence of a wound received in the Penobscot expedition, under Gen. Lovell.

185. V. David Alden, Northport, Me. son of David, (83) m.

CHILDREN

1. David. 2. Dau. ___, m. ___ Doyle, Northport. 3. Dau. ___, m. ___ Atkins, Portland. 4. Dau. , m. ___ Trowbridge.

186. V. James Alden, Portland, Me. son of David, (83) b. 1776, m. Elizabeth, dau. of Robert Tate of Portland.

CHILDREN

1. Robert Tate, 1805. (356)	2. Mary, 1807. (357)	4. Delia (359)
	3. James. (358)	5. Eliza (360)

187. V. Benjamin Alden, Baltimore, son of David, (83) 13 dead; m. had 2 or 3 ch.

188. V. John Alden, Portland, Me. son of David, (83) b. at Cape Elizabeth, 1770, m. 1792, Mehetabel Webb, who d. 14 May, 1852, a. 75.

CHILDREN

1. *John, 5 Jan. 1793, d. 3 Aug. 1813. 2. Benjamin. 20 Feb. 1795. (361) 3. * ___, b. 12 July, 1797, d. 23 Sep 1825. 4. *Jacob W. 6 Feb, 1799, d. 8 May, 1802. 5. *Franklin, 18 Feb. 1802, d. 11 Jan. 1820. 6. *Louiza, d. May, 1837. 7. *Caroline, 13 Dec, 1806, d. 10 Mar. 1811. 8. *Mehetabel, 28 Jan. 1809, d. 22 Nov. 1850. 9. Albert, 5 Mar. 1811. (362) 10. Caroline, 11 July, 1813, d. July, 1845. 11. John, 4 March, 1815.

189. V. Benjamin Alden of Duxbury, son of Bezaleel, (84). A faithful and efficient school master; was for many years Town Clerk; never married; d. 8 Jan. 1835, a. 85.

190. V. Isaiah Alden of Duxbury, son of Bezaleel, (84) was b. 26 Nov. 1758, d. 19 Mar. 1845, a. 86; m. 1 Jan. 1787, Mary Weston, who was b, 2 June 1767.

CHILDREN

1. Ichabod, 4 Nov 1788, (363)	5. Martha, 22 Feb 1796.
2. Isaiah. 17 Dec. 1789. (364)	6. Ruth, 14 Nov. 1799.
3. Mary, 4 July, 1792.	7. Peleg, 6 June, 1806, (366)
4. Benjamin, 22 Mar. 1794. (365)	8. James, 20 Apr. 1808. (367)

191. V. Bartlett Alden, Duxbury, son of Wrestling, (8.5) was received into Marshfield Church in 1817. *Marshfield Rec.*

152. V. Rebecca Partridge Alden, Duxbury, dau. of "Wrestling, (85) was b. 1769, m. 1791, John Sampson.

193. V. Abigail Alden of Duxbury, dau. of Samuel, (91) was b. about 1780, and m. Ebenezer Waterman.

194 V. Lucy Alden of Duxbury, dau. of Samuel, (92) m. Michael Soule.

195. V. Captain John Alden of Duxbury, son of Col. Ichabod, (92) was b. 25 Nov. 1774; lived near Captain's Hill; m. 26 Mar. 1801, Ann Hall, who d. 15 Dec. 1833, a. 56.

CHILDREN

1. Deborah, 30 Jan. 1802, d, 16 May 1804.
2. Ichabod, 30 Mar. 1806. (368)
3. Samuel, 21 Apr. 1808. (369)
4. Deborah, 5 June, 1815. (370)

196. V. Rebecca Partridge Alden, dau. of Col. Ichabod Alden, (92) was b. 7 Aug. 1777: and m. Constant Sampson.

197. V. John Alden, Needham, son of John, (90) was b. 9 Oct. 1731. and went to Vermont. I have no account of his descendants.

198. V. Alice Alden, dau. of John, (94) was b. 1733, and m. Jonathan Capron of Attleborough, Mass.

199. V. Henry Alden, Needham, son of John, (94) was b. 1734, d. 1812, a. 78; m. Thankful Parker, b. 1730, who d. 3 Feb. 1814.

CHILDREN

1. William, 1 July, 1761. (371) perhaps more.

200. V. Dea. Silas Alden, Needham, son of John, (94) was b. 1736, d. 1826, a. 90; m. Margaret Capron.

CHILDREN

1. Moses. (372)
2. Elizabeth. (373)
3. Paul. (374)
4. Silas. (375)
5. Amasa. (376)
6. Lydia, (377)
7. Rebecca. (378)
8. Simeon. (379)
9. Samuel. (380)
10. George. (381)

201. V. Samuel Alden, Needham; son of John, (94) b. 1743, d. 1797; m. Susanna Coller.

CHILDREN

1. Hannah, 1772.
2. Susanna, 1774, d. 1775.
3. Abigail, 1776.
4. Susanna, 1777.
5. Sarah, 1778.
6. *Priscilla, 1779; d. young.
7. Samuel, 1792.

202. V. Thomas Alden, Middlebury, Vt. son of John, (94) was b. 1743, d. 1797; m. Polly Cheney.

203. V. Thankful Alden of Needham, Mass. dau. of John, (94) m. a Pratt.

204. V. Mary Alden of Needham, dau. of John, (94) m. Samuel Paine of Roxbury.

Sixth Generation

205. VI. Nathan Alden, Esquire, East Bridgewater; farmer; son of Nathan, (99) was b. 2 July, 1751, d. 6 Nov. 1842, a. 91; was a very worthy man; m. 1776, Sarah, dau. of William Barrell, who d. 1816, a. 61.

CHILDREN

1. Mary, 1777. (401)
2. Lydia, 1779. (402)
3. Marcus, 1782. (403)
4. Isaac, 1786. (404)
6. Sarah, 1792. (405)
6. Lucius, 1796. (406)

He m. 2, in 1819, wid. Joanna Soule of Middleboro'.

206. VI. Isaac Alden of E. Bridgewater, son of Ezra, (100) was b. 1763, d. 1827, a. 64; m. 1781, Mary, dau. of Thomas and Abigail Russell. She d. 1814, a. 47.

CHILDREN

1. *Agnes, 1787, d. a. 2 mo.
2. Ezra, 1788. (407)
3. Thomas Russell, 1790. (408)
4. James Sullivan, 1801. (409)
5. A ch. 1807; m. 2, Betsey, dau. of Daniel Willis; had
6. Benjamin. (410), perhaps others.

207. VI. Abigail Alden, dau. of Isaac, (101) was b. 1757, m. 1778, Joseph Whiting.

208. VI. Mehetabel Alden, dau. of Jonathan, (102) was b. 15 Sept. 1767; m. Henry Jackson of Minot, Me.; had children, seven sons and four daughters.

209. VI. Isaac Alden of E. Bridgewater, son of Jonathan, (102) was b. 1772, and d. 20 Mar. 1832, a. 60; m. 1794, Ruth, dau. of Joseph Byram. After her husband's death she m. 2,. Alpheus Fobes.

CHILDREN

1. Joanna, who m. 1818, Wm. Bird. (411)
2. Nabby. (412)
3. Lewis. (413)

210. VI. Daniel Alden of Auburn, Me. son of Jonathan, (102) was b. 31 March, 1773; m. Deborah, dau. of Jonathan Fulington.

CHILDREN

1. Elvira. 2. Hannah. 3. Cyrus. 4. David. 5. John. 6. Mehetabel.

211. VI. Ezra Alden, E. Bridgewater, farmer, son of Jonathan, (102) was b. 15 July, 1774, d. 26 June, 1861, a. 87; m. 1798, Abigail, dau. of William Vinton, b. 1783, d. 1865, a. 82.

CHILDREN

1. Edward Vinton, 25 June, 1799, d. Tinm. 1822.
2. William Vinton, 4 Aug. 1809. (414)

212. VI. John Alden, E. Bridgewater, and Auburn, Meson of Jonathan, (102) was b. 15 Dec. 1775; m. Deborah, dau. of Benjamin Robinson.

CHILDREN

1. Benjamin. 2. Mary 3. Alvina. 4. Charles; all born in E. Br. of whom I have no further account.

213. VI. Samuel Greene Alden, son of Jonathan, (102). was b. in 1778, and was killed at Eastport, Me. by the bursting of a cannon, 14 June, 1836; m. 1804, Rhoda, dau. of Benjamin Richards.

CHILDREN

1. *Benjamin. 2. Samuel Greene, 3. Bartlett Richards. One account says, Robert B. who d. June 5, 1814.

214. VI. Cyrus Alden, North Auburn, Me. son of Jonathan. (102) was b. 30 May, 1783; m. 19 Sept. 1808, Nabby Keith, dau. of Capt. David Kinsley.

CHILDREN

1. Mary Kinsley, 1809.
2. Hannah Greene, 1811,
3. Nabby Vinton, 1813.
4. Jane Gary.
5. William Ladd.

215. VI. Mary Albert, dau. of Jonathan, (102) m. 1810,. Abel Barren, E. Br.
They had children, 1. Hannah Greene, 1811, who m. John Reed. 2. ilarianne, who m. B. G. Studley of Hingham, Mass. 3. Martha, who m. Nathaniel Vaughn of E. Br. 4. *George Whitfield, who d, 1841, a. 16. 5. Thomas White, who m. E. Ryder, W. B.

216. VI. Jonathan Alden, son of Jonathan, (102) went to the State of New York.

217. VI. Levi Alden, Claremont, N. H. farmer, son of John, (103) was b. prob. abt 1772, d. of *enteritis* in 1845; m. 1800, Baodicea Warner.

CHILDREN

1. Louiza, 30 Nov. 1800, (415)
2. Albert G, 3 Apr. 1804. (416)
3. Thomas W. 2 June, 1807. (417)
4. John, 26 Dec. 1809, (418)
5. James Madison, 9 Feb, 1813, (419)
6. Levi, 1815. (420)
7. Lucinda, 21 July. 1818. (421)
8. Alfred, 14 June, 1822. (422)

218. VI. John Alden, Greensboro', Vt. son of John, (103) m.; no ch.

219. VI. Charity Alden, Claremont, N. H. dau. of John (103) m. Samuel Blodgett, who is dead. She is blind; has no children.

220. VI. Mary Alden, dau. of John, (103) m. William Pettigree of Weathersfield, Vt. who d. 1816. She d. at Claremont, N. H. 1850.

They had children, 1. Thomas. 2. Alden. 3, William. 4. Mary, 26 May, 1813. who m. 26 Sept. 1839, Rev, Mr. — Keyes. She went with her husband on a mission to the Holy Land; had a son born on Mt. Zion at Jerusalem, who was baptized with the water of the Kidron. She embarked 24 Jan, and arrived at Beirut, 1 Apr, 1840; lost a second child at Beirut in 1842, — relieved, 12 Nov. 1844.

221. VI. Elizabeth Alden, dau. of John, (103) m. David Pettigree.

222. VI. Jonathan Phinney Alden, M. D. Cambridge, Mass. M. M. S. S. son of John, (103) was b. 12 Sept. 1793, d. 7 Sep. 1863, a. 70; m. 20 Sept. 1825, Esther Cecilia Alden, dau. of Col. Joseph Alden, (224a) son of James, (104).

CHILDREN

1. Caroline Frances, b. 13 Nov. 1826, m. John Franklin Hall, went to California; has 1 dau. Norma Frances, b. 29 Apl. 1847. (423)

223. VI. Chester Alden, Woodstock, Vt. son of James, (104) m.

CHILDREN

1. Chester, Woodstock, Vt. (424)
2. Alvan, Woodstock, Vt. (425)
3. Samuel H., Janesville, Wis. (426)
4. Sophia, m. Levi Judkins. (427)
5. Catherine, m. James M. Alden. (419)

224. VI. Samuel Alden, Janesville, Wis. son of James, (104).

224a. VI. Col. Joseph Alden of Claremont, N. H. and Woburn, Mass. son of James, (104) b. 26 Nov. 1779, d. 7 Oct. 1847, a. 68; m. Lucy Warner, b. 9 Feb. 1772, d. 9 Dec. 1849, a. 66.

CHILDREN

1. * Louiza Villars, 1798, d. a. 2 V.
2. Hiram Orlando, 1800. (427a)
3. Esther Cecilia, 21 Feb. 1802. (427b)
4. Emily Ormand, 1803, m. William Kendall; he is dead; Milford N. H. (427c)
5. * (Harry.)
6, * (George.)
7. Caroline Frances, 6 Dec. 1806. (427d)
8. Joseph Warren, 3 Jan. 1808. (427e)
9. Lucy Catharine, 30 Nov. (427f)
10. Cynthia Louiza, (427g)
11. James Franklin, 1 Jan. (427h)

225. VI. Adam Alden, Stowe, Vt. son of Benjamin, (105).

CHILDREN

1. Ezra B. 2. Joseph. 3. Leslie. 4. John.

226. VI. Zen AS Alden, Lebanon, N. H. farmer, son of Joseph, (106) was b. 1 July, 1748, d. 1833, a. 85; m. Lydia Finney, who was b. 19 July, 1753, d. 1839, a. 86.

CHILDREN

1. A son; d. same day.
2. Lydia, who m. a Balch. (428)
3. *Zephaniah, d. a. 2 years.
4. Ziba. (429)
5. Lucinda. (430)
6. Susanna. (431)

7. Eliab, d. a. 3 years.
8. *Joseph, d. soon.
9. Zenas Phelps. (432)
10. Rosamond, m. a Gale of Royalton, Vt. (432a)

227. VI. Capt. Joseph Alden, Stafford, Ct. son of Joseph, (106) m. Lydia Hyde of Stafford.

CHILDREN

1. Martha. (433)
2. Clarissa. (434)
3. *Joseph.
4. Joseph.
5. Lydia. (4365

6. Horatio, 1 May, 1792. (436)
7. Hannibal, d. 1820.
8. Levi H. d. 24 Jan. 1812, a. 13.
9. Zephaniah
10. Almida. (437)

228. VI. Benjamin Alden, Stafford, Ct. son of Joseph, (106) m. went to Maine, had 10 ch. *Mrs. Zenas Alden.*

229. VI. Rev. Abishai Alden, Willington, Ct. Congregational minister, son of Joseph, (106) was b. 1765, d. 1833, a 68; gr. Dart. Coll. 1787; was ordained in Willington, Ct. in 1T91; dds. 1802, installed pastor, Montville, formerly New London, North, in 1803; dismissed Apr. 1826; minister at Grassy Hill, Lyme, Ct. from May, 1830 to May, 1831.

He m. Betsey Parker and had eight children, of whom I know only the names of Almira, Augustus, James Hillhouse, Betsey.

230. VI. Martha Alden, dau. of Joseph, (106) m. Oliver Pinney of Stafford, Ct. and had ten children.

Mrs. Zenas Alden.

231. VI. Sarah Alden of Stafford, Ct. dau. of Daniel, (107) m. Noah Davis of Stafford, Ct.

They had children, 1. Daniel, who m. a Chapin, and was rep. in 1812, 2. Sarah, who m. Abel Parsons of Somers. 3. Asenath, who m. Asa Patten of Stafford.

232. VI. Hannah Alden of Stafford, dau. of Daniel, (107) was b. in 1750; m. Moses Hibbard of Lebanon, N. H.

They had children, 1. *Moses, who d. in infancy. 2. Hannah, 21 Jan. 1789. She m. in 1812, Seth Estabrook of Lebanon, N. H. who went to Alden, N. Y. They had six children.

233. VI. Abigail Alden of Stafford, Ct. dau. of Daniel, (107) was b. Oct. 1750, and d. May, 1814, a. 64. She m. abt 1772, Jude Converse.

They had children, 1. Silence, who d. in 4 days. 2. Dorothy, 1774; m. Asaph Hyde, and had seven children. 3. Howard, 1776, d. at New Orleans, 1816. 4. Seth. 1778, who d. in Illinois abt 1823. 5. Jude, 1780, d. in Illinois 1816. 6. Abigail, 1782. who m. John Mansfield and had a family, 7. Daniel, 1784, who settled in Waterloo, Ill. where he d. much respected, in 1858, leaving a widow but no children. 8. Hannah, 1786, who m. 1805, Samuel Blodgett of Randolph, Vt., Royalton, Vt., where he kept a celebrated Hotel and finally removed to Brandon, Vt. They had 9 children. He d. in 1800; she d. in 1859. She m. 2, in 1790, Aaron Eaton of West Stafford, Ct. and had children, 59. Joshua Wells. 10, Luther, 1792. 11. Sarah, 1795.

234. VI. Daniel Alden, Stafford, Ct. and Lebanon, N. H, farmer, son of Deacon Daniel, (107) b, 1753, and d. of paralysis agitans, 27 Jan. 1817, a. 64. He was much respected.

He m. Sarah, dau. of Dea. Ezra Alden of Greenwich, Mass. (116) who was b. 1761, and d. 2 Dec. 1817, a 56.

CHILDREN

1. Daniel, 11 Feb. 1786, (438)	9. *Seth Turner, 5 Mar. 1800, d. 2 Aug. 1804.
2. Ezra, 8 Dec. 1787. (439)	
3. *John, 2 July, 1789 d, 3 Sept. 1789.	10. *Dorothy, 1 Apr. 1802, d. Aug. 1803.
4. Sally, 1 Nov. 1790. (440)	
5. *Roxana, 7 June, 1792: d. May, 1812, a. 20.	11. *Dorothy, 19 Jan. 1804, d. 3 May, 1804.
6. Elam, 22 Mar. 1794, (441)	12. * William, 1 Mar, 1806, d. same day.
7. Julius, 4 Jan. 1796. (142)	
8. Luther, 9 Aug. 1798. (443)	

235. VI. Dr. Ebenezer Alden, Randolph, Mass. Physician, son of Daniel, (107) was b. at Stafford, Ct. 4 July 1755; d. of typhoid fever at Randolph, 16 Oct. 1806, a. 51.

He received his academical education at Plainfield, Ct. under the tuition of Ebenezer Pemberton, Esq. and pursued his medical studies with Dr. Elisha Perkins, on the completion of which, he was invited to settle in Randolph, Mass. then the South Precinct in Braintree. He accepted the invitation, and from 1781, to the time of his death, a period of twenty-five years, he sustained an excellent reputation, and received his full share of medical patronage. A tribute to his memory written by his pastor. Rev. Jonathan Strong, D. D., may be seen in Alden's Epitaphs, vol. 3, art. 488, from which I extract the following paragraphs. "The duties of his profession he discharged with reputation to himself and great usefulness to his employers. His circle of business, although small at first, gradually increased until it became very extensive. As a physician he was remarkably prudent, attentive, and successful. During the latter part of his life, his advice was much sought, and respected by his brethren of the Faculty in his vicinity. No physician in this part of the country possessed the love and confidence of his patients to a higher degree. This was evident from the universal sorrow felt at his decease."

He was admitted a member of the Congregational Church in Randolph on the first Sabbath in June, 1788, and maintained a consistent religious profession until his death. He was a punctual attendant on public worship; never absenting himself from the House of God, except as required by the most urgent necessity. He was eminently a child of the covenant, his parents and grand parents and theirs' on both sides down to the first ancestors who came in the May Flower, having all been members of the Congregational church: and so far as is known, having honored their Christian profession.

Among his pupils may be named Doctors Isaac Alden, Darius Hutchins, Ziba Bass, Nathan Perry, Samuel White Thayer, and Jonathan Wild, H. U. 1804. He was a good instructor, as well as physician, performing the duties of every relation in life punctually and with the most scrupulous exactness.

He m. Apr. 1787, Sarah Bass, dau. of Col. Jonathan Bass. She was b. 24 Jan. 1760; d. 2 Dec. 1833, a. 74, and was a lineal descendant from Hon. John Alden, (1) through his dau. Ruth, (7) who m. John Bass, son of Dea. Samuel Bass, who came to Roxbury in 1630, and early removed to Braintree. She possessed great energy and decision of character; made a public profession of her faith in Christ at the same time with her husband, and was one of the best of mothers.

CHILDREN

1. Ebenezer, 17 Mar. 1788. (444)
2. Henry Bass, 7 June, 1791. (445)

3. Susanna, 7 Sept. 1793, who is (1866) unm. and resides on the old homestead.

236. VI. Jesse Alden, Cornish, N. H. farmer, son of Daniel, (107) was b. 30 May, 1762; d. of epidemic spotted fever, 2 Apr. 1813, a. 51. He m. Sarah, dau of Samuel Rice, who was b. 9 Feb. 1764, d. ___.

CHILDREN

1. Samuel Rice, 7 May, 1793, (446)
2. Amanda, 14 Dec. 1795, (447)
3. Sarah, 9 Jan. 1797, (448)
4. Jesse, 26 Nov. 1798, (449)
5. Harvey, 7 Jan. 1802, (450)
6. *David, 6 Mar. 1804, d. 17 May. 1806.

7. Hannah, 31 July, 1805 (451)
8. Betsey, 31 July, 1805 (452)
9. Mary, 30 Jan. 1808, unm. (1866) and resides at Lebanon, N. H. in the family of Col. Ezra Alden.

237. VI. Samuel Alden, A. M., Hanover, N. H., Druggist and trader, son of Daniel, (107) was b. at Stafford, Ct. 1768, d. at Hanover, N. H. of dropsy, 1842 a. 74. He grad. at Dartmouth College in 1795; engaged in commercial pursuits, first in his native town, in company with his brother in law, Dr. Samuel Willard, and afterwards at Hanover, N. H. where he passed the greater part of his life. In both places he was highly esteemed as an upright merchant and useful citizen. At one period his business was extensive as a druggist as well

as general trader. He was a member of the College Church at Hanover. He m. Abigail, dau. of Rev. John Willard, D. D. Harv. Coll. 1751, pastor of the Cong. Church at Stafford, Ct. She was an eminent Christian and d. of cancer, 13 Sept. 1832, after protracted suffering.

CHILDREN

1. Abigail Willard, 28 Oct. 1809, (453).

He m. 2, Mrs. Sarah Boardman, who survived her husband but a short time, dying in Ohio while on a visit to her son by a former husband.

238. VI. Dr. Isaac Alden, Plainfield, N. H. son of Daniel, (107) was b. at Stafford, Ct. 11 Feb. 1770; d. 25 Aug. 1845, a. 75.

He studied the profession of Medicine under the tuition of his brother Dr. Ebenezer Alden of Randolph, Mass. (235) and settled as a physician in Orange, Vt. and afterwards in Chelsea, Vt. where he was much respected as a citizen, and as a man, but never acquired an extensive practice. At length he relinquished medical pursuits and devoted himself to agriculture, removing to Plainfield, N. H. where he died. He was a modest, retiring man, but had many virtues, which were appreciated by those who knew him intimately. He m. Hannah Perry, b. in 1779, who survived him several years, being over eighty at the time of her death.

CHILDREN

1. Roxinda, 20 Mar. 1803, (454)
2. Fidelia, 12 Aug. 1805, (455)
3. Sarah Bass, 1 July, 1807, (456)
4. Lewis 20 Apr. 1811: d. 2 May, 1811.

5. Eliza Jane, 4 Mar. 1813: d, unm. abt. 1860.
6. Henry Bradley, 7 Aug. 1805, (457)

239. VI. Col, Amos Alden, Enfield, Ct., son of Jonathan, (112) m. Hannah Bush.

CHILDREN

1. Mary, 2. Hannah, 3. Amos, 4. Seth, 5. Lovice.

He m. 2 Elizabeth, clau. of Lemuel Kingsbury, widow of Elisha Pitkin of Hudson, N. Y.

240. VI. Jonathan Alden, son of Jonathan, (112) m. Mary: Merrill of Stafford, Ct.

241. VI. Mary Alden, dau. of Jonathan, (112) m. Stone, son of Simeon Stone, and went to Ruport, N. Y.

242. VI. Azubah Alden, dau. of Jonathan, (112) m. Ramsdale, son of Jacob Ramsdale.

243. VI. Huldah Alden, dau. of Jonathan, (112) m. Rufus Bush of Enfield, Ct.

244. VI. Dr. Howard Alden, Suffield,. Ct., son of Jonathan, (112) m. Rhoda, dau. of Consider Williston.

CHILDREN

1. Sarah. 2. Sidney. 3. Edwin. 4. Delia. 5. Leonard. 6. Howard. 7. Eliza Pitman. 8. George Williston. 9. Sarah King. 10. Julia.

I regret that I have received no further particulars of this family.

245. VI. Experience Alden, dau. of Jonathan (112) m. Randall Wheeler, of Greenwich, Mass.

246. VI. Martha Alden, dau. of Eleazer, (113) was b. 1752; d. 1802, a. 50. m. Sylvanus Blossom.

They had children, 1. Alden. 2. Libbeus.. 3. Sarah, who m. William Snell, Jun. Thayer.

247. VI. Abigail Alden, dau. of Eleazer, (113) was b. 23 Aug. 1756; m. William Snell, Esq.

They had children, William, Seth, Smerdis, Eleazer, Alden, Martin. Thayer.

248. VI. Hannah Alden, dau. of Eleazer, (113) was b. 1762; m. Levi Latham.

They had children, Nathaniel, Cyrus, Susanna, *Marcus, Robert, Marcus, Lewis, Hannah.

249. VI. Eleazer Alden, son of Eleazer, (113) was b. 21 Mar. 1767; m. Deborah Churchill, who d. 4 June, 1804.

CHILDREN

1. Lewis. 2. Isaac. 3, Rebecca.

250. VI. Isaac Alden, son of David, (44) was a magistrate, and d. in Warren County, Pa. a. 80. He m. Irene, dau. of Rev. Ebenezer Smith, a Baptist minister.

CHILDREN

1. Philander.	5. Isaac, (460)	9. Philo.
2. Philomela, (458)	6. Hiram. (461)	Thayer.
3. Joshua, (459)	7. Richard, (462)	
4. Pliny.	8. Enoch.	

251. VI. David Alden, Middlefield, O. son of David, (114) was m. 27 May, 1783, to Susanna Ward of Buckland, dau. of John Ward and his wife Mary Torrey.

CHILDREN

1. Ezra. 2. Lucy, (463). 3. Chandler, 4. Mary, 5. Lydia, 6. Enoch, 7. Susanna, 8. Hannah, 9. Sarah.

252. VI. Rev. John Alden, Ashfield, minister of the Baptist persuasion, son of David, (114) was b. 1761; d. 1842, a. 81, and inherited the paternal estate. He was a man of piety and respectable attainments, but the subject of some eccentricities of character. He m. Nancy, dau. of Jonathan Gray of Pelham Mass, who. was b. 23 Dec. 1771, and d. Mar. 1813, a. 42.

CHILDREN

1. Arion. | 2. Elizabeth, 7 Mar. 1789.

3. Eunice, 12 Sept. 1790;
4. Nancy, 10 Feb. 1792.
5. Armilla, 3 Dec. 1793.
6. Cyrus, 15 Aug. 1795, (464)
7. Lucy, 5 July, 1797.
8. Willard, 24 April 1800, (465)

9. Minerva, 1 June, 1802.
10. Habilla, 3 June, 1804.
11. John, 10 Jan. 1806, (466),
12. Sophronia, 23 Sept. 1808.
13. Lucy, 23 Aug. 1810.
14. David, 10 Feb. 1813, (467)

253. VI. Lydia Alden, dau. of David, (114) m. Jonathan Gray.

They had children, Elias, Irene, David, Lucy, Lydia, Levi, Nancy and Naomi.

Thayer.

254. VI. Dr. Enoch Alden, Rome and Redfield, N. Y., son of David, (114) m. Lucy Elmor. "He was a man of superior ability, — a great student, and for many years considered, while in Rome and Redfield, one of the best surgeons in the State of New York." *Rev, John Alden.*

255. VI. Sarah Alden of Greenwich, Mass. dau. of Dea. Ezra Alden, (116) m. Daniel Alden of Lebanon, N. H. (234).

256. VI. Judith Alden, dau. of Ezra, (116) nil. James Stone of Phillipston.

They had children, James, a physician, Jemima. Meriam, Abigail, Elizabeth, Sarah.

257. VI. Eunice Alden, dau. of Ezra, (116) was b. 13 Nov. 1766, d. 17 May, 1854; m. Capt. Abijah Powers, who was b. 18 Mar. 1761, d. 1814.

They had children, 1. John, 4 Apr. 1787. 2. Sally, 25 July, 1789, who m. 1813, Capt. Joseph Powers, and d. 16 Dec. 1865. 3. Benjamin, 10 May, 1792; d. 1855. 4. Horace, 29 July, 1794. 5. Alvah, 2 Aug, 1796; d. 23 Sept. 1824. 6. Cyrus, 16 Dec. 1804.

258. VI. Ezra Alden, Greenwich, Mass., farmer, son of Ezra, (116) was b. 25 July, 1769, d. 23 Nov. 1846, a. 77, of disease of the heart; m. Acsah, dau. of Dea. Nehemiah Stebbins, who d. 15 May, 1851.

CHILDREN

1. Pliny Allen, 1 Apr. 1792. (468)
2. Samuel, 25 Aug. 1793. (469)
3. Alma, 26 Aug. 1795. (470)
4. *Jason, 26 June, 1797; d. same day.
5. Abel, 23 July, 1799. (471)
6. Emery, 2 July, 1801. (472)
7. James, 10 Mar. 1804, d. 13 Mar. 1844.

8. Sally Colburn, 30 July, 1805, d. 31 Jan. 1809.
9. Festus, 5 May, 1808. (473)
10. James Milton, 21 June, 1810. (474)
11. Lyman, 31 Aug. 1812. (475)
12. Sarah, 13 Apr. 1818. (476)

259. VI. Dorothy Alden, dau. of Ezra. (116) m. Ebenezer Eaton of Danville, Vt. brother of Gen. William Eaton, and had three children.

260. VI. Anna Alden, dau. of Ezra, (116) m. Rev. Caleb Knight of Stafford, Ct. who gr. at Wms. Coll. 1800 j was a Congregational minister, who settled in Hinsdale, Mass. from whence he removed to the State of New York, where he d. in 1854, a. 83.

They had a son Charles Backus, and other children.

261. VI. Alice Alden, dau. of Ezra, (116) m. Eli Snow of Greenwich and Ware, Mass.

They had two daughters and one son who became a minister.

262. VI. Meriam Alden, Greenwich, Mass. dau. of Ezra, (116) m. Dea. — Gaston, and is supposed to be living in Illinois: has no children.

263. VI. Rev. Timothy Alden, D. D. Portsmouth, N. H. Meadville, Pa. son of Rev. Timothy Alden, (117) was b. in Yarmouth, Mass. 28 Aug. 1771; d. at Pittsburg, Pa. 5 July, 1839, a. 68. At the age of eight years he went to live with his uncle, Lt. Joshua Alden of Bridgewater, who offered to make him the heir of his farm; where he continued seven years. But as he manifested a much stronger inclination for literary than for agricultural pursuits, by his uncle's advice he relinquished farming, and commenced his studies preparatory to college with his father, which he completed at Phillips Academy, Andover. There, it is believed, he received his first religious impressions; and there he laid the foundation of those classical attainments for which he was distinguished. He entered Harvard College, in 1790, where he held a high rank as a scholar, especially in the ancient languages, and delivered a Syriac Oration when he graduated.

After he left College he instructed an Academy in Marblehead, pursuing simultaneously his studies for the ministry. For a time he was a resident graduate at Cambridge, receiving instruction from David Tappan, D. D., Professor of Theology in the University. In 1799, having been invited to preach at Portsmouth, N. H. he was ordained, 20 Nov. colleague with the venerable Samuel Haven, D. D. In 1800, he opened a school for young ladies in Portsmouth, which he continued during the summer months until he resigned his pastorate, 31 July, 1805, and then devoted his whole time to it, until 1808. In that year he removed to Boston and commenced a school, where his labors were highly appreciated, and he received the patronage of many respectable families. About this time he was appointed Librarian of the Mass. Historical Society and with great labor prepared a Catalogue of its books and pamphlets which was printed in 1811. Here also he had an opportunity of gratifying his antiquarian tastes. To the regret of many friends, in 1810 he left Boston to accept an appointment as instructor in the Young Ladies' Department in the Academy at Newark, N. J. From Newark he removed to the city of New York, where he opened a school for Young Ladies, in which he continued until his attention was arrested by a proposal to establish a College at Meadville, Pa. of which he was elected President, 28 July, 1817. Here he became interested in the condition of the Indians, and occasionally labored as a missionary among the Seneca and Mungee tribes. His last missionary tour was made in 1820.

In 1831 he resigned his connection with the College, and in 1832 opened a boarding school in Cincinnati. In 1833 he removed to East Liberty, near Pittsburgh Pa. and took charge of an Academy. During the year preceding his death he preached as a stated supply to the people in Sharpsburg, His last sermon was from 1 Pet. iv, 7; *But the end of all things is at hand.* His health, which had been good, about this time began to fail, and after a few weeks of intense suffering, mental and physical, he became calm, and died peacefully at the house of his daughter in Pittsburg. Rev. Mr. Todd preached his funeral sermon, and his remains were deposited in the burying ground at Sharpsburg, where he had commenced his labors one year before. A full obituary notice of him may be found in Rev. Dr. Sprague's Annals of the American Pulpit, vol. 2, p. 449-454.

He was a man of rare endowments, living in the past and future rather than in the present, — ardent in his feelings, enthusiastic in whatever employments he was engaged, yet easily discouraged; ready to embark in new schemes, then suddenly abandoning them; ever desirous of doing good, but often by methods which seemed to others, and proved to be impracticable. He m. Elizabeth Shepard, dau. of Capt. Robert Wormsted of Marblehead. She d. 3 Apr. 1820.

CHILDREN

1. Martha Wright, 1798. (477)
2. Elizabeth Shepard Wormsted, 1800. (478)
3. Timothy Fox, 1802. (479)
4. Robert Wormsted, 1804. (480)
5, Sarah Weld Josephine, Nov. 1812. (481)

He m. 2, in 1822, Sophia Louiza L. Mulcock of Reading, Pa., who is deceased and left one daughter, 6. Caroline, who m. has had four daughters, all now residing in Minnesota.

264. VI. Isaiah Alden, Yarmouth, son of Rev. Timothy, (117) was b. 22 Sept. 1772; gr. at Harv. Coll. 1799; d. 1843, a. 71. In 1817 he went to Meadville, Pa. where he was engaged in the instruction of youth. In 1801 he preached a Sermon on the death of Abraham Hedge, which was published. His name is not italicised on the Harvard Triennial, and it is believed that he was never ordained, devoting himself mainly to the instruction of youth.

He m. Susanna Hedge, dau. of Barnabas Hedge, Esq. of Yarmouth.

CHILDREN

1. Betsey. (482)
2. Eunice Weld.
3. Sarah Weld. (483)
4. Weld Noble.

265. VI. Rev, Martin Alden, Yarmouth, son of Rev. Timothy, (117) was b. in 17 Oct. 1773; gr. Harv. Coll. 1799, d. 1838, a. 65. He m. Mary Kingman.

CHILDREN

1. Albert. (484)
4. Timothy. (485)
5. *Caleb Holmes.
5. Isaiah. (486)
3. *Mary Kingman, 1813.
6. * Martin Luther.

266. VI. Oliver Alden, Charleston, S. C. son of Rev. Timothy, (116) was b. 9 Mar. 1775; was a merchant in the house of Crocker and Sturgis, and for many

years a magistrate. In 1829 he removed to Aldinia, a new village pleasantly situated on the Western shore of Konneyaut lake, Pa. He m. Lucy dau. of David Alden (251) of Williamstown, Mass. and afterwards of Batavia, O.

CHILDREN

1. Mary Ward.	4. Oliver Noble. (488)	7. Lucy.
2. Julia Ann.	5. Henry Williams. (489)	8. Clinton. (491)
3. David Chandler. (487)	6. Charles Fox. (490)	

267. VI. Sarah Weld Alden, Yarmouth, dau. of Her. Timothy, (117) was b. 17 Dec. 1776, d. July, 1847, a. 71; m. Capt. Isaac Matthews of Yarmouth, his 2 wife, who d. at sea, 5 Oct. 1827. They had no issue.

268. VI. Martha Shaw Alden, Yarmouth, dau. of Rev. Timothy, (117), was b. 8 Jan. 1778, d. 1857; m. Capt. Jeremiah Taylor, who having relinquished a seafaring life, settled on a farm in Hawley, Mass. where he d. 5 June, 1820, a. 53; leaving to a widowed mother in rather straitened circumstances, the maintenance and education of a large and interesting family of children, to which she proved herself fully competent. Four sons were educated for the ministry and became pastors of Congregational Churches, and adorned their profession.

Her children were, 1. Rev. Oliver. Alden, b. at Yarmouth, Mass. 18 Aug. 1801. and d. at Manchester, Mass. 18 Dec. 1801, a. 50 years and 4 months. He gr. at Union College in 1825, and at the Theological Institution, Andover Mass. in 1829. "He was a careful French, German, Latin, Greek, and Hebrew scholar; had studied the Rabbinic literature, and was no mean proficient in the Arabic." He spent several years at Andover in literary pursuits, preaching occasionally, as opportunities occurred. His publications, original and translated, mostly in the periodicals of the day, were numerous. While at Andover he prepared with great labor and accuracy, a Catalogue of the Seminary Library, which was printed in 1838. In Sept, 1839, he was installed pastor of the Congregational Church in Manchester, Mass. having previously received ordination as an evangelist, where he continued until his death. He m. in 1843, Mary, dau. of Nehemiah Cleaveland, M. D. of Topsfield. His library was rare and valuable. In 1853, a memoir of his life was published by his brother Rev. Timothy Alden Taylor, and subsequently an obituary notice of him by Rev. William B. Sprague, D. D, in his Annals of the American Pulpit. 2. *Myra, who d. a. 4 years. 3. Sarah, who m. Amariah D. Sproat of South Deerfield, and had seven children. 4. Martha, a teacher. 5. Mary Fox, who d. a. 2 years. 6. Rev. Timothy Alden, who was b. at Hawley, Mass. 7 Sept. 1809, and magnified his office, holding forth the word of life and giving it utterance kindly but with great plainness of speech. In his hands the silver trumpet never gave an uncertain sound. In him was most happily combined the pastor and scholar. He wrote much for various periodicals, also a Memoir of his elder brother. In 1850 he published an extended treatise on some of the doctrines, duties, and dangers of the Christian Pilgrim, entitled Zion's Pathway, which he dedicated to his three brothers in the ministry, of which it has been truly said, — "It is a pleasant, practical and complete compendium of systematic Theology, popularly stated and illustrated." At the time of his death he was preparing a Memoir of his honored mother, whom he survived but a few months. His funeral sermon was preached by the venerable Thomas Shepard, D. D. of Bristol, R. I., who also preached his ordination sermon. His people testified their respect for his memory by erecting over his grave a beautiful monument of Italian marble. The Congregational Quarterly for 1859, to which I am indebted for some of the preceding facts, contains (a more extended notice of his life and labors. 7. Rev. Rufus Taylor, Shrewsbury, N. J. gr. Amh. Coll. 1837; studied theology at Princeton, N. J.; was ordained at Shrewsbury, 10 Nov. 1840. dis. Apr. 1852; installed at Manchester, Mass. 6 May, 1852, dismissed Dec. 1857. He is now (1866) District Secretary of the Am. and For. Uh. Union at Philadelphia; his residence at Princeton. N. J. He m. Esther, dau. of Dea. Daniel Williams, Ashfield Mass. has children, the eldest of whom is expected to graduate this month, June 1866, at Nassau Hall. 8. Mary Joice, living in Plainfield, Mass. 9. Mira, who m. Joseph W. Russell, and resides in Dalton, Mass. 10. Rev. Jeremiah, D. D., b. 11 June, 1817; gr. at Amherst College, 1843; was ordained pastor of the ancient church in Wenham, Mass. 27 Oct. 1847, his three brothers being present and assisting in his induction into the pastoral office; was dismissed 19 Aug. 1856, installed pastor of the first church in Middletown, Ct. 1 Oct. 1856, where he still resides. Hem. 1849, Elizabeth, dau. of Dr. William Pride, of Springville. Pa. and has children.

269. VI. Daniel Alden, North Bridgewater, Mass., carpenter, son of Samuel, (121) b. __, d. 10 Sept. 1799; m. 18 Dec. 1786, Sally, dau. of Jonathan Gary, who d. 5 Mar. 1846, a. 83.

CHILDREN

1. Otis. (492)
2. Daniel, 10 June, 1791. (493)
3. Sally. (494)
4. Alpheus, 16 Apr. 1798. (495)

270. VI. Deacon Silas Alden, Jay, Maine, carpenter and farmer, son of Samuel, (121) b. 5 Aug. 1765, d. 18 Apr. 1842, a. 77; m. Charity Staples of Falmouth, Me.

CHILDREN

1. Sybil, b. 29 Apr. 1798. (496)
2. *Samuel, d. 1799.
3. Hannah, 31 July, 1799, d. young
4. Sylva, 30 Jan. 1801. (497)
5. *Charity, 11 Jan. 1803, d. young
6. Silas, 3 Oct, 1804. (498)
7. Eliza, 17 Mar. 1806. (499)
8. Williams, 11 Oct. 1807. (500)
9. *Isaiah, 11 Mar. 1809, d. young.
10. * Male inf. 2 Aug. 1810.
11. Winslow, 1 June, 1812. (501)
12. Lovina, 5 July, 1814. (502)
13. *Lucinda, 21 Oct. 1816, d. 1827.
14. Male, 5 Mar. 1818, d.
15. Eleanor Quint, 16 Oct. 1820. (501)

271. VI. Joseph Alden, Jay, Maine, carpenter and farmer, son of Samuel, (121) b. __, d. 1851, a. over 80. An obituary notice was published in Zion's Advocate, which I have not seen. He m. Prudence Macomber.

CHILDREN

1. Betsey. (504)
2. Lucy. (505)
3. Joanna, d. unm.
4. Joseph. (506)
5. Mary. (507)
6. Elijah. (508)
7. Almira. (509)

272. VI. Samuel Alden, Abington, Mass., farmer, lived on the homestead of his father, Samuel Alden, (121) b. __, d. 20 May, 1857; m. 1799, Sally, dau. of Mark Ford, who d. 10 Aug. 1847.

CHILDREN

1. Sanford. (510)
2. Mehetabel. (511)
3. Hannah. (512)
4. Sally. (513)

273. VI. Williams Alden, North Bridgewater, carpenter and farmer, son of Samuel, (121) b. 1772. d. 16 Feb. 1856, a. 84; m. 1803, Thankful, dau. of Dea, William Linfield of Randolph, d. 20 Aug. 1847.

CHILDREN

1. Mary. 1805. (514) | 2. Lavinia, 1807. (515) | 3. Clarissa, 1809. (516)

274. VI. Hannah Alden, dau. of Samuel, (121), m. Seth. Copeland of W. Bridgewater, and had three children.

275. VI. Deacon Seth Alden, East Stoughton, Mass. carpenter, son of Samuel, 121, b. 3 Nov. 1777, d. 3 June, 1838, a. 61; a deacon in the Baptist church; m. 11 Jan, 1802, Harmony, dau. of Perez Southworth, who was b. 1781, d. 24 May, 1823.

CHILDREN

1. *Lysander, 12 Aug. 1804, d. 28 Nov. 1808.
2. Eunice, 27 Nov. 1806. (517)
3. Azel, 1 Mar, 1809. (518)
4. and 5. * Twins, 22 Feb. 1811, d. same day.
6. Lysander, 21 Jan. 1812. (519)
7. Samuel, 12 Sept. 1814. (520)
8: *Adoniram Judson, 30 May, 1817 h d. burned to death, 22 Nov. 1819.
9. Adoniram Judson, 25 Nov. 1819. (521)
10. Southworth, 13 May, 1825 (522)
11. Seth, 13 May, 1826, 1825.

He m. 2, Betsey,, dau. of Nathaniel Littlefield, who was b. 3 Oct. 1790, and d. 28 Jan. 1842.

12. Ann Amelia. 3 Aug. 1826. (524)
13. Nathaniel Littlefield, 13 June, 1828. (525)
14. Isaac, 10 Dec. 1830. (526)
15. James. 7 Sept. 1835. (527)

276. VI. Hosea Alden, Abington, Mass. farmer, son of Samuel, (121) who d. 5 Mar. 1837, m. 1817, Mille, dau. of William Edson, who d. 1851.

CHILDREN

1. Daniel (528) | 2. Abigail (529) | 3. Luther Edson. (530)

277. VI. Elijah Alden, Brimfield, Ludlow, son of Josiah, (122) was a soldier in 1775, in the eight months' service; was a prisoner in Quebec, 31 Dec. 1775. See Gen. Reg. 1852, p. 133; m. Rebecca Fuller.

CHILDREN

1. Martha. 2. Elijah. 3. Marilla. 4. Sophronia.

278. VI. Azel Alden, or Hazael, Ludlow, carriage maker, son of Josiah, (122) b. 1770, d. 1854, a, 84; m. 1791, Bethany Wilbor.

CHILDREN

1. Stillman. (531)	4. Bethany. (534)
2. Lovina. (532)	5. Solomon. (535)
3. Josiah. (533)	6. Mary. (536)
m. 2, Cynthia Snell.	

279. VI. Abiah Alden, dau. of Josiah, (122) m. Benjamin Winchester.
280. VI. Charity Alden, dau. of Josiah, (122) m. Peter Trask of Randolph, Vt.
281. VI. Josiah Alden", Ludlow, farmer, son of Josiah, (122) b. 1773, d. 3 Sept. 1833, a. 80; m. Olive Brown.

CHILDREN

1. Azel. (537)	5. Washington Brown. (541)	9. Oranius. (545)
2. Justin. (538)	6. Charles. (542)	10. Eunice. (546)
3. Charity. (539)	7. John. (543)	He m. 2, Wid. Mary
4. Zenas. (540)	8. Mary. (544)	Bates; had no children.

282. VI. Lucy Alden, dau. of Josiah, (122) m. Amos Fletcher, tailor.
They had children, 1. Bathsheba. 2. Charity, twins. 3. Erastus. 4. Zebina. 5. Amos. 6. Nathan.
283. VI. Rebecca Alden, dau. of Josiah, (122) m. Benjamin Snow, farmer, Belchertown.
They had children, 1. James, deaf mute. 2. Rebecca. 3. Isaac. 4. Lucinda. 5. Lois. 6. Ambrose.
284. VI. Benjamin Alden, son of Josiah, (122) m. Polly Hodges.

CHILDREN

1. Mary. (547)	4. David. (550)	7. Eliza. (553)
2. Jefferson. (548)	5. Dexter. (551),	
3. Caroline. (549)	6. Lucinda. (652)	

285. VI. Simeon Alden, Randolph, Mass., currier, son of Simeon, (123) b. 29 Feb. 1764, d. 2 Apr. 1843, a. 79; m. 1785, Rachel, dau. of Joshua French of Randolph, who was b. 30 June, 1765, d. 22 Feb. 1844. a. 79.

CHILDREN

1. Horatio Bingley, 16 March, 1786. (554)
2. *John, 1787, d. 14 Oct. 1798.
3. Hosea. 1789. (555)
4. Rachel, 1792. (556)
5. Pally, 1797. (557)
6. John, 1799. (558)
7. Hiram, 1804. (559)
8. *Isaac, 1807, d. 19 Mar. 1827.

286. VI. Alpheus Alden, Newton, Boston, Randolph, bootmaker, son of Simeon, (123) was b. 27 Apr. 1765, d. 24 Mar. 1820. a. 55; m. Betsey Smith of Boston, who was b. June, 1773.

CHILDREN

1. Simeon, 14 Apr. 1793. (560)
2. Betsey, 1795, d. 1802.
3. Lucinda, 1797. (561)
4. Alpheus, 1800, d. 1802.
5. Elizabeth, 18 Dec. 1803, unm.

287. VI. Silas Alden, Randolph, boot-manufacturer, son of Simeon, (123) was b. 29 June, 1766, d. — May. 1845, a. 79; m. Polly, dau. of Thomas French, 3; who was b. 1765, d. 14 Oct., 1810, a. 45.

CHILDREN

1. Silas, 1786. (562)
2. Calvin, 1788. (563)
3. Samuel, 1790. (564)
4. Polly, 1792. (565)
6. *Adoniram, 1794, d. 24 Apr. 1816.
6. Leonard, 1796. (566)
7. Thomas, 1798, d. 1820.
8. *Cynthia, 1801, d. 1805.
9. Melinda, 1803. (567)
10. Sally French, 1803, unm.
11. Sukey French, 1803, unm.
12. Cynthia, 1808. (568)
13. Silence, 1810. (569)
He m. 2, Wid. Charlotte Thayer; no children.

288. VI. Solomon Alden, Lynn, Saugus, son of Simeon, (123) b. 1767, d. Lynn, 4 May, 1815, a. 48; m. 1795, at Newton, Hannah, dau. of John Stone, Jun.

CHILDREN

1. Hannah, 10 Oct. 1795. (570)
2. Betsey, 25 May, 1796. (571)
3. John, 23 Feb. 1799. (572)
4. Joseph, 25 Aug. 1801. (573)
5. Solomon, 16 Apr. 1803. (574)
6. Mary, 29 Sept. 1806. (575)
7. Davul, 17 Dec. 1808. (576)
8. William, 30 May, 1810. (577)
9. Martha, 16 June, 1813, d. 25 Nov. 1813.

289. VI. Mary Alden, dau. of Simeon, (123) was b. 1769, d. 1847; m. a Chamberlain of Roxbury.

Had a daughter, 1. *Betsey. She m. 2, Martin Conning of Boston, baker. They had children, 2. Mary. 3. Maria, who m. Mr. Taylor of Boston. 4. Isaac. 5. Henry.

290. VI. David Alden, Boston, son of Simeon, (123) was b. 1771, d. 1801, a. 30; m. Rachel ___.

CHILDREN

1. John Adams, (578)

2. David Tolman, (579)

291. VI. Jonathan Alden, Watchtown, Randolph, Baltimore, merchant and accountant, son of Simeon, (123) was b. 6 Apr. 1775, d. 13 Mar. 1820,m. 1797, Beulah Crafts, dau. of Joseph Crafts.

CHILDREN

1. Sally, 29 June, 1797, (580)
2. Nancy, 30 Jan. 1799, (581)
3. Jonathan, (582)
He m. 2 Mehetabel, dau. of Capt. John Tolman, had ch.
4. John Tolman, 1806, (583)
5. David, 1807.

6. Mehetabel, 1809, d. Fairhaven, Vt. 18129.
7. Elizabeth Fisher, 1811, d. Fairpoint, Vt. 16 Jan. 1836.
8. Caroline, (585)
9. Gilbert, 1815, d. Fairhaven, Vt. 24 Nov. 1830.
10. Susan, June, 1819, (586)

292. VI. Isaac Alden, Walpole, Mass., son of Simeon, (123) b. 1777, d. Apr. 1846, in Boston. In 1802, taught a singing school in Randolph, Mass. It is understood that he was twice married and left children, whose names, if received in time, will be entered at no's. 587-589.

293. VI. Lot Alden, Salem, Mass., son of Simeon, (123) b. 1781, d. Salem, 29 Aug. 1854, a. 73 V. 5 mo; m. Susan Richards of Newton, Mass., who d. 30 July, 1859, a. 77.

CHILDREN

1. Granville, (590)
2. Warren, (591)
3. Putnam d. in West Indies.

4. Bradford, d.
5. Dudley, d.
6. Julia Ann, (592)
7. *A son.

8. Miranda, (593)

294. VI. Caleb Alden, Bridgewater, son of Oliver, (124) b. 14 Nov. 1766, d. 20 Apr. 1846; m. 1790, Sally, dau. of Benjamin Hayward, who d. 29 Oct. 1847, a. 79.

CHILDREN

1. Oliver, 30 Aug. 1792, (594)
2. Sally, 25 Feb. 1794, (595)
3. Mehetabel, 25 July, 1795, (596)

4. Susan, 22 April, 1798. (597)
5. Cromwell, 22 Sept. 1800, (698)
6. Mary, 2 Aug. 1806.

295. VI. Experience Alden, dau. of Oliver, (124) b. 25 Feb. 1779, d. 3 Mar. 1861; m. 1800, Sylvanus Pratt.

They had children, 1. Experience, 21 July, 1804, who m. Benjamin Pope. 2. Mary W. 1 May, 1809, who m. B. Crocker.

296. VI, Seth Alden, Bridgewater, son of Seth, (125) removed to Maine; m. Sally, dau. of William Snell.

CHILDREN

1. William Snell, b. in South Bridgewater in 1840. (599)

297. VI. Mehetabel Alden, dau. of Joseph, (126) b. 28 Oct. 1776, d. 6 Mar. 1813; m. 1797, Thomas Mitchell of Enfield, Mass., who was b. 1765, d. 24 Mar. 1843.

They had children, 1. Sally, 1798. 2. Calvin, 1800, whose name was changed to Marcus Milton, and d. 1839. 3. Alden, 1804. 4. William, 1806. 6. George Washington, 1808, d. St. Augustine, 10 Mar. 1836. 6. Jane, 1811.

298. VI. Capt. Joseph Alden, Bridgewater, farmer, son of Joseph, (126) b. 24 May, 1777, d. 20 Dec. 1852, a. 75; m. 1800, Polly, dau. of Amos Hay ward. She d. 31 July, 1842, a. 69.

CHILDREN

1. Addison. 27 Sept. 1801 (600)
2. Almeda, 24 July, 1803. (601)
3. Amelia, 11 July, 1806, d. 19 Aug. 1848.
4. Amos, 29 June, 1808. (602)
5. Amanda, 12 June, 1811.
6. Alexander, Sept. 1814. (603)

299. VI. Daniel Alden, Belchertown, farmer, son of Joseph, (126) b, 29 Jan. 1780, d. of schirrus stomach, 15 Oct. 1856, a. 76; m. Joanna, dau, of Ephraim Tillson, who was b. 17 Nov. 1784, d. 26 Sept. 1856, a. 72.

CHILDREN

1. Daniel, 23 Feb. 1806, (604)
2. Joanna, 17 May, 1807.
3. Orlando Tillotson, 29 Sept. 1808. (605)
4. Freeman, 21 Dec. 1809. (606)
6. Bethiah Carver, 22 Dec. 1811.
6. Joseph, 18 June, 1813. (607)
7. Emily, 16 June, 1815. (608)
8. Thomas, 21 June, 1817. (609)
9, Maria, 16 Mar. 1819, d. 10 May, 1863, a, 44.
10. Cornelia, 29 Jan. 1821, d. 26 Sep. 1823.
11. Caroline, 29 Jan. 1821; resides in Roxbury.
12. Sarah Church, 22 Mar. 1823, teacher.

300. VI. Thomas Alden, Bridgewater, farmer, son of Joseph, (126) b. 6 Dec. 1782, d. 27 Oct. 1850, a. 68; m. 1815, Matilda, dau. of Daniel Copeland, who d. 1 June 1849.

CHILDREN

1. *Thomas, 21 Aug. 1816, d. 7 Mar. 1817.
2. Matilda Copeland, 18 April 1818, (610)
3. Elizabeth Brown, 4 Feb. 1820, (611)

301. VI. Cyrus Alden, Esq., Boston, Fall River, attorney at law, son of Joseph, (126) b. 20 May, 1785, at Bridgewater d. Tiverton, R, I. 29 Mar. 1855, a. 70.

He gr. at Brown U. in 1807; pursued the studies of the law with Judge Rice, Litchfield, Ct., and with Hon. William Baylies of West Bridgewater, Mass., and was admitted to the bar at Plymouth, Mass. in 1810. He commenced the practice of law the same year at Wrentham, Mass., where he pursued his profession six years and then removed to Boston where he continued six years, and then went to Fall River. In 1837 he represented that town in the Legislature. In 1819 he published a work entitled "Abridgement of Law with practical Forms," 8 vo. 800 pages.

In 1849 he made an unsuccessful effort to secure a meeting of the descendants of Hon John Alden with a view of erecting a monument to his memory.

He went so far as to suggest an inscription for the monument which he proposed should be erected in Bridgewater, rather than in Duxbury, as being more accessible and in his view quite as appropriate. It was substantially as follows:

Hon, John Alden,
Born in Old England in 1599,
Died in New England, 1687,
First of the Pilgrim Band to tread on Plymouth Rock 1620.
For many years one of the Governor's Assistants,
The greater portion of his life an efficient Magistrate;
A christian in whom was no guile.
As a neighbor, the good Samaritan;
As a civil officer, without reproach.
His mortal remains rest in Duxbury.
This monument erected to his memory by his descendants, 1852.

From a letter received from him at that time, several of the preceding facts were obtained. He was a worthy man and had a good reputation in his profession.

He m. 24 May, 1813, Mary Margaret, dau. of Alexander and Mary Farquhar Jones of Providence, R. I.

CHILDREN

1. Mary Jones, 13 Mar. 1811. (612)
2. Charles James, 18 Mar. 1816. (613)
3. Caroline Perkins. (614)
4. Jane Frances, 4 Oct. 1821. (615)
5. *William Baylies, 30 July, 1828, d. 8 June, 1829.
6. Eliza Wood, 21 May, 1826. (616)
7. Harriet Farquhar, 14 April, 1829. (617)
8. *Alexander Joseph, 25 Feb. 1834 d. 28 June, 1835.

302. VI. Eunice Alden, dau. of Joseph, (126) b. 1788, d. unm. 30 Mar. 1830, a. 42.

303. VI. Bethiah Alden, dau. of Joseph, (126) b. 14 June, 1790; m. 1813, Alfred Arnold of Enfield, Mass.

They had children, 1. William Frederic. 2. Eunice Alden. 3. Eliza Ann. 4. Frances Maria. 5. Sarah Jane. 6. Mary Miles.

304. VI. Rev. Seth Alden, Marlborough, Mass., clergyman, son of Joseph, (126) was b. in Bridgewater, Mass., 21 May, 1793, d. suddenly 13 Nov. 1853.

He gr. at Brown U. 1814, was ordained in Marlborough, W. Par. 3 Nov. 1819; was dismissed Apr. 1834. Am. Qu. Reg. 11. 250. He afterwards preached in Brookfield, Southborough, and Lincoln; in the latter about five years. While supplying a pulpit in Westborough on the Sabbath Nov. 13, as above, he fell back suddenly and expired. Ch. Register. He m. Mary D. Miles, dau. of Rev. John Miles, who d. 1825, a. 26.

CHILDREN

1. John Carver, 29 July, 1823. (618)   2. *William Bradford, 1825, d. 1825.

He m. 2, Persis, dau. of Dea. Benjamin Rice of Marlborough, who was b. 1804.

3. Mary-Denny, 23 Nov. 1832. (619)
4. Benjamin Franklin Rice, 9 Dec. 1834. (620)
5. *William Bradford.
6. Edward Winslow, 24 Oct. 1840. (621)
7. Adeline Augusta, 21 Sept. 1842. (622)
8. Susan Elizabeth, 12 Sept. 1343.

305. VI. Betsey Alden, dau. of Joseph, (126) was b. 13 Oct. 1796, d. 24 Apr. 1838, a. 42; m. 23 Nov. 1823, Joseph Hooper, Jun., b. 1793.

They had children, 1. Betsey, 6 June, 1827. 2. Eunice Alden, 4 Dec. 1830' who m. Albert H. Blanchard, and has four children.

306. VI. Sarah Alden, dau. of Solomon, (127) b. 1756 m. Azel Shaw, Bridgewater.

They had children, Alexander, Soranus, Charles, Azel, and others.

Hist. Bridgewater.

307 VI. Solomon Alden, Esq. Bridgewater, farmer, son of Solomon, (127) b. 1757, d. 28 Aug. 1852, a, 94 V. 8 mo. 20 days; m. 1782, Patty King.

CHILDREN

1. Solomon. 1787. (623)
2. Mary, 1789. (621)
3. *Nancy, 1793, d. 1800.
4. Sarah, 1795. (625)
5. Lewis Thomas, 1798. (626)

308. VI. Noah Alden, Bridgewater, son of Solomon, (127) m. Elizabeth Miller of Middleborough and went to Illinois.

CHILDREN

1. Noah.   2. Hiram.

309. VI. Alexander Alden, Bridgewater. son of Solomon, (127) went to Maine; m. 1792, Lucy Leonard.

310. VI. Amasa Alden, Bridgewater, son of Solomon, (127) m. 1799, Sally Hathaway.

CHILDREN

1. Abigail, who m.	2. Sarah, who m. Darius Dunbar.

311. VI. Hannah Alden, dau. of Solomon, (127) m. 1796. Seth Miller, Esq.

312. VI. Bethany Alden, dau. of Solomon, (127) m. Eliphalet White.

313. VI. Mary Alden, dau. of Solomon, (127) m. Elijah Alden, (151).

314. VI. Caleb Alden, Lyme, N. H., farmer, son of Dea. David, (128) was b. 26 Oct. 1759, and d. 20 Jan. 1802, a. 42 y. 2 m. 29 d.; m. 1788, Susanna, dau. of Jesse Dunbar, who was b. 1763, d. 1834, a. 71.

CHILDREN

1. Jesse, 1 Aug. 1789. (627)	3. Ezra, 1791. (629)	7. Susan. (633)
2. Caleb, 30 Jan. 1790. (628)	4. Betsey. (630)	8. Azubah. (634)
	5. Martha. (631)	
	6. David. (632)	

315. VI. Rufus Alden, Middleboro', Mass., son of David, (128) m. Sally Shaw of Raynham.

CHILDREN

1. *Ezra, d, young.	5. Darius. (636)	9. Rufus, (639)
2. Apollos, (635)	6. Abigail (637)	10. Rhoda, d. unm.
3. Silas, (635)	7. Sally, d. unm. 1857.	
4. Enoch.	8. Chloe. (638)	

316. VI. David Alden, Middleboro', Mass., farmer, son of David, (128) b. 30 June, 1767, d. 13 Mar. 1850. He m. 1788, Betsey, dau. of Levi and Molly Hathaway of Middleboro'. She was b. 21 Feb. 1771, d. 27 Oct. 1852.

CHILDREN

1. David, 10 Oct. 1789. (639a)	2. Oliver Hathaway. (639b)

317. VI. Andrew Alden, North Middleboro', son of David, (128) m. Silence Fobes.

CHILDREN

1. Jason Fobes, 22 Jan. 1792. (640)	2. Philander. (641)	4. Horatio H. (643)
	3. Andrew L. (642)	5. Josiah Vaughn. (644)

318. VI. Huldah Alden, dau. of David, (128) m. Zachary Weston and had five children.

319. VI. Rhoda Alden, dau. of David, (128) m. — Yaughn.

320. VI. Job Alden, North Middleboro', Mass., son of Job, (131) was b. 29 Nov. 1768; m. Lydia Shaw, had ten children, of whom eight lived to adult age. Mrs. Z. Alden.

CHILDREN

1. Peter. (645)
2. Paraclete. (646)
3. Zephaniah Shaw. (647)
4. Lois. (648)
5. Lydia. (649)
6. Lucy. (650)
7. Mary, d. Tinm. Hallowell, Me.
8. Maria Otis, unm.

321. VI. Peter Oliver Alden, Middleboro', Mass., son of Job, (131) was b. 20 Aug. 1772; gi\ Bro. Un. 1792. He is not starred in the Triennial of 1860, but if living, his residence is not known to me.

322. VI. Ebenezer Alden, Union, Me., son of Job, (131) was b. 20 Sept. 1774, d. 10 Aug. 1862, a. 88; m. Patience Gilmore; was many years post master.

CHILDREN

1. Horatio, 1800. (651)
2. Louiza, 1802. (652)
3. Silas, 1804. (653)
4. *Selina, 1806, d. 1807.
5. Lyman, 1808. (654)
6. Melina, 1811. (635)
7. Augustus, 1814. (656)
8. Ebenezer, 1816. (657)
9. James Gillmor, 1819. (658)
10. Edward, 1821. (659)
11. *Henry, 1824, d. 1847.
12. *George Adelbert, 1818, d. 1829.

323. VI. Spooner Alden, Bangor, Me., or vicinity, son of Job, (131) b. 13 Sept. 1779; m. and had four children whose names, if received in time, will be inserted at no's. 660-663.

324. VI. Augustus Alden, Esq. Hallowell, Me. attorney at law, son of Job, (131) b. 16 June, 1781; gr. Dart. Coll. 1802, d. 1850, a. 69; m., no children.

325. VI. Eliab Alden, Cairo, N. Y., son of Eliab, (145) m. Mehetabel Stevens.

CHILDREN

1. Amanda. (664)
2. Abner. (665)
3. Charles. (666)
4. John. (667)
5. La Fayette. (668)
6. Henry. (669)
7. Oramel. (670)

326. VI. Abner Alden, M. D. Bridgewater, Mass., physician, son of Eliab, (145) was b. 1790, d. at Bridgewater, 1818, a. 28. He was a promising young man: received his medical education in the city of New York; and had just commenced the practice of his profession, when he was stricken down by a fever then prevalent, which proved fatal.

327. VI. Levi Hathaway Alden, Windham, N. Y., blacksmith, son of Eliab, (145) was b. at Wareham, Mass., 28 Aug. 1793: went early with his father to Cairo, N. Y.: learned the trade of a blacksmith, which he pursued at Windham, N. Y., with which he connected brick making and accumulated considerable

property. In 1812 he was drafted as a soldier, and was appointed sergeant. At the close of the war he returned to his employment, which he continued in connection with carriage building until 1836. He then engaged in farming and the lumbering business. In 1841 he purchased a site for a tannery in Wayne Co. Pa., and committed to two of his sons the charge of erecting buildings. The place was named Aldenville, and one of his sons was appointed postmaster. In 1850 he visited his sons, also a sister of his wife resident at Carbondale, Pa., where after a brief illness he died of typhoid fever, 5 Aug. 1850, a. 57. He was buried at Aldenville, and a suitable monument placed over his grave by his sons.

In 1828 he was appointed Justice of the Peace, and in 1840 Associate Judge to fill a vacancy in Greene County, N. Y. He was an enterprising man of business, of sober life and conversation; and an Episcopalian by religious profession which he adorned, and his end was peace.

He m. 23 Jan. 1817, Amanda, dau. of Jahiel Tattle,, who was b. 7 Jan. 1798: d. 9 Mar. 1864.

CHILDREN

1. James M. 21 Apr. 1818. (671)
2. Julius Tattle, 18 Feb. 1821. (672)

3. Levi Hathaway, 1 Jan. 1825. (673)

328. VI. Rev. Charles Henry Alden, Chaplain U. S. N., son of Eliab, (145) was b, at Lyme, Ct. 17 June, 1798: d. Pensacola, Florida, 24 Sept. 1846. He was fitted for College, but prevented by continued ill health from pursuing a collegiate course. In 1820 he went to Rhode Island and studied Theology with Bishop Griswold, teaching during the time in Bristol: was ordained by him in 1823, and for more than two years taught a classical school in Greenwich, R. I., preaching in a small church there. In 1825, he removed his school to Providence, that he might supply the church in Bristol during the Bishop's absence on official duty; but he was soon obliged from sudden, severe attacks of illness to relinquish preaching. In 1829 his health so utterly failed that his school was given up, and a change of climate and entire rest from all mental labor was decided to be the only chance of recovery, or of life. The winter of 1829-30 was passed in Savannah, Ga. In June he returned much benefitted. Physicians, advising him to try a milder climate than New England, after teaching a year in Princeton, N. J., he opened a High School for young ladies in Philadelphia, on an extended and liberal plan, preaching frequently on the Sabbath. In the midst of great success his health again failed, and, hoping that a sea life would improve it, he obtained a chaplaincy in the Navy. In 1841, he joined the Flag Ship Delaware, and went with the squadron to S. America, where he remained eighteen months, then to the Mediterranean, visiting several important places in Spain, Portugal and Italy. During his absence he wrote for the North American, published in Philadelphia, and his letters were highly appreciated. Nothing beautiful or rare escaped his notice. On his return, after remaining with his family about a year, he was ordered to Pen-

sacola, Fa. Here his duties were very arduous. It was during the war with Mexico, and the sick were constantly brought to the hospitals, and on the Sabbath the beautiful little chapel at the Navy Yard was filled with attentive listeners. A Sabbath school, singing school and library were commenced, and when each day his labors seemed more abundant and more blessed he was called away to a higher and more glorious life; his faith was triumphant, and he felt that to die was gain. At his request a *post mortem* examination was made, and it was found that his protracted sufferings were not occasioned by dyspepsia, but by an unusual disease of the heart. Tumors had formed within it and had nearly stopped the circulation of the blood. The immediate cause of death was yellow fever. To the bereaved consort I am indebted for the principal facts contained in the preceding statement, which I could not well condense. In the Providence Journal an obituary notice of Mr. Alden, written by Gov. Anthony, now U. S. Senator, was published soon after his death. After reciting several of the preceding facts, he thus concludes: "Mr. Alden was a fine scholar, and a man of excellent literary taste; of polished manners, and of true kindness of heart. As an instructor he leaves but few equals behind him. His excellence consisted not only in his singular capacity for imparting knowledge, and impressing it upon the youthful mind, but in his captivating manners, and the confidence and affection which he never failed to inspire, in all who came under his teaching. This brief notice is written by one who bears grateful recollection of his fidelity as an instructor, and who knew his worth as a man, and who tenders to his stricken family the sympathy of one who can well appreciate the loss of such a husband and father. He m. 9 June, 1825, Alice Burrington Wight, dau. of Rev. Henry Wight, Bristol, R. I. She was b, 10 Feb. 1800. Her mother descended from John Alden, and often said "she was more proud of her puritan descent, than if she had been heir to a kingdom." Her mother Abigail Alden was dau. of David of Middleboro', and m. Z. Leonard, and had several children, one of whom lived over one hundred years. Mrs. Wight d. in Georgia in Sept. 1865, at the age of 93, "true to her country and its flag," retaining her faculties to the last, and dying a most triumphant death.

CHILDREN

1. Abby Frances, b. Providence, R. I. July, 1826.
2. Georgie Anna, b. Savannah, Ga. 12 Apr. 1830.
3. Charles Henry, b. Philada. 28 Apr. 1836. (674)

329. VI. Mary Alden, dau. of Eliab, (145) m. James Kortz of Catskill, N. Y. They had children, 1. Charles. 2. John.

330. VI. Rev. Joseph Alden, D. D., New York City, son of Eliab, (145) was b. 4 Jan. 1807; gr. Un. Coll. 1828; studied divinity at Princeton, N. J.; was ordained pastor of the Congregational church at Williamstown, Mass. 3 July, 1834; dismissed on account of a failure in his voice after six months. In 1835 he was elected Professor of Rhetoric, Political Economy and History, in Williams College, from which office he retired in 1852; was soon after appointed Pro-

fessor of Moral Philosophy and Metaphysics in Lafayette Coll. Pa., and was six years President of Jefferson College, Pa.

He has written many juvenile books and much for the public papers, particularly for the New York Observer; and more recently a work on Mental Philosophy, which has been highly commended, entitled "Elements of Intellectual Philosophy;" also "The Science of Government in connexion with American Institutions," and "Christian Ethics, or the Science of Duty." He received the degree of D. D. at Union Coll., and L. L. D. at Columbia Coll.

He m. in 1834, Isabel Graham, dau. of Rev. Gilbert R. Livingston, D. D., of Philad. b. 14 Oct., 1817.

CHILDREN

1. *Ida Livingston, 18 Mar. 1835; d. 20 Oct. 1843.
2. William Livingston, 9 Oct. 1837. (675)

331. VI. Mary Alden, dau. of John, (146) m. Rev. Isaac Tompkins of Haverhill, Mass.

They had seven children. 1. Lois. 2. Sally. 3. Isaac. 4. Christopher. 6. Mary. 6, Samuel Sprague. 7. Abigail.

332. VI. Capt. John Alden, Fairhaven, Mass., farmer, s. of John, (146) was b. 9 Sept, 1771, d. 8 Aug. 1843, a. 72; m. 5 Dec. 1793, Ruth, dau. of Samuel Pope, who was b. 14 Mar. 1773, and d. 18 Sept. 1845.

CHILDREN

1. Ebenezer, 30 July, 1794. (676)	4. Lois, 1 June, 1803. (677)
2. Elizabeth, 19 Feb. 1796, d. 8 June 1819.	5. Ruth, 9 Nov. 1805. (678)
	6. John, 17 July, 1807. (679)
3. Samuel, 17 Apr. 1799, d. Jamaica, W. I. 14 July, 1825.	7. Abigail Pope. (680)
	8. William Pope, 21 May, 1810. (681)

333. VI. John Alden, Middleboro', Mass., son of Nathan; (148) b. 6 Dec. 1767, d. 20 Oct. 1841; m. 1790, Susanna Dunham, b. 20 May, 1763, d. 2 Jan. 1814, a. 51.

CHILDREN

1. Andrew, 30 Dec. 1790, d. 1792.	3. Susanna, 14 Dec. 1794.
2. Priscilla, 25 Jan. 1793.	4. Sally, 3 June, 1797.

334. VI. Otis Alden, Middleboro', Mass., son of Nathan (148) was b. 6 Dec. 1767, m. 17 March, 1796, Abigail Barrows.

CHILDREN

1. Jason, 19 July, 1798.	3. Otis, 22 Apr. 1803.
2. Lois Jacobs, 14 Sept. 1800.	4. Abigail, 31 Aug. 1805.

316. VI. Earl Alden, Middleboro', farmer, son of Nathan, (148) b. 2 Nov. 1778; d. 18 June, 1864, a. 85 V. 7 mo. 16 d.; m. 9 Apr. 1801, Nancy, dau. of Rev. Samuel Nelson, b. 22 Apr. 1775, d. 14 Aug. 1856, a. 81.

1. Abner, 16 Aug. 1801. (685)
2. Charity Haskell, 29 July, 1803. (686)
3. Mary Miller, 5 Mar. 1806. (687)
4. Milton, 14 Sept. 1807. (688)
5. Elbridge Gerry, 4 April, 1810. (689)
6. Anne Nelson, 27 July 1812. (690)

7. Samuel Nelson, 1 Feb. 1815. (691)
8. *Priscilla Miller, 8 May, 1817, d. young.
9. Sarah Rounseville, 5 Feb. 1820. (692)

Hem. 2, a. 80, 31 Mar. 1858, Catherine A. Armstrong, a. 26, and had 1 ch.

336. VI. Nathan Alden of Middleboro', Mass., son of Nathan, (148) was b. 20 June, 1788; m. 4 July, 1809, Betsey Shaw of Middleboro'. They had 1 s. b. 25 Apr., 1815.

337. VI. Israel Alden, Middleboro', Mass., farmer, son of Elijah, (151) was b. 1780., d. 5 Sept. 1836, a. 56.

337a. VI. Serena Alden, Mid., dau. of Elijah, (151) b. 1786, d. 1834; m. 9 Mar. 1828, Eli Shaw.

They had children, 1. Serena, who m. Edward N. Barrows, and has 9 ch. 2. Louiza. 3. Charles. 4. Albert. 6. Nathaniel. 6. Julia Mary. 7. Willie. 8. Eugenie. 9. Inf.

338. VI. Elijah Alden, Mid. Mass., farmer, son of Elijah, (151) b. 10 June, 1790; m. Lucinda P. Robinson, who d. 20 Dec. 1857, a. 62.

CHILDREN

1. Emeline, 23 Jan. 1818, now of Fairhaven.
2. William Henry, 21 Sept. 1820. (693)

3. James Monroe, 9 Nov. 1823. (694)
4. John Francis, 1 Jan. 1826. (695)
5. Charles Frederic, 1 Dec. 1803. (696)

He m. 2, 16 Dec. 1858, Eliza Wetherell.

339. VI. Daniel Alden, Middleboro', Mass., farmer, son of Elijah (151) b. 1796: m. 25 Dec. 1822, Lucy, dau. of Daniel Hartwell, b. 2 Oct. 1796.

CHILDREN

1. Lucy Hartwell, 21 Feb. 1824. (697)
2. *Daniel Frederick, 29 Nov 1825.
3. Elizabeth M. 7 June 1829. (698)
4. Vienna, 3 July, 1832. (699)

5. Jared Foster, 18 Apr. 1836. (700)
6. *Alexander Morton, 18 July, 1840, who d. 18 Nov. 1852.

340. VI. William Alden, Meshoppin, Pa., son of Mason Fitch, (164) was living in 1859, an old man; his wife was dead: they had several children. s. p.

341. VI. Sarah Alden, dau. of Mason Fitch, (164) m. Abraham Pike; was dead in 1859, had one or two gr. children living in the West. s. p.

342. VI. Abigail Alden, dau. of Mason Fitch, (164) m. a Mowbry: had ch. one of whom has been in the Legislature of Pennsylvania. s. p.

343. VI. Austin Alden, son of Josiah, (176) b. 3 Nov. 1784: m. Anna Lord.

344. VI. Salome Alden, dau. of Josiah (176) b. 12 Nov. 1786: m. Solomon Davis.

345. VI. Capt. Charles Alden, Portland; Me. son of Josiah (176) b. 20 Jan. 1789; was living in 1859, m. Nancy Quimby: had ch. Sarah and Charles: both dead.

346. VI. Nancy Alden, dau. Josiah (176) was k 13 Feb. 1793; d. 1859 in Bangor, Me., m. 1 — Parker of Buxton: had 2 ch; m. 2 Warren Nickerson, Bangor: no ch.

347. VI. Gardner Alden, Gorham, Me., son of Josiah (176) b. 13 Jan. 1795, d. 8 Sept, 1831; m. 1822 Martha Chick.

CHILDREN

1. Henry, 1823. (701) | 2. Clarissa, 1823; twins.

348. VI. Lucia Smith Alden, Duxbury, Mass., dau. of Judah (181) b. 5 Dec. 1780, d. 2 Feb. 1858; m. 1804 Capt. Sylvanus Smith, of Duxbury who d. 1865, a. 85; no ch.

349. VI. John Alden, Duxbury, trader, son of Judah (181) b. 1784; m. 1811, Mary Winsor.

CHILDREN

1. Mary 1811, (702) | 2. John 1813, (703) | 3. Henry 1815, (704)

350. VI. Briggs Alden, Duxbury, Mass., son of Judah (181) b. 8 Oct. 1786, d. 4 Jan. 1840 a. 5 4; m. Hannah D. James.

CHILDREN

1. Judah, 22 July, 1820, d. 18 Aug. 1823. 2. William James, 22 April 1822, (705) 3. Lucia P., 20 Apr. 1824. 4. Judah, 24 Aug. 1825, (706) 5. Samuel, 28 Apr. 1827, (707) 6. Amherst, 15 May, 1832, (708)

351. VI. Mercy Alden, Duxbury, Mass. dau. Judah (181) b. 1788; d. 1840, a. 53, m. 14 June 1812, Henry R. Packard, of Baltimore, who d. at sea 1834, a. 50.

They had children, 1. Marcia, who married Capt. Robert Welsh. 2. Hannah James, the young poetess, b. 1815: d. 1831, a. 16.

352. VI. Welthea Alden, Duxbury, Mass., dau. of Judah, (181) b. 1792, m. William James of Scituate, who is dead; had 10 children.

353. VI. Samuel Alden, M. D., Bridgewater, son of Judah (181) b. 24 Jan. 1803; gr. Harv. Coll. 1821; M. D. Dartmouth Coll. 1825. M. M. S. S. m. 29 Jan. 1829, Mary Angier, dau. of Ezra Hyde. She was b. 12 Jan. 1806.

CHILDREN

1. Ezra Hyde, 16 Sept. 1830, expressman, m. Mary Smith, 2. Samuel. I Mar. 183.3, d. Mar. 1835. 3. William, 11 Oct. 1836. Lost at sea 6 May 1856, 4. Lucia Smith, 3 May 1839. 5. *Frank, 23 June 1841, d, 5 Oct. 1847. 6. Alice Wadsworth, 5 Sept. 1843, m. 15 Aug. 1866, Edward Hutchins Cutler, of Providence, R, I. 7. Mary Angier, 20 Oct, 1845, 8. *Martha, 21 Oct, 1847, d. 1849. 9. Samuel, 17 Mar. 1852.

354. VI. Samuel Alden, son of Nathaniel (182) b, 19 July 1785, m. Hannah, dau. of Stephen Reed.

CHILDREN

1. Amherst, 1808, (709) 2. Joanna, 1810. S. Stephen, 1812, d. 23 Sept, 1846, a. 34. 4. Mary G. 1817, (710) 5. William Ripley, 1819, (711) 6. Lucia Smith, 1822. 7. Samuel G. 1827, (712) 8. Julia F. 1829.

355. VI. Welthea Alden, Freeport, Me., dau. of Nathaniel (182) b. Dec. 1788, d. 24 Nov. 1834; m. Jeremiah Winslow: had no children.
356. VI. Robert Tate Alden, Boston, sail maker, son of James (186) b. 1805, m. 1832 Sarah Brewer Taylor.

CHILDREN

1. James. 2. Anna. 3. Mary. 4. Sarah. 5. Adaline Roberts, 1840.

357. VI. Mary Alden, dau. of James (186) m. William Bradley of Portland, Me. and d. without issue.
358. VI. James Alden, Charlestown, Mass., ship carpenter, son of James (186) m. 1838 Thompson: no ch.
359. VI. Delia Alden, dau. James (186) m. Henry or Harvey Henderson of Baltimore, Md., has 6 children.
360. VI. Eliza Alden, dau. of James (186) m. S. T. Arthur, Philadelphia, has 5 ch.
361. VI. Benjamin Alden, Texas, son of David, probably (185) b. 20 Feb. 1795, resides in Texas; m. and had one son.
362. VI. Albert Alden, Delafield, Waukesha Co. Wis., son of John (188) b. 1811, m. Dec. 1843, Caroline Fairservice of Summit, Waukesha Co., Wis.

CHILDREN

1. Albert, 28 Aug. 1844. 2. Theodosia, 12 Sep. 1845. 3. Agnes Mary, 1 May 1848. 4. Caroline Louiza, 20 Mar. 1852.

363. VI. Ichabod Alden, Duxbury, son of Isaiah, (190) b. 4 Nov. 1788, m. Abigail, daughter of Nathaniel Delano. No children.
364. VI. Isaiah Alden, Scituate, son of Isaiah, (190) b. 17 Dec. 1789, d. 18 Nov. 1831, a. 42: m. Mercy, dau. of Lemuel Vinal.

CHILDREN

1. Isaiah, 1 Sept. 1819, d. 28 June, 1848. 2. Mercy, 20 April, 1821. 3, Thomas. 4. Lydia.

364.a VI. Martha Alden, Duxbury, Mass., dau. of Isaiah, (190) b. 22 Feb. 1796, m. 2 Dec. 1824, Elijah Delano, of Duxbury, Mass.

CHILDREN

1. Anna, 2 Sept. 1825, m. 1855, Thomas J. Elliott, Charlestown. 2. Martha Jane, 7 Oct. 1828, m. 1854 Alvan Baker, Duxbury. 3. Mercy Maria, 31 Oct. 1831. 4. Henry Mudge, 28 June, 1837.

365. VI. Captain Benjamin Alden, Duxbury, farmer, surveyor, magistrate, son of Isaiah (190) b. 22 March, 1794: Nov. 18, 1832 m. Martha Chandler, dau. of Bradford Sampson, b. 22 Feb. 1804; had 1 ch. Rebecca, 28 Oct. 1833, who d. 28 April, 1861, unm.

366. VI. Peleg Alden, Duxbury, Mass., a teacher, son of Isaiah (190) b. 6 June, 1806, d. in Fredericksburg, Va., 21 Sept. 1831, a. 25 years, unm.

367. VI. James Alden, Boston, hatter, son of Isaiah (190) b. 20 April. 1808, m. Anna, dau. of Nathaniel Bickford, of Waterborough. Me.

CHILDREN

1. Peleg J. 24 Aug. 1835. 2. James, 5 Dec. 1837. 3. Sophia, 8 Sept.; d. 16 Sept. 1844. 4. Ruth A. 28 Jan. 1843, d. Dec. 9, 1844. 6. Benjamin F. 25 Sept. 1846, d. 3 Feb. 1849. 6. Ruth S. A. O. 11 Oct. 1849, d. Feb. 22, 1850.

368. VI. Ichabod Alden, Charlestown, Mass., ship carpenter, son of Capt. John (195) b. 30 Mar. 1806, m. 3 Sept. 1829, Margaret Morgan: has had 12 children; of these,

Anner, b. 3 Sept. 1829. Margaret, 8 Sept. 1832.

369. VI. Samuel Alden, Duxbury, Mass., ship carpenter, son of John (195) b. 21 April 1808, m. June 20, 1841, Myra Torrey.

CHILDREN

1. Charles Edwin, 1842, d. in army. 2. Samuel Wakefield, 1844, m. Torrey. 3. Mary Wyman, 1846. 4. George Lothrop, 184S. 5. Walter.

370. VI. Deborah Alden, dau. of John (195) b. 5 June, 1815, m. 8 April 1841, John Ford, had 1 ch.

Deborah, 24 Jan. 1842, who is dead.

371. VI. William Alden, Calais, Vt., son of Henry (199) b. 1 July, 1761, d. Calais, Vt., 27 Sept. 1822, a. 61: m. Susanna, dau. of Jason Whitney, of Natick, Mass. She was b. 9 Dec. 1766: d. 27 Feb. 1844, a. 78.

CHILDREN

1. Isaac, 19 Mar. 1789, (713) 2. William, 22 Aug. 1791, (714) 3. Asa, 25 Sept. 1794, (715) 4. George, 30 May 1797, (716) 5. Elizabeth W. 9 July, 1802, (717) 6. Hannah, 13 Sept. 1806, (718).

372. VI. Moses Alden, Marlboro, N. H., farmer, son of Silas (200) b. 1760, d. in Walpole, N. H. 1833, a. 73: m. Elizabeth, dau. of Isaiah Whitney, who was b. 18 May, 1764, d. 1833, a. 69.

CHILDREN

1. Reuben, (719) 2. Alvan, 1791, (720) 3. Betsey, (721) 4. Moses, (722) 5. Sarah, (723) 6. Dexter, (724) 7. William, (725) 8. Maria, (726).

373. VI. Elizabeth Alden, dau. of Silas (200) m. Enoch Mills, of Watertown, Mass., who went to South Carolina and had 2 children.

374. VI. Paul Alden, Newton, Mass., farmer, son of Silas (200) "a man much respected," b. 27 April, 1767: d. 3 Dec. 1815, a. 48; m. '21 April, 1796, Rebecca, dau. of Ebenezer Newell, b. 19 Feb. 1773.

CHILDREN

1. Lucinda, 23 Jan. 1797,(727) 2. Elizabeth, 14 Oct. 1798, (728) 3. Roxana, 26 April. 1800, d. unm. 2 June. 1853. 4. Rebecca N. G April. 1802, (729) 6. Nancy, 4 Nov. 1804, (730) 6. Paul, 18 July, 1807, (731) 7. Silas, 8 July, 1809, (732) 8. Ebenezer N. 22 Dec. 1811, d. New Orleans, unm. 11 Nov. 1832.

375. VI. Silas Alden, Templeton, Mass., farmer son of Dea. Silas, (200) b. 21 April, 1767: d. 13 Dec. 1840, a. 76; m. 1790 Mary, dau. of Jonathan Gay: b. 24 Aug. 1770: d. 7 Apr. 1847.

CHILDREN

1. Marshall. 13 Mar. 1791, (733) 2. Luther, 20 Mar. 1793, (734) 3. Harvey, 12 Jan. 1798, (730) 4. Priscilla, E. 24 Feb. 1804.

376. VI. Amasa Alden, Dedham, Mass., farmer, son of Silas (200) b. 29 March, 1772, d. Dec. 7, 1857, a. 86; m. 1793 Martha Davenport, dau. of Benjamin Davenport.

CHILDREN

1. Francis, 1793, (736) 2. Leonard, 1796, (737) 3. George, 1804, (738) 4. Amasa, 1812, (739). Mr. A. Alden.

377. VI. Lydia Alden, dau. Silas (200) m. Fuller Mills, of Boston. They had children,
1. Richard. 2. Lydia. 3. A son — perhaps more.

Mr. A. Alden.

378. VI. Rebecca Alden, dau. of Silas (200) m. Timothy Pike, of Dudley, Mass., and had one son, Dexter.

379. VI. Simeon Alden, Newton, Mass., farmer, son of Silas (200) m. Elizabeth Cook, had 2 sons and 2 dau.: perhaps more.

380. VI. Samuel Alden, Newton, Mass., son of Silas (200) m. ___.

CHILDREN

1. Simeon, boot manufacturer, Milford, Mass. (740) 2. A dau. deceased.

381. VI. George Alden, Needham, son of Silas (200) m. had a son George; all dead, parents and child.

382. VI. Elisha Alden, Stafford, Ct., farmer, son of Lt. Elisha, (158a) was b. 1767, d. 1846; m. 6 Oct. 1793, Clarissa Barker, of Coventry Ct., who d. 25 June, 1800; m. 2, 25 Oct. 1800, Pamelia Shepherd of Tolland, Ct., who d. Oct. 30, 1848.

CHILDREN

1. Anna Richardson, 5 Aug. 1794, m. Samuel Chapman, (741) 2, Jolm, 18 Dec. 1795: d. 28 Mar. 1797. 3. John, 5 Feb. 1798, d. unm. 4. Clarissa, 12 Jan. 1800, m. Simeon Horton, of Stafford, Ct., (742) 5. Desire West, 25 Aug. 1801, d. 21 Aug. 1829. 6. Austin, 1 May, 1803, m. Nancy Oker, (743) 7. Augustus, 23 July, 1804, m. Deborah Crowell, (744) 8. George, 15 Feb, 1806. d. 24 Aug. 1825. 9. Seymour, 27 Aug 1807: d. 14 May, 1808. 10. Francis Seymour, 15 March, 1809: d. 16 Jan. 1840. 11. Pamelia Ann, 31 Aug. 1810: d. 21 Mar. 1827. 12. Alonzo Erskine, 8 Mar. 1812, (745) 13. William Chauncey, 21 June 1813; m. 1 Sophia Smith, m. 2, Hannah Ballard, (746) 14. Lydia Shepherd, 30 Sept. 1815, m. Henry Wilson, of Ellington Ct., (747) 15. Elisha, 24 Nov. 1817, (748) 16. Washington, 7 April, 1821, m. Jane Barrows, (749).

383. VI. Nathan Alden, Wilbraham, Mass., farmer, son of Elisha (158c) son of Noah (68) was b. 1768, d. 9 Nov. 1840; m. Sarah Beston (?) 14 March, 1791, who was b. 24 Nov. 1766: d. 16 Aug. 1847.

CHILDREN

1. Noah, 1792, (750) 2. *Horace b. 9 April, 1793, (751) 3. *Horace, 1794, d. 1795. 4. Sally, 12 Jan. 1796, (752) 5. Marcia 12 Jan. 1796, (753) 6. Cyrus, 1799, (754) 7. Laura. 8. Nathan. 9. Nathan, (755).

384. VI. Simeon Alden, son of Elisha (158c) son of Noah (68) m. 1 Polly Preston, m. 2 — Hurd.

385. VI. Samuel Alden, son of Elisha (158c) son of Noah (68) m. 1 Marion Glazier, m. 2 Keziah Blodgett.

386. VI. Darius Alden, son of Elisha (158c) son of Noah (68) m. Matilda Els worth.

387. VI, Spencer Alden, Springfield, Mass., son of Elisha (158c) son of Noah (68) was b. 1780, m. Mary Ann Rockwell.

388. VI. Serena Alden, dau. of Elisha (158c) son of Noah (68) m. Joseph Merrick.

389. VI. Fear Alden, dau. of Elisha (158c) son of Noah (68) m. David Glazier.

390. VI. Joanna Alden, dau. of Elisha (158c) son of Noah (68) m. 1 Leonard Holt, m. 2 —.

Seventh Generation

401. VII. Mary Alden, E. Bridgewater, dau. of Nathan, (205) bapt. 22 June, 1777; d. 13 Dec. 1799, a 22: m. 1797, Capt. William Vinton, who d. 1841, a. 66.

They had ch. 1, b. 1798, d. same day. 2. Mary Alden, 29 Nov. 1799, who m. 1820 Ebenezer Tolman, Esq. of Stoughton.

402. VII. Lydia Alden, dau. of Nathan, (205) was b. 29 Aug. 1779, d. 18 Dec. 1843, a. 64; m. June, 1801, David Keith Jun. of E. Br.

They had ch. 1. Julia Alden, 1802, who m. Francis Packard of N. Br. his 2 wife. 2. Mary Russell, 1804, who m. Alfred Brown of Abington. 3. Lydia, 1806, who m. David Dunbar. 4. David Noble, 1808, who d. 1844. 5. Abigail, 1810.

403. VII. Marcus Alden, New York, music teacher, son of Nathan, (205) was b. 9 Aug. 1782, d. in New York, 25 Aug. 1848, a. 64; m. Apr. 1808, Salome, dau. of Col. Aaron Hobart of Abington, Mass., and was for a time engaged in mercantile pursuits.

CHILDREN

1. Aaron Hobart, Aug. 1809, who d. in Brooklyn, N. Y. unm. a. abt, 50. 2. Susanna Hobart, 1815, who m. Seymore Hoyt of N. Y.: residence, Stamford, Ct.

404. VII. Isaac Alden, Esq., East Bridgewater, Mass. farmer, son of Nathan, (205) was b. 3 Sept. 1786, d. 20 Dec. 1843, a. 57; m. 21 Nov. 1811, Clarissa, dau. of Lieut. Ephraim Whitman of Abington, whose mother was Abigail Alden, (108).

CHILDREN

1. William Barrell, May 1813. 2. Henry, Apr. 1817, (760).

405. VII. Sarah Alden, E. Br. dau. of Nathan, (205) b. 13 Sept. 1792; m. 2 Apr. 1818, James Penniman Tolman of E. Stoughton, who d. 1844, a. 49.

They had children, 1. James Winchell, 17 Sept. 1820, who m. Lucretia Stockbridge; went to Ill. 2. Nathan, 19 Mar. 1823; m. L. A. Belcher; resides in Randolph, Mass, 3. Sarah Barrell, 31 Oct. 1825, m. Samuel Packard. 4. Henry, 11 Dec. 1828; m. Kate Lang. 5. Marcus Alden, 15 Oct. 1832, a clergyman, m. Hannah Billings Goldthwait.

406. VII. Rev. Lucius Alden, Newcastle, N. H. congregational minister, son of Nathan, (205) was b. in E. Bridgewater, Mass. 18 June, 1796. At the age of twenty he became the subject of deep religious impressions in connection with the death of his mother, which issued in his hopeful conversion, public profession of his faith, and the consecration of himself to the ministry. In Feb. 1818, he entered Brown University at an advanced standing of six months, and graduated in 1821 with high honors. After graduation he was invited to a

tutorship in Columbia College, which he declined, and commenced his Theological studies at Andover, where he continued until he had completed the usual course. In July, 1825, he was approbated as a preacher, and on the 29 Sept. ordained at the Old South Church, Boston, as a missionary to Indiana. In this service he continued nearly five years, assisting in organizing churches, establishing and supervising various sabbath schools in the district to which he was assigned.

In 1830, having returned to visit his friends in New England he was invited to preach for the people in East Abington, where his labors as a stated supply were much blessed, and he was ultimately persuaded to become their pastor, being installed 5th Dec. 1834, and relinquishing, at what he deemed a call of duty, his cherished purpose of devoting himself to missions in the west.

In 1843, owing to a failure of his health and the great increase of his labors, he requested a dismission from his people in E. Abington, which was voted by advice of council June 27. After a relaxation of several months he returned to his home in E. Br., preaching occasionally, superintending the public schools, and making himself generally useful, until the close of the year 1845, when he was requested to visit Newcastle, N. H. He engaged to supply the people there for six months. His labors have been much blessed and his engagement has been renewed from time to time, to the mutual satisfaction of all parties, and still continues. His congregation is both sea-faring and military. During the late war fifteen hundred officers and soldiers of the U. S. Army were stationed there. Mr. Alden is still able to perform his duties. He never married; has competent means of support, and is universally respected.

407. VII. Ezra Alden, Abington, Mass., son of Isaac, (206). b. 1788, m. 31 Jan. 1813, Susan, dau. of Lieut. Bela Dyer.

CHILDREN

1. Bela, 11 Nov. 1813. (701). 2 and 3. Twins, d. soon. 4. Mary. 14 Feb. 1817. (762) 5. Jared. 17 June, 1821. (763) 6. Susan, 17 Mar. 1826. (764) 7. Hannah, 29 Dec. 1829; umn. 8. A ch. 30 July, 1832; d. 6 Apr. 1834.

408. VII. Thomas Russell Alden, son of Isaac, (206) b. 1790: d. Mar. 1830: m. 1813, Jane, dau. of Matthew Allen, who d. 1827; m. 2 Dorothy, dau. of Stephen Hearsey.

CHILDREN

1. Lucius, 1815. (765) 2. Russell, 1821. (766) 3. Allen, 1823. (766a) 4. Mary Jane, 1825. (767) 5. Edward, 1829. (768)

409. VII. James Sullivan Alden, Bridgewater, Mass., painter, son of Isaac, (206) m. Ann E. Washburn, dau. of Jeremiah. She was b. 8 June, 1810: d. 30 Aug. 1860.

CHILDREN

1. James Elbridge, 28 Apr. 1831. (769) 2. George Thomas, 2 Feb. 1835. (770) 3. Isaac Russell, 30 May, 1844. 4. Frederic Clinton, 6 May, 1849.

He m. 2, 21 Nov. 1863, Sarah, dau. of Levi Leach; no ch.

410. VI. Benjamin Alden, Bridgewater and Dubuque, Iowa, son of Isaac, (206).

CHILDREN

1. *A dau. d. young. 2. Edmund. 3. A son, d. young.

411. VII. Joanna Alden, dau. of Isaac and Ruth, (209) m. 1818, William Bird.

412. VII. Nabby Alden; dau. of Isaac, E. Br.

413. VII. Lewis Alden, E. Bridgewater, son of Isaac, (209).

414. VII. William Vinton Alden, Boston, merchant, son of Ezra, (211) b. 4 Aug. 1809, d. 24 Oct. 1862, a. 53. He was a worthy member of Essex St. Congregational Church, and for more than twenty years its clerk. He m. in 1833, his second cousin Nancy Adams, dau. of Dea. Josiah Vinton, who was b. 26 Oct. 1807.

CHILDREN

1. William Edward, 17 June, 1837. 2. Leonard Case, 22 Dec. 1839. (771)

415. VII. Louisa Alden. dau. Levi, (217) b. 30 Nov. 1800. m. Jacob 11. Peterson.

416. VII. Albert G. Alden, Washington City, son of Levi, (217) b. 3 Apr. 1804, m. Mary Parmenter.

417. VII. Thomas W. Alden, Claremont, N. H,, son of Levi, (217) b. 2 June, 1807; m. 1833, Hnldali Blodgett.

418. VII. John Alden, son of Levi, (217) b. 2 G Dec. 1809: d. 15 June, 1845; m. Caroline Pearce.

419. VII. James Madison Alden, Janesville, Wis., son of Levi, (217) b. 9 Feb. 1813: m. in 1837, Catharine, dau. of Chester Alden, (223).

420. VII. Levi Alden, Janesville, Wis., son of Levi, (217) b. 24 July, 1815: m. 26 July, 1843, Sarah Ann Leach, dau. of Winslow Leach, of Fleming, N. Y.

CHILDREN

1. Mary E. 21 July, 1844. 2. Francis B. 10 June, 1846. 3. Louiza J. 9 June, 1848. 4. Sarah L. 9 Feb. 1850.

421. VII. Lucinda Alden, dau. Levi, (217) b. 21 July, 1818, m. 1842, Henry Baker, who d.; m. 2, Horace Baker, Goshen, N. Y.

422. VII. Alfred Alden, Janesville, Wis. son of Levi, (217) b. 14 June, 1822.

423. VII. Caroline Francis Alden, dau. of Dr. Jonathan P. Alden of Cambridge Port; (222) m. John Farnham Hall, who went to California; had 1 ch. Norma Frances.

424. VII. Chester Alden, Woodstock, Vt. son of Chester, (223) prob. has a family.

425. VII. Alvan Alden, Woodstock, Vt. son of Chester, (223) prob. has a family.

426. VII. Samuel H. Alden, Janesville, Wis. son of Chester, (223) prob. has a family.

427. VII. Sophia Albert, Woodstock, Vt., dau. of Chester, (223) m. Levi Judkins.

427a. VII. Hiram Orlando Alden, Esq., Belfast, Me., a distinguished telegraph operator, son of Joseph, (224a) b. in 1800, m. Emily Bingham of Claremont, N. H., and had three sons and two daughters.

427b. VII. Esther Cecilia Alden, of Claremont, N. H., dau. of Joseph, (224a). m. Dr, Jonathan P. Alden, (222.)

427c. VII. Emily Ormond Alden, dau. of Joseph (224a). No further particulars.

427d. VII. Caroline Frances Alden, dau. of (224a) m. Norman Robbins, Belfast, Me., and had one son, Norman.

427e. VII. Joseph Warren Alden, merchant, Boston and New York, now, 1866, resident in Elizabeth, N. J. son of Joseph, (224a) b. 1808: m.l8 Oct. 1830, Emily, dau. of Dea. David Gillmor, of Jaffrey, N. H. She was b. 13 Apr. 1811: d. 11 Apr. 1834. He m. 2 Lucy Ripley, (widow) sister of his former wife, who was b. 30 Sept. 1801.

CHILDREN

1. Emily Gillmor, 21 Jan. 1834: now (1866) Associate Principal in the Castleton Seminary, Castleton, Vt. 2. Ann Frances, 19 July, 1836: d 26 Sept. 1S36. 3. Joseph Henry, 21 Aug. 1838: d. 2 Sept. 1838. 4. James Birney, 4 Sept. 1841; now (1866) in mercantile business in New York. From 23 Sept. 1861, to 22 Sept. 1864 he was a soldier in the 1st Mass. Cavalry, and was a sergeant; and one year from Oct. 1, 1864 to 1 Oct. 1865 was in the subsistence Department of U. S. Volunteers.

427f. VII. Lucy Catherine Alden, Claremont, N. H., dau. of Joseph, (224a) m. Perley Morse, Methuen, Mass., and had one son, Edward.

427g. VII. Cynthia Louiza Alden, Claremont, N. H., dau. of Joseph, (224a) m. Miles Griffin, had three sous, and one daughter who is dead.

427h. VII. James Franklin Alden, New York City, son of Joseph, (224a) has a wife and three children.

428. VII. Lydia P. Alden, dau. of Zenas, (226) b. 1781, d. June 1814, m. 1799, Abner Balch, b. 1770, d. July 1817.

They had ch. 1. Alden, 1800, d. 1815. 2. Abner, 1804— lives in Bath, N. H. 3. Eliza, 180.5, m. 1821, Aaron Hayes: d. in 1826. 4. Lydia P., b. 1807, m. Aaron Hayes: d. in 1830. 5. Albert, b. 1809, d. 1863. 6. Almira, b. 5 Aug. 1811, m. 1853, Frank Roel, or Rowel, an artist, resides in Boston. 7. Albert Allen, b. 3 Dec. 1813; m. Lois Balcom, who d, 1840; k. at St. Johnsbury, Vt. by cars, Mar. 1864.

429. VII. Ziba Alden, Lebanon, N. H., son of Zenas, (226) m. Sybil Allen.

CHILDREN

1. Phineas Allen, (772) 2. Lydia Pinney, (773) 3. Delia Allen, (774) and three others who d. young.

430. VII. Lucinda Alden, Lebanon, N. H., dau. of Zenas, (226) m. Benjamin Fuller, of Hardwick, Vt.

431. VII. Susanna Alden, Lebanon, N. H., dau. of Zenas, (226) m. 1, Cady Allen; m. 2, Capt. — Parkhurst of Royalton, Vt., no children.

432. VII. Zenas Phelps Alden, Lebanon, N. H., son of Zenas, (226) was an invalid and is dead; m. Mary White, of Lebanon, N. H.

CHILDREN

1. Zenas, who served three years in the army. 2, A daughter.

432a. VII. Rosamond Alden, Lebanon, N. H., dau. of Zenas, m. Samuel Gage of Randolph, Vt.

433. VII. Martha Alden, Stafford, Ct., dau. of Joseph, (227) m. Dr. Josiah Converse, Stafford, Ct., and was living in 1864: had a son, E. A. Converse, in Stafford.

434. VII. Clarissa Alden, Stafford, Ct., dau. of Joseph,

(227) m. Stoddard Elsworth, of East Windsor, Ct.

435. VII. Lydia Alden, of Stafford, Ct., dau. of Joseph, (227) m. Jabez White Giddings, Hartford, Ct.

436. VII. Horatio Alden, Hartford, Ct., merchant, son of Joseph, (227) b. 1 May, 1792; d. 5 Mar. 1858, a 66, inconsequence of a fall and fracture of the thigh; m. Philura, dau. of Silas Deane: b. 1798.

CHILDREN

1. Philura Deane, 15 Feb. 1816, d. 18 Dec. 1820. 2. Adeline Eliza, 9 Dec. 1818, (775) 3. Jesse Deane, 12 Oct. 1820, (776) 4. William Gumming, 17 July, 1826, (777) 5. Isabella Graham, 31 July, 1828, (778).

437. VII. Almida Alden, dau. of Joseph, (227) m. David Tryon Child, E. Haddam, Ct.

438. VII. Dr. Daniel Alden, Cabot, Vt., physician, son of Daniel, (234) b. 11 Feb. 1786: studied his profession under the direction of Dr. Jacob Holmes', of Athol, Mass. and at Dartmouth College Medical Institution; settled at Cabot, Vt., where he had just commenced the practice of his profession with fair prospects, when he was arrested by typhoid fever, and died August 1813, a. 27 years.

439. VII. Lt. Colonel Ezra Alden, Lebanon, N. H., farmer, son of Daniel, (234) b. 8 Dec. 1787: m. 26 Jan. 1826, Sarah, dau. of Jesse Alden, (236) of Cornish, N. H. She was b. 9 Jan. 1797, and d. suddenly 27 Mar. 1865: both were members of the Cong. Church, and highly respected. He was commissioned Lt. Colonel in 1822. They had no ch.

440. VII. Sally Alden, of Lebanon, N. H, dau. of Daniel, (234) b. 1790: m. Dea. Stephen Tracy of Cornish, N.H., who d. Oct. 1865, having sustained the office of deacon in the Congregational church forty-nine years.

They had children, 1. Alden. 2. Caroline.

441. VII. Elam Alden, Windsor, Vt., farmer, son of Daniel, (234) b. 22 Mar. 1794; m. 5 May, 1829, Sarah, dau. of Asaph Hyde, who d. 15 Oct. 1856, a. 59. An obituary notice of her life and character was published in the Vermont Chronicle, 5 Nov. 1856. He m. 2, in 1862, Mrs. Harriet Gould.

CHILDREN

1. Jane Blodgett, 12 Aug. 1825. 2. Ellen Maria, 16 Aug. 1827. 3. Mary Anna, 6 March, 1829. 4. *George William, 14 Oct. 1830, d. 10 June, 1851. 5. *Horace Elisha, 28 June, 1832, d. 1855. 6. Edwin Hyde, 14 Jan 1836, (779) 7. *Henry Abbott, 22 May, 1838, d. 1 Sept. 1841.

442. VII. Julius Alden, Waterville, Maine, trader, son of Daniel, (234) b. 4 Jan. 1796; m. 1820, Elizabeth Louiza, dau. of David Nourse.

CHILDREN

1. *Sarah Elizabeth. June 11, 1827, d. June 19, 1856. 2. Frances Louiza, Apr. 1829. 3. *Henry Augustus, 13 June, 1833, d. 14 Aug. 1833. 4. Charles Henry, 13 Apr. 1836. 5. Arthur Julius, 23 Apr. 1838. 6. Edward Clarence, 1 Sept. 1841, d. 26 Oct. 1844. 7. Clara Theresa, 13 June, 1848.

443. VII. Brig. Gen. Luther Alden, Lebanon, N. H., son of Daniel, (234) deacon Cong. Chh. 1856, b. 19 Aug. 1797, m. 16 Sept. 1824, Susan, dau. of Capt. Joseph Wood of Lebanon, N. H. who was b. 8 Nov. 1759, and was present at a meeting in Lebanon, 8 Nov. 1859, and took part in the exercises and d. in Dec following.

CHILDREN

1. Joseph Wood, 9 Sept. 1826, (780) 2. Sarah Jane Wood, 3 Feb. 1828, (781) 3. Charles Henry, 14 Dec. 1832, d. in Minnesota. 4. Francis Elizabeth, 23 Oct. 1842.

444. VII. Ebenezer Alden. M. D. Randolph, Mass. son of Ebenezer, (235) b. 17 Mar. 1788; gr. Harv. Coll. 1808; pursued his professional studies with Nathan Smith, M. D. at Dartmouth College, where he received the degree of M. B. in 1811; then attended the Lectures of Drs. Rush, Barton, Wistar, Physick, and others in Philadelphia, and received the degree of M. D. from the University of Pennsylvania in 1812. He settled as a physician in his native town, where he still (1866) continues to reside.

He m. 14 Apr. 1818, Anne Kimball, dau. of Capt. Edmund Kimball, of Newburyport, Mass. b. 14 June, 1791.

CHILDREN

1. Ebenezer, 10 Aug. 1819, (782) 2. Mary Kimball, 27 Apr. 1822: d. 18 Aug. 1860. 3. Edmund Kimball, 11 Apr. 1825, (783) 4. Henry Augustus, 8 Aug. 1826,

(784) 5. Sarah Bass, 21 May, 1828. 6. Anne Kimball, 15 Aug. 1833: d. 28 Dec. 1854.

445. VII. Henry Bass Alden, Esq. Randolph, Mass. farmer, son of Dr. Ebenezer, (235) b. 7 June, 1791; d. suddenly of disease of the heart, 24 June, 1851, a. 60.

He occupied the homestead of his father; gr. at Harv. Un. in 1812; was never married; lived with his sister Susanna. He was much respected; was frequently elected to office in the town, and represented it in the Legislature.

446. VII. Samuel Rice Alden, Cornish, N. H. farmer, son of Jesse, (236) b. 7 May, 1793; m. in Grafton, Vt. and went to Granville, N. Y.

441. VII. Amanda Alden, Cornish, N. H. dau. of Jesse, (236) b. 14 Mar. 1795, d. 5 Dec. 1840; m. Rufus Beane.

Children: 1. Sarah Anna, 10 Aug. 1830: was a member of the family of Col. Ezra Alden, (439) where she d. after a protracted sickness, 8 May, 1866. 2. Jesse Alden. 3. Henry Eastman, Dec. 1834. 4. Carlos Tyler, 1836. 5. Ellen Francis, 9 Aug. 1838: d. 9 Feb. 1800, at Lebanon, N. H. 6. Harvey, 20 Sept. 1841: was in the U. S. Army, 5th. N. H. Reg.

448. VII. Sarah Alden, Corni.sh, N. H. dau. of Jesse, (236) m. Col. Ezra Alden, (430) of Lebanon, N. IT, which see,

449. VII. Jesse Alden, Cornish, N. H. son of Jesse, (236) b. 26 Nov. 1798; went to Monte Bello, III. where he d. young.

450. VII. Harvey Alden, Cornish, N.H. farmer, son of Jesse, (236) was b. 7 Jan. 1801, d. 9 July, 1835, a. 34; m. Anna B. Holbrook, dau. of Joseph, Braintree, Mass.; had no ch. After his decease she m. 1836, Alvan Snell of Randolph, Mass.

451. VII. Hannah Alden, Cornish, N. H. dau. of Jesse, (236) b. 31 July, 1805, d. 21 Mar. 1832; m. Benjamin Ayers of Cornish; left two ch. George and Harvey.

452. VII. Betsey Alden, dau. of Jesse, (236) b. 31 July, 1805; m. Abner Flanders.

Children: 1. John. 2, Joseph. 3. Mary. 4. Julia Marion.

453. VII. Abigail Willard Alden, dau. of Samuel, (237) b. 28 Oct. 1809. d. at Freehold, N.J. of cancer, Oct. 1855, a. 46; m. Otis R. Freeman, M. D., Hanover, N. H. who went to Freehold, N. J.

Children: 1. Samuel Alden, 25 Jan. 1838, gr. Lafayette College. 2. Abby Willard, 11 Mar. 1840. 3. Charles Otis, Feb. 1842. 4. Mary Russell, 1844: d. 26 June, 1863, a. 19.

454. VII. Roxinda Alden, dau. of Isaac, (238) b. 20 Mar. 1803: was living in 1860: m. a White: went to Illinois; had 3 daughters.

455. VII. Fidelia Alden, dau. of Isaac, (238) b. 12 Aug. 1805: d. Apr. 1864, a. 59; m. Moses Chase, of Cornish, N. H.

3. They had ch. John, Helen, Adelia, Ormond, Byram.

456. VII. Sarah Bass Alden, dau. Dr. Isaac, (238) b. 1 July, 1807: d. 1861, in Illinois; m. a Morton.

456a. VII. Eliza Jane Alden, Lowell, Mass., dau. of Dr. Isaac, (238) d. Lowell, 8 Sept. 1860. Application for Probate of her estate made 25 Sept. 1860. Inv. $1020. Left mother Hannah, and sisters Fidelia A. Chase, Cornish, N. H., Sarah B. Morton and Roxinda White and br. Henry B. Alden, of ___.

457. VII. Henry Bradley Alden, Plainfield, N. H., son of Isaac, (238) b. 7 Aug. 1815; went to Illinois: m. had a family, was living in 1860.

458. VII. Philomela Alden, dau. of Isaac, (250) m. Dr. ___ Rathbone, Cambden, N. Y.

459. VII. Joshua Alden, son of Isaac, (250) was many years in the service of the patriots in South America.

460. VII. Isaac Alden, son of Isaac, (250) owned and occupied an extensive plantation in Louisiana, 30 miles from Natchitoches.

461. VII. Dr. Hiram Alden, Ripley, N. Y., son of Isaac, (250) a physician. I have obtained no account of his family.

462. VII. Richard Alden, Esq., Pine Grove, Pa., son of Isaac, (250) b. 1794: m. Betsey Newman; had four daughters who d. young, and one son Isaac S. b. 1830, (785).

463. VII. Lucy Alden, Middlefield, Ohio, dau. of David (251) m. 25 Mar. 1769, John Spooner, Dartmouth, Ms., had ch, John and Thomas.

463a. VII. Armilla Alden, Ashfield, Mass., dau. of Rev. John, (252) b. 3 Dec. 1793; m. Aaron Lyon, Esq., of Cassadar ga, Chatauque Co., N. Y.

464. VII. Dea. Cyrus Alden, Ashfield, Mass., farmer, son of Rev. John, (252) b. 15 Aug. 1795: was twice m.

465. VII. Willard Alden, Cazenovia, N. Y., son' of Rev. John, (252) b. 24 Apr. 1800. I have no further account of him.

466. VII. Rev. John Alden, Providence, R. I., son of Rev. John, (252) was b. 10 Jan. 1806, was first settled at Shelburne Falls, Mass., where he was also Principal of Franklin Academy for six years, holding the double relation of pastor and teacher. He continued with the church another year. His pupils numbered over 2000: about two hundred of whom had the ministry in view. He then went to North Adams, where he ministered six years, and over two hundred were added to the church. He was pastor after this in Southboro' and Westfield, Mass., and in Windsor, Vt., where he was chaplain to the State Prison, and in all these places precious revivals were enjoyed.

He was then agent for the Foreign Missionary Society in Northern New England; and for the past six years has been, and now, (1866) is agent for the American and Foreign Bible Society. Mr. Alden has published several pamphlets, among others a poem at the centennial celebration in Ashfield, (his native town,) in June, 1865.

He m. 23 Nov. 1833, Ann M. C. Chamberlain, dau. of Ephraim Chamberlain, Cambridgeport, Mass.

CHILDREN

1. Augustus E. b. 22 Feb. 1837, (786) 2. Francis Howard, 7 Jan. 1839, d. 19 July 1844. 3. Adoniram Judson, 21 Nov. 1844.

466a. VII. Sophronia Alden, of Ashfield, Mass., dau. o Rev. John, (252) was b. 20 Sept. 1809; m. 19 Apr. 1834, Edward Griffith Miner, banker, Winchester, Ill., b. 21 Jan. 1809.

They had children, 1. James, 16 Jan. 1835, who m. 17 April 1861, Ellen Thomas: is a physician, and was surgeon in the 101st Reg. Ill. Volunteers. 2. Henry, 10 Jan. 1837. 3. Anna Judson, 5 Sept. 1839, who m. 22 May, 1866, Charles B. Hubbard. 4. Lucy Alden, 30 Oct. 1841. 5. John Howard, 24 May, 1844, who was killed in the U. S. Army in Mississippi, 14 Sept. 1862. 6. Mary Ellen, 19th Aug. 1847, d, 28 Aug. 1848. E. G. Miner.

466b. VII. Lucy Thomas Alden, dau. Of Rev. John, (252) was b. 23 Aug. 1810: m. 16 Jan, 1834, Dr. Chenery Puffer, of Shelburne Falls, Mass., who was b. 22 Jan. 1804.

They had children, all b. in Coleraine, Mass. 1. Henry Marvin, 1 Jan. 1835, gr. Rochester U. 1860, studied law. 2. Samuel Willis, 8 Jan. 1837, gr. Rochester U, 1860, st. law. 3. Charles Chenery, 15 June, 1841, gr. Rochester U. 1863. 4. Lucy Maria, 5 Dec. 1842; d, 10 Feb. 1846. Dr. P. has been President of the Franklin Dist. Med. Soc., and in 1863 Rep. to G. C. of Mass.

46 T. VII. David Alden, Kewanee, Ill, teacher and farmer;, son of Rev. John, (252) b. 10 Feb. 1812, d. 24 Nov. 1864, gr; Brown U. 1838: resided in Ashfield, Mass., Kalamazoo, Mich., Shelburne Falls, Mass., held the office of deacon seventeen yrs: was a justice of the peace and much employed in public business. After his death an obituary notice of his life and character was published, which I have not seen. He was killed by his carriage coming into collision with the engine in crossing a railroad.

He m. 1, 19 Feb. 1839, Tirzah Maria Hart, who d. at Kalamazoo, Mich., 16 July, 1840: m. 2, 29' Aug. 1842, Esther Wells' Blackington, North Adams, Mass., who d. 3 Jan. 1845: m. 3, 27 Aug. 1846, Mary Bliss, dau. of Asa Ingraham, of North Adams, Mass.

CHILDREN

1, Isabel Maria, 12 July 1844: d. 6 Feb. 1848. 2. Francis Hearsey, 18 May, 1847. 3. James Willie, "3 Nov. 18+9; 4. Mary Isabel, 10 Jan. 1852: d. 23 Sept. 1854. 5. Charles David, 16 Aug. 1855. 6. Edward Miner, 15 Mar. 1857 r d. 13 Oct. 1859. 7. Harry Bartlett, 14 Sept. 1859: d. 13 Aug. 1862. 8. Frederick F. 14 Nov. 1861: d. 2 Sept. 1862. 9. Flora Grace, 23 Nov. 1864.

468. VII. Pliny Allen Alden, Hardwick, Mass., carpenter, Bon of Ezra, (258) b. 1792, m. 1828, Elizabeth Works.

CHILDREN

1. Cornelia, 10 Oct. 1829. 2. Mary E. 23 July, 1831. 3. John Pliny, 4. Julia, 20 Dec. 1834, (twins).

469. VII. Samuel Alden, Greenwich Mass., son of Ezra, (258) b. 8 Feb. 1791, went to the State of New York; m. Fanny Andrews.

CHILDREN

1. Samuel Ezra, 15 Dec. 1819, (787) 2. James Milton, 1 Jan. 1822, (788) 3. Fanny Emeline, 27 Sept. 1823, (789) 4. Franklin, 21 Nov. 1825, (790) 5. Emma Charlotte, 25 Feb. 1829, (791) 6. Alma Jane, 21 Dec. 1831, (792).

470. VII. Alma Alden, dau. of Ezra, (258) b. 1795, d. in Petersham, Mass., 21st June, 1855: m. Orrin West, of Greenwich, Mass., son of Roger West, Esq.

They had ch. 1. Harriet Newell, 11 Mar. 1818. 2. Lorenzo West, 11 Mar 1820. 3. Adalinc Frances, 11 Mar 1834. [It is remarkable that they were all born in the same month in the year, and on the same day of the month.]

471. VII. Capt. Abel Alden, Greenwich, Mass., farmer, son of Dea. Ezra, (258) b. 23 July, 1799: m. March, 1823, Eveline, dau. of Jacob Thompson, Esq., of Monson, Mass.

CHILDREN

1. Ursula Maria, 4 Nov, 1823, (793) 2. Francis Eveline, 7 Feb. 1827, (794) 3, William Thompson, 15 Jan. 1830, (795) 4. Julietta Florence, Aug. 25, 1832. 5. Harriet Hadussa, 14 Nov. 1835. 6. Augustus Dewey Alden, 20 Sept. 1842. 7. *Charles L. Alden, 5 Feb. 1845, d. 12 June 1849. 8. Henry LeRoy, 8 May, 1847.

472. VII. Emery Alden, Greenwich, Mass., son of Ezra, (258) b. 2 July, 1801, d. 23 April, 1865, a 64; m. 21 April, 1824, to Susan Reed, (b. Abington, Mass., 22 March, 1866,) by Rev. Joseph Blodgett of Greenwich.

CHILDREN

1. Addison Franklin, 9 Dec. 1824, (79f3) 2. Charles Milton, 20 May, 1807, d, 28 Feb. 1829, 3. Caroline Cordelia, 27 Jan. 1829, (797) 4. Julius Emery, 12 May, 1832, (798).

473. VII. Festus Alden, Hardwick, son of Ezra, (258) b. * 5 May, 1808; m. 28 Apr. 1831, Fanny N. Gibbs; d. 19 Oct. 1838; m. 2, 10 Sept. 1840, Sylva Terry of Hardwick, Mass.

CHILDREN

1. Angelina, 29 Nov. 1832, (799) 2. Theodore F. L. 17 May 1841, (799a) 3. George A. 11 Feb. 1846, d. 9 Sep. 1846. 4. Harrison F. 20 April, 1848, d. 2 Dec. 1849. 5. Ezra P. S. 27 Oct, 1851, 6, Fanny L. 12 May, 1854.

474. VII. James Milton Alden, Greenwich, Mass. son of Ezra, (258) b. 1810; m. 20 Nov. 1834, Elizabeth B. Root, b. 11 Apr. 1814, d. 18 May, 1858, a. 44.

CHILDREN

1. Sarah E. 24 Aug, 1835 (799b). 2. *James H. 25 June, 1837, d. 17 Feb. 1839. 3. James M. 26 Feb. 1839. (799c). 4. Mary E. 14 Mar. 1844, (799d) and 5. Achsah E.

15 March, 1844, (twins). 6. Edwin M. 8 Jan. 1846. 7. *Henry M. 12 Mar. 1849, d. 14 Aug. 1849. 8. Inf. son 1851. 9. Dwight Erving. 1 Jan. 1856. He m. 16 Nov. 1860, Hannah Richardson, who was b. in London, Eng. 19 Feb. 1826.

475. VII. Lyman Alden, Greenwich, Mass. son of Ezra, (258) b. 21 Aug. 1812; m. 9 Mar. 1843, Dorcas Marsh, dau. of Jacob Marsh of Ware Mass.

CHILDREN

1. Alonzo Lyman, 19 July, 1845. 2. Harrietta Augusta, 23 Sep. 1848. 3. Lorin Howard, 21 Sept. 1850.

476. VII. Sarah Alden, dau. of Ezra, (258) b. 13 Apr. 1814; m. 19 Feb. 1851, Erastus Blodgett, Greenwich, Mass. only son of Rev. Joseph Blodgett; no ch.

477. VII. Martha "Wright Alden, dau. of Rev. Timothy, (263) was b. 19 May, 1798; m. Hon. Patrick Farrelly, Meadville, Pa. (his 2d wife) who d. at Pittsburg, Pa. on his way to Congress, 12 Jan. 1826.

They had ch. 1. A dau. d. in infancy. 2. Patrick Alden, 12 Aug. 1821, who was killed by a fall from his horse. She m. 2, Mr. Fadden.

478. VII. Elizabeth Shepherd Wormsted Alden, dau. of Rev. Timothy, (263) was b. Portsmouth, N. H. 23 Nov. 1800; m. John Gibson of Meadville, Pa., merchant.

They had 5 ch. Elizabeth Shepherd and 4 who d. in infancy. Elizabeth m. John Craighead and had 8 children: 4 sons and 4 daughters. "Frank was a noble lad, was in the 100 Pa. Reg. of Volunteers, and d. at City Point, a. 17."

479. VII. Timothy Fox Alden, Pittsburg, Pa., lawyer, son of Timothy (263) was b. Portsmouth, N. H. 12 Apr. 1802; d. 1856, a. 54; gr. Alleghany Coll. Pa. in the first class, 1821; A.M. 1824; studied law; settled in Meadville, Pa.; m. Priscilla Dunn Van Home, 1828, who was living in 1865.

CHILDREN

1. Timothy Cornelius Wormsted Farrelly (799e). 2. Josephine Willis. (799f) 3. Cornelius Van Home, 1828, d. Jan. 1834. 4. Harriet S. (799g).

480. VII. Robert Wormsted Alden, son Timothy, (263) was b. Portsmouth, N. H. Jan. 1804; gr. Alleghany Coll. 1821; was a midshipman in U. S. Navy, several years; then went into the whaling service; was unm; and it is supposed was lost at sea.

481. VII. Sarah Weld Josephine Alden, dau. of Rev. Timothy, (263) b. Newark, N.J. 30 Dec. 1812; m. 6 Nov. 1832. Peter Joseph Maitland, Pittsburg, Pa. who d. 17 Sept, 1840; m. 2, Dr. Thomas P. Dale of Alleghany City, Pa. where (1866), he is in full practice and much respected.

Children, 1. Mary, b. 28, Dec. 1833. 2. Josephine Alden, who m. Thomas Bakewell, Jun. and has two sons. 3. John Alden, who went to sea in 1806, and no tidings have been received from him since Dec. 1857.

482. VII. Betsey Alden, Meadville, Pa. dau. of Isaiah, (264) m. Augustus Bradley of Meadville; had ch. Adeline Elizabeth, Warren Hedge, Augustus, Susanna, and Harriet who d, in infancy.

483. VII. Sarah Weld Alden, Meadville, Pa. dau. of Isaiah, (264) m. Rev. James Grier Wilson.

484. VII. Hon. Albert Alden, Barre, Mass. son of Martin, (265) b. 26 Aug. 1811; has a family, but the particulars have not been received; was a member of the Senate of Mass. in 1852.

485. VII. Timothy Alden, New York City, printer, son of Martin, (265) b. 1809; d. 4 Dec. 1848, a. 39; was the inventor of the wonderful type-setting and distributing machine, to which he devoted twenty years of his life. Since his death it has been much improved by Henry W. Alden, Esq. and is now owned by a company incorporated for the purpose.

486. VII. Isaiah Alden, carpenter, son of Martin, (265). No particulars.

487. VII. David Chandler Alden, son of Oliver, (266).

488. VII. Oliver Noble, son of Oliver, (266).

489. VII. Henry Williams Alden, City of New York, printer; interested in the famous type-setting and distributing machine; v. supplement.

490. VII. Charles Fox Alden, son of Oliver, (266) v. sup.

490a. VII. Lucy Alden, dau. of Oliver, (266) m. a Mr. Enos of Neenah, Wis.

491. VII. Clinton Alden, son of Oliver, (266); v. sup.

492. VII. Otis Alden, North Bridgewater, Mass. son of Daniel, (269) b. 1788, d. 9 Sept. 1825, a. 37; m. Harriet, dau. of Rev. Joseph Adams of Jay, Me. She d. 7 Dec. 1825, a. 35.

CHILDREN

1, Sally, 29 Sept. 1810, d. at Plymouth, Mass., 18 May, 1842, a, 32. 2. Harriet, 4 Mar. 1812, (800) 3. Otis Gary, 4 July, 1814, (801) 4. Albert, Oct. 1817, (802) 5. *Joseph Adams, Oct. 1824, d. 1826.

493. VII. Dea. Daniel Alden, Randolph, Mass., carpenter son of Daniel, (269) b. 10 June, 1791; m. 11 Dec. 1815, Eunice, dau. of Perez Southworth, who d. 8 July, 1817, a 24: m. 2, Olive, dau. of Samuel Tucker, of Canton, who d. 4 Sep. 182G, a. 33; m. 3, 10 Dec. 1828, Abigail Marsh, of Hiugham, who d. 8 Oct. 1839; m. 4, 26 May, 1843, Mrs. Grace Ide Peabody, widow of Rev. Charles H. Peabody, pastor of the Baptist Church, Randolph, who d. 21 April, 1842, a. 43, much respected.

CHILDREN

1. Daniel, 1 July, 1817, who d. num. 14 Dec. 1844, a 27. 2. Olive, 5 Nov. 1820, (803) 3. Ann Judson, 20 Feb. 1822, (804) 4. Lucia Ware, 13 April, 1825. (805) 5. Abigail Amanda, 2 Sept. 1829, (806) 6. Mary Marsh, 27 Nov. 1830, (807; 7. Francis Wayland, 23 Sept. 1834, (808) 8. Lucas Wales, 29 Aug. 1836, (809).

494. VII. Sally Alden, North Bridgewater, Mass. dau. Daniel, (269) m. Dea. Jonathan Burr, Worthiugton, Mass.; no eh.

495. VII. Dea. Alpheus Alden, North Bridgewater, Mass. carpenter, son of Daniel, (269) b. 1798; m. 1826, Charlotte, dau. of Jeremiah Tucker; m. 2, 1844, Priscilla Crosby; m. 3, Alice Bass of New Sharon, Me.

CHILDREN

1. Addison Tucker (8 10) 2. Sarah Ann, (811) 3. Charlotte; all by first wife.

496. VII. Sybil Alden, Jay, Me. dau. Silas, (270) b. 1798; m. Abijah Reed, Wilton, Maine.

Had ch. 1. Amos, 1825, soldier in U. S. A., k. a. 40. 2, Alden, conductor on O. C. & N. R. R., lives in Bridgewater. 3. Elvira Ann, d. young. 4. John Reed, Wilton, Me., farmer. 5. Augustus, Jay, Me., farmer. G. Winslow, m. wife dead. 7. Lucy Ann, m. B. Macomber, Jay, Me.

497. VII. Sylva Alden, Jay, Me. dau. Silas, (270) b. 1801, d. 1842; m. John Packard, Readfield, Me.; now lives in Jay, Me.

Children, 1. *Augusta, d. 2. Albion, carpenter, Winthrop, Me. 3. Otis, carpenter, unm. 4. Louis, do. Winthrop, Me. 5. Sewall, farmer, Jay, Me. 6. Winslow, U. S. A., killed in army. 7. Cary.

498. VII. Silas Alden, Winthrop, Me. son of Silas, (270) b. 1804; m. Polly Morrison of Fayette, Me.; m. 2, Mary Page of Winthrop, Mo.

CHILDREN

1. Montgomery Morrison, 15 Dec. 1833, (812) 2. Columbus, (813) S. Emily, (814) 4. Ellen, (815) (twins) all by the first wife.

499. VII. Eliza Alden, Jay, Mc. dau. Silas, (270) b. 1806, d. 18 Apr. 1856; m. Nathaniel Noyes, Jay, Mc.; m. 2, Noah Thayer, Randolph, Mass.; no ch.
Children, 1. Nathaniel, who m. Martha A. Dyer, Randolph, Mass. 2. Hosca, m. a Fisher of Weymouth, d. 3. *Emery, all by her first husband.

500. VII. Williams Alden, Winthrop, Me, farmer, son of Silas, (270) b. 1807; m. Louisa Reynolds of Jay, Me.

CHILDREN

1. Harriet Ann, (816) 2. Rutilus, (817)

501. VII. Winslow Alden, Randolph, Mass. carpenter, son of Silas, (270) b. 1812; m. 17 Oct. 1839, Hannah, dau. of Oliver Fuller of Jay, Me. She was b. 5 Sept. 1807; had a son Ausou, b. 5 Oct. 1840, who d. 3 1865, a. 25.

502. VII. Louisa Alden, Jay, Me, dau. Silas, (74) b. 5 July, 1814, m. Louis Packard, Redfield, Me.; has three dau.

503. VII. Eleanor Quint Alden, Jay, Mc. dau. of Silas, (270) b. 20 Apr. 1820, d. June 13, 1864, a. 44: m. 1843, Linus Belcher. Randolph, Mass, carpenter; had one dau. Eleanor Alden, 9 July, 1845.

504. VII. Betsey Alden, Jay, Me., dau. Joseph, (271) m. Gilbert Eustis: had 3 children: m. 2, Nathan Walker, Peru, Me. no ch.

505. VII. Lucy Alden, Jay, Mc., dau. of Joseph, (271) m. Thomas Macomber, of Sangerville, Me., 1 ch.

506. VII. Joseph Alden, Jay, Me., son of Joseph, (271) has had three wives and several children.

507. Mary Alden, Jay, Me., dau. of Joseph, (271) m. Danel Dathry, and had 6 ch.

508. VII. Elijah Alden, Jay, Me., son of Joseph, (271) m. Prudence Alden.

509. VII. Almira Alden, Jay, Mc., dau. Joseph, (71) m. Samuel Alden, (520) son of Seth, (275). After his death, m. a Torrey, of Abington, Mass., who is dead, and she is now (1866) a widow.

510. VII. Sanford Alden, North Bridgewater, son of Samuel, (272) m. Eliza Keith of Easton, Mass., who d. 9 Feb. 1857, m. 2. Widow Pitts, of New Bedford.

CHILDREN

1. Sanford Otis. 2. Samuel Ford, b. 23 Aug. twins, 1829, (818) (819) 3. *Eliza Jane. 4. Sarah, (820) 5. Hannah Copeland,(821) 6. *Williams, d. 1857.

511. VII. Mehitabel Alden, North Bridgewater, Mass., dau. Samuel, (272) m. "Williams Gary.

512. VII. Hannah Alden, North Bridgewater, Mass., dau. Samuel, (272) m. Seth Copeland.

513. VII. Sally Alden. dau. Samuel, (272) m. Walter Keith; had 4 eh.

514. VII. Mary Alden, North Bridgewater, Mass., dau. Williams, (273) b. 1805, m. 1829 Francis Gary, N. Br. who d, 1834; no issue. She d. 24 Feb. 1856, a. 50.

515. VII. Lavina Alden, North Bridgewater, Mass., dau. of Williams, (273) b. 1807: m. 31 Dec. 1828, Albert Kingman.

They had ch. 1. Ellen, 5 July, 1831, who m. 4 Jan. 1853, T. Emerson Gurney; he d. 15 Jan. 1855: m. 2, 1 Sept. 1857, Elisha H. Joslyn: they have one ch. Albert K. b. 30 Mar. 1865. 2. Mary G. b. 4 July, 1836, who m. 1 Sept. 1863, Harvey Tolman. 3. Lizzie Alden, 31 Oct. 1841.

516. Clarissa Alden, N. Br. Mass., dau. of Williams, (273) b. 1809: d. 23 Nov. 1860; m. 1831, Dr. Abel W. Kingman, N. Br. who first settled at Dartmouth, Mass.

They had ch. 1. *Francis Williams 1833; d. 1840. 2. Clara Clifford, 8 Jan. 1836, who m. 20 June, 1858, Capt. Alexander Wheldon; have 1 dau. 3. Abel Willard, 8 July, 1838, a merchant, Boston. 4. Hannah Williams, 1840: d. 1841. 5. Thomas Sewall, 8 Apr. 1843. 6. Helen, 1846: d. 1847, a. 7 mos. 7. Barton Elliot, 19 Aug. 1848. Dr. K. m. 2, Olive Alden Packard, wid. of E. T. Packard, who d. 1856, dau. of Daniel Alden, (493).

517. VII. Eunice Alden, East Stoughton, Mass. dau. of Seth, (275) b. 27 Nov. 1806: m. 1824, Howard Alger, of West Bridgewater, Mass. b. 1792.

They had ch. 1. A son, 13 Jan. 1827. 2. Harmony, 7 July, 1828: d. 13 Aug. 1852. 3. Henry Howard, 27 July. 1830; has a family. 4. Eunice, 27 Jan. 1835, m. Winchester Turner. 5. Sarah Jane, 7 May, 1838: m. Robert Freeman Fuller. 6. Hannah, 5 Sept. 1842: m. Volney Howard of South Randolph, Mass. 7. Daniel Everett, 5 Mar. 1846: d. 15 Oct. 1863.

518. VII. Azel Alden, Hartford, Mc., shoemaker, son of Seth, (275) was b. 1 Mar. 1800: m. 15 Oct. 18-37, Mary dau. or Seth Harris, of Turner, Me., b. 21 April, 1807.

CHILDREN

1. Eunice A. 17 June 1838. 2. Seth Harris, 10 Dec. 1810, farmer. He enlisted Aug. 1862, and served during the war in the 16th Reg. of Mc. Vol.; was twice wounded. 3. Lucy E. 19 Aug. 1843. who m. 27 Dec. 1860, Samuel A. Nelson of Livermore, Me. 4. Southworth, 4 Mar. 1847: d. 14 Jan. 1853. 5. Isaac B. 9 Nov. 1852: d. 10 Jan. 1854.

519. VII. Lysander Alden, East Stoughton, 'Mass., son of Scth, (275) b. 21 Jan. 1812, m. 22d Feb. 1830, Louisa Harris Ross, b. 6 Oct. 1810.

CHILDREN

1. Mary Ann, 6 July, 1830, (822) 2. Samuel Bingley, 12 May, 1833, (823) S. Betsey Jane, 29 Oct. 1835. 4. Betsey Jane, 29 Oct. 1835, (824) 4. Ellen Augusta, d. 1859, (825) 5. Susan Maria, (826) 6. Ann Amelia, (827) 7. Rodana Laura.

520. VII. Samuel Alden, E. Stoughton, Mass., shoemaker, son of Seth, (275) b. 1814: d. 24 May, 1853; m. Elmira, dau. of Joseph Alden, (271) had ch.: *Eleanor, who d. young, and John, who has a family. She m. 2, Jesse Torrey, of Abington, Mass., who is deceased.

521. VII. Adoniram Judson Alden, East Stoughton, Mass., farmer, son of Seth, (275) occupies the homestead, b. 25 Nov. 1819: m. 1841, Almira Whiting, b. 1819.

CHILDREN

1. Sophronia Ann, 6 Oct. 1843. 2. Adoniram, 29 June, 1846.

522. VII. Southworth Alden, East Stoughton, Mass, son of Seth, (275) b. 1823: m. 10 July, 1850, Elizabeth Curtis, dau. of George Winchester.

CHILDREN

1. Rhoda Ann, 18 Jan. 1852: d. 17 April, 1853. 2. Mary Elizabeth, 27 Nov. 1854. 3. Edward Southworth, 26 Oct. 1859.

523. VII. Seth Alden, E. Stoughton, Mass., son of Seth, (275) b. 15 May, 1823, has removed to Cleaveland, Ohio, m. Polly Jones: had no ch.; m. 2, Augusta Blanchard, Salisbury. N. H. They have two sous, Frank and Frederick.

524. VII. Ann Amelia Alden, E. Stoughton, Mass., dau. of Seth, (275) b. 3 Aug. 1826: m. 9 May, 1846, Isaac Blanchard, East Stoughton, boot manufacturer.

They had children: 1. Addie Louiza, 7 Feb, 1849, 2. Flora Williams, 24 Feb. 1854. 3. Isaac Lawrence, 10 May, 1860.

525. VII. Nathaniel L. Alden, Dubuque, Iowa, merchant, son of Seth, (275) h. 13 June, 1828: m. 13 Aug. 1847, Mary Jane, dau. of Consider S. Andrews, of West Harwich, Mass. She was b. 10 May, 1829.

CHILDREN

1. Frank Fillmore, 24 Aug. 1850. 2. Emma Louiza, 26 Mar. 1855, 3. Isaac, 11 Oct. 1857. 4. Ella Sabra, 16 Nov. 1859. 5. James, 8 Jan. 1862.

526. VII. Isaac Alden, E, Stoughton, Mass., now, (18G6), in Malcom, Iowa, son of Seth, (275) m. Hannah M. Rice.

CHILDREN

1. Clara Florence. 2. Charles and two others.

527. VII. James Alden, E. Stoughton, Mass., son of Seth, (275) b. 7 Sept. 1835; has been in the oil regions: is now, (1866), in Cambridge, Mass., an innkeeper: has no family.
528. VII. Daniel Randall Alden, North Bridge water, son of Hosea, (276) b. 1825, d. 1842.
529. VII. Abigail Williams Alden, North Bridgewater dau. of Hosea, (276) was b. Aug. 1820, m. 1842, Judson Loring.
530. VII. Luther Edson Alden, North Bridgewater, shoe cutter, son of Hosea, (27G) was b. 24 Sept. 1830: m. 17 Dec. 1854, Amanda, dau. of Marcus Copeland, who was b. 9 Aug. 1833: was in the army four years.

CHILDREN

1. Frank Williams, 14 Aug. 1855. 2. Daniel Herbert, 19 Aug. 1857. 3 Frederic Shelton, 17 Shelton, 17 July, 1859. 4. Herman Luther, 21 Oct. 1861.

531. VII. Stillman Alden, Bridgewater, son of Azel, (278), m. Amanda Beebe; no ch.
532. VII. Lovinia Alden, Ludlow, Mass., dau. of Azel. (278) m. Ira Barker.
Children: Addison Atwood. 2. Almon Alden. 3. Rebecca, 4. Paulina, 5, Sophia.
533. VII. Josiah Alden, Springfield, Mass., in U. S. Armory, son of Azel, (278).

CHILDREN

1. Harriet. 2. Caroline. 3. James.
534 VII. Bethany Alden, Ludlow, dau. of Azel, (278) Mass., m. Henry Shumway, Belchertown, Mass., a millwright, his second wife: no children.
535. VII. Solomon Alden, Cummington, Mass., son of Azel, (278) carriage maker, m. Loraine Claiborne; no ch.
536. VII. Mary Alden, dau. of Azel, (278) m. William E. Smith, piano forte maker.
537. VII. Azel Alden, Ludlow, Mass., son of Josiah, (281) b. 12 Aug. 1792; d. of cancer, 22 Oct. 1860; m. 20 May, 1821, Mary, dau. of Jesse Brainard, of East Haddam, Ct. She was b. 7 Sept. 1796.

CHILDREN

1. Sarah Sophia, 17 Mar. 1822, (828) 2, John Brown, 11 Feb. 1825, (829) 3. Anna Newell, 31 May, 1834, 4. Azel Brainard, 11 Mar. 1838: d. 20 Sept, 1838.

538. VII. Justus Alden, Ludlow, Mass., farmer, son of Josiah, (281) b. 15 Sept. 1793: d. 30 May, 1831: "as a great sufferer from rheumatism; was confined to his bed eight years before his death, his limbs drawn up to his body: his ankle, knee and wrist joints drawn out of place; his eyes distorted in their sockets, so that he was totally blind for two years preceding his death. He was emaciated to a skeleton: and it was necessary to cut the cords of his limbs before he could be placed in his coffin." — J. B. A. He m. Betsey Porter.

CHILDREN

1. Josiah, resides in Wilbraham, Mass., millwright. 2. George, res. in Bridgeport, Ct. 3. Betsey, res. at Indian Orchard, Springfield, Mass. 4. Olivet, m. Austin Morse, of Ludlow, Mass., who is d. 5. Norman, res. in South Belchertown, Mass. 6. Justus, res. in Ludlow; employee on Western railroad. 7. Charity, m. 1, George Sherbrooks, 2. — Worthington, of Holyoke, Mass. 8. Jemima, m. George Lisherness, of Maine, who went into the army in 1861 or 1862, and has not been heard from. She resides at Indian Orchard. 9. d. in infancy.

539. VII. Charity Alden, Ludlow, Mass., dau. of Josiah, (281) b. 5 June, 1797, d. 11 Aug. 1829, unm.

540. VII. Zenas Alden, Ludlow, Mass., and Springfield, son of Josiah, (281) b. 1 Nov. 1795, d. Jan. 1840; m. Betsey Taylor, Hartford, Ct.

CHILDREN

1. George Washington, d. Springfield, 1863 or 1864, 2. Henry, India rubber manufacturer, Waterbury, Ct. 3. Charles, Hartford, Ct. 4. Jane. 5. Caroline, m. a Mr. Taylor, Hartford, Ct. 6. William, resides in Springfield.

541. VII. Washington Brown Alden, M. D., Ludlow, Mass. son of Josiah, (281) b. 14 July, 1799, d. 5 Aug. 1859. Received the degree of M. D. at the Berkshire Med. Ins. 1828: "Was Town Clerk, Treasurer, and school committee fifteen out of twenty five years." He m. 4 Oct. 1830, Hannah B. Bartlett, b. 25 Dec. 1805.

CHILDREN

1. Helen C. 19 July, 1831. 2. Mary S. 7 Aug. 1834: d. Springfield, 24 Sept. 1864. 3. Philo W. 30 Oct. 1836.

542. VII. Charles Alden, Ludlow, Mass. son of Josiah, (281) b. 6 Dec, 1803, d. 22 May, 1862, having held the office of Justice of the Peace eighteen years; m. 1, 20 Nov. 1831, Lydia, dau. of George and Ruth More, who d. 1 July, 1841; m. 2, Margaret More, who d. Feb. 1852: m. 3, Louiza, dau. of Jonathan and Sally Paine.

CHILDREN

1. Charles Wesley, 7 Nov. 1832, (830) 2. Elizabeth Jane, 29 Mar. 1834, (831) 3. Fletcher Clark, 22 Mar. 1836, (832) 4. *Francis Washington, 23 Feb. 1845, d. young. Mrs. Louiza Alden.

543. VII. John Brown Alden, Ludlow, Mass., farmer, son of Josiah, (281) in early life taught various schools with success: was for a time a resident in Weathersfield and Hartford, Ct.; m. 17 June, 1827, Huldah Wright, dau. of Capt. John Clapp, of Weathersfield, Ct.

CHILDREN

1. Jane Olivet, 12 March, 1828, who m. Pliny Robinson of Holyoke, and resides in Southampton, Mass. 2. Eunice Brown, 19 June, 1829: m. Chester Canterberry of Belchertown; resides in Springfield, Mass. 3. John Brown, 1 June 1831; res. in Worcester. 4. Clarissa Ann, 25 Aug, 1833; d. 29 Sept. 1833. 5. Arthur Rowley, 5 Aug. 1834: d. 30 Dec. 1834. G. Sarah Elizabeth, 26 Oct, 1835: m. Richard L. Frost, of Springfield, Mass. 7. James Henry, b; 6 Nov. 1837: d. 30 Dec. 1837. 7. Birdsey Brainard, 12 Feb. 1839: resides in Strathalbyn, South Australia. 9. Preston Dwight, 25 Feb. 1841: res. in Worcester. 10. James Henry, 12 Feb. 1845: d. 21 Feb. 1845. 11. Albert Leslie, 16 May, 1846: d. 25 Aug. 1849. 12. Edwin Herbert, 27 June, 1848. 13. Frances Marion, 4 Dec. 1850: d. 22 May, 1852.

544. VII. Mary Needham Alden, Ludlow, Mass., dau. of Josiah, (281) b. 13 Sept. 1810; m. 27 Oct. 1831, Henry Fuller of Ludlow, Mass., farmer.

They had children, 1. Mary Newell, 1 Aug. 1832: m. Henry Collins of Ludlow. 2. Henrietta Susan, 15 Dec. 1833: m. Edwin Chapin. 3. Olivet Brown, 1 May, 1835: m. Henry Charles Frost. 4. Henry Seymour, 5 Feb. 1837: d. 1 Sept. 1843. 5. Edward Everett, 25 May, 1839: m. 20 Nov. 1862, Delia Jane Prentice. 6. Emma Asenath, June 1841. 7. Henry Seymour, 27 Aug. 1843: m. 16 Dec. 1862, Elizabeth Munsing. 8. Francis Starkey, 27 April, 1846. 9. Fanny Virginia Adelaide, 17 Oct. 1848: d. 17 Jan. 1866. 10. Lillian Eliza, 22 Sept. 1850. 11. Hattie Beecher, 16 Feb. 1854: d. 1 Feb. 1857.

"Henry Seymour, was killed instantly while driving a span of horses which became frightened, throwing him from a load of wood, and both wheels passing over him."

645. VII. Orsamus Alden, Ludlow, Mass., farmer and mi-owner, — lives on the old homestead — son of Josiah, (281) b. 5 June, 1808: m. 28 June, 1842, Eliza Ann, dau. of Samuel Lemmon, of Ware, Mass., b. 18 May, 1818.

CHILDREN

1. and 2. died in infancy. 3. Myraetta, 22 Oct. 1844, d. 27 Oct. 1861. 4. Georgianna, 7 July, 1846, d. 25 Sept. 1862. 5. Elliot C. Gillvary, 5 Feb. 1848. 6. Emera Francelia, 7 Nov. 1849. 7. Ida Alberta, 25 Aug. 1851. 8. Albert Prince, 14 June, 1853. 9. Arthur Ovilla, 21 Oct. 1855. 10. Marcena Melvin, 5 Dec. 1857. 11. Isabella Emeretta, 19 May, 1869. 12. Clarence Elma, 20 May, 1861.

546. VII. Eunice Brown Alden, Ludlow, Mass, dau. Josiah (281) b. 23 Dec. 1813, m. 24 Mar. 1833; Marvin King of Long meadow; resides in Ludlow, farmer. They have ch.

1. Mary Medelia, 9. Feb. 1834; m. 26 Nov. 1852, Justus Alden. 2. Marvin Henry, 5 Apr. 1835. 3. Ann Frances, 28 Feb. 1837: m. Charles Henry Knapp, Northampton. 4. Samuel Alden, 15 Dec. 1838: magistrate: served as sergeant in the late war four years: was seven times wounded. 5. Julia Isadora, 22 Mar. 1841. 6. Arthur Delano, 13 May, 1843: corporal in the army fifteen months. 7. Homer Washington, 8 Dec, 1844: d. 5 Sept. 1845. 8. Homer Rising, 4 June, 1846, resides in Denver City, Colorado, with others from Ludlow. 9. Olive Eugene, 14 May, 1848. 10. Frank Emmit, 26 May, 1850; d. 1 Oct. 1852, 11. Frederic Augustus, 17 Nov, 1852. 12. Lelia Imogen, 23 Dec. 1854.

547. VII. Mary Alden, Ludlow, Mass, dau. Benjamin (284) b. 17 Feb. 1806, m. Martin Richardson, who is dead. She resides in Salisbury, Ct.

548. VII. Jefferson Alden, Ludlow, Mass, son of Benjamin, (284) b. 26 Jan. 1804; 1858 m Hospital for Insane at Worcester, Mass.

549. VII. Caroline Matilda Alden, dau. Benjamin, (284) b. 26 June, 1815; m. 27 Dec. 1861, Artemas Harmon Whitney of Ludlow; no ch.

550. VII. David Alden, Enfield, Conn, son of Benjamin, (284) b. 17 May, 1807, m. had

CHILDREN

Lucius D. (833) and others.

551. VII. Dexter Alden, New Haven, Ct., merchant, son of Benjamin, (284) b. 13 Oct. 1812.

552 VII. Lucinda Marilla Alden, Ludlow, Mass., dau. Benjamin, (284) b. 4 Dec. 1817; m. Amos Josiah Gardner of Spring. field, Mass.

553. VII. Eliza Ann Alden, Ludlow, Mass., dau. Benjamin, (284) b. 8 July, 1822; m. Samuel Gay of Springfield, Mass, who is dead.

554. VII. Horatio Bingley Alden, Randolph, Mass., boot manufacturer, son of Simeon, (285) b. 16 March, 1786; m. 1812, Mary, dau. of Ephraim Belcher, b. 30 Sept, 1795.

CHILDREN

1. *Mary, 23 Dec, 1812, d. 6 Jan. 1813. 2. Mary Belcher, 25 Jan. 1816, (834) 3. Horatio Bingley, 8 Apr. 1820 (835)

555. VII. Hosea Alden, Randolph, Mass, boot maker, son of Simeon, (285) b. 1789; d. 26 May, 1835, a. 46; m. 1811, Martha, dau. of Silas Howard, of N. Bridgewater, who d. 23 Feb. 1858, a. 63.

CHILDREN

1. Mary, (836) 2. *Louiza. 3. Rachel, (837) 4. Henry Averin, 10 Nov. 1813, (838) 5. Jane, (839) 6. Emily Howard, (840) 7. Martin, (841) 8. Eliza Ann, (842) 9. Hosea, lost at sea. 10. Martha, (843) 11. Albert, (844). 2. *Isaac.

556. VII. Rachel Alden, Randolph, Mass, dau. of Simeon, (285) b. 26 May, 1792; d. 30 Dec. 1837; m. 1816, Capt. Samuel Thayer, Randolph, Mass.

CHILDREN

1. Henry Dearborn, m. Sarah Clark. 2. Sarah, m. Elbridge Arnold.

557. VII. Sally Alden, Randolph, Mass. dau. of Simeon, (285) was b. 20 Apr. 1797; d. 22 Feb. 1844; m. 1818, Adam French of Braintree.
Had 8 ch.: Alden, Rachel, Sarah, Mary, Ann, Robinson, who was lost at sea, Horatio, John Jarvis.

558. VII. John Alden, boot manufacturer, Randolph, Mass., son of Simeon, (285) was b. 15 Dec. 1799; m. 20 Mar. 1831, Mary Dunbar, dau. of Caleb Copeland, W. Br. b. 1 Apr. 1809.

CHILDREN

1. John. 15 Feb. 1832, d. 4 Sept. 1850. 2. Frederick Hart, 7 Jan. 1839. 3. Mary Copeland, 14 Apr. 1843.

559. VII. Hiram Alden, Randolph, Mass, boot cutter, son of Simeon, (285) b. 14 Nov. 1804; m.29 Feb. 1824. Mary, dau. of Isaac Tower.

CHILDREN

1. Julia Ann, 1825, (845) 2. Hiram Carroll, 1826, (846) 3. Charlotte Augusta, 1831, (847) 4 Margaret. 1833, (848) 5. *Caroline Francis. 1835, d. 1856. 6, *Mary Celestina," 1837: d. 1840. 7. William Hart, 1839, (849)8. Celestina Justina, 1841: d. 1842. 9. Mary Justina, 1846.

560. VII. Simeon Alden, Baltimore, merchant, son of Alpheus (2 86) b. 14 April, 1793, d. 9 Nov. 1858, a. 65; m. abt. 1822, Mary, Ann McElroy; no ch.

561. VII. Lucinda Alden, dau. Alpheus, (286) b. 1797; m. John Stoddard of Boston.
Children, 1. John, 1821. 2. William Henry. 3. Alpheus Alden. 4. Mary Elizabeth: m. Daniel D. Grover, of Boston. 5. Simeon Alden, 1834: d. 1866.

562. VII. Silas Alden, Randolph, Mass, boot manufacturer, son of Silas, (287) b, 24 Oct. 1786; d. 19 Jan. 1855; m. 26 Mar. 1809, Harriet, dau. of Thomas French Esq. b. 11 July, 1792; d. 1835.

CHILDREN

1. Charles, 28 Feb, 1810, (850) 2. George, 8 May, 1812, 1851) 3. *Harriet, 7 Apr. 1814. 4. Clementina L. 7 Feb. 1816, (852) 5. Harriet French, 14 June, 1818. 6, Julia Ann, 28 Dec. 1820, 7. Caroline, 19 Feb. 1823: d. 21 Nov. 1848. 8. Helen Augusta, 3 Aug. 1825, (854) 9, Hannah French, 6 Aug. 1828.

563. VII. Calvin Alden, Randolph Mass, boot maker, son of Silas, (287) b. 1788; d. 1825, a. 37; m. 1809, Martha, dau. of Eben'r Hayden of Stoughton, who m. 2, 1835, Col. Cyrus Porter.

CHILDREN

1. Calvin, 1809, (855) 2. Martha Hayden, (856) 3. Mary French 1813, (857) 4. Lewis, 1815, (858) 5. Lucy Ann, 1819, (859) 6. *Adoniram, d. a. 4 y. 7. *Eliza Jane, d. a. l y. 3m. 8 Adoniram, 1824, d. 21 Aug. 1859, (860)

564. VII. Samuel Alden, Philadelphia and N. Orleans, merchant, son of Silas, (287) b. 1790, d. 1838, a. 48; m. Mary Ann McDonald in Louisiana. She d. of cholera in Aug. 1832.

CHILDREN

1. Charles James, (861) 2. Samuel, twins, b. 6 Jan. 1S15; d. a. 6 w. 3. Mary Ann. d. Tuscaloosa, Al. a. 5 yrs. 4. Virginia Rose, b. Richmond Va, d. Wilmington, N. C., a. 17. 5. William Parris, b. Tuscaloosa, living in 1852. 6. Ann Eliza, 7. Carolina, d. of cholera. 8. Samuel, d. a. 4 mo.

565. VII. Polly Alden, Randolph, dau. of Silas, (287) b. 1792: m. 7 June, 1812, Dr. Ephraim Wales of Randolph, b. 11 Nov. 1787: d. of senile gangrene, 5 March, 1863: M. B. Dart Coll. 1810.
They had ch. 1. Peter, 1813, who m. Maria Ann Downs in 1837, and had three ch. 2. Mary, 1815, d. unm. 1851. 3. Lawrence, 1817, d. 1818. 4. Ephraim, 1819, M. D. Harv. 1844. 5. Sally. 1821. 6. Thomas Beal, 1823, gr. Mid. Coll. M. D. Harv. 1847, d. 2 Feb. 1861. 7. Ann Maria, 1832.
566. VII. Leonard Alden, Easton and Randolph, boot maker, son of Silas, (287) b. 1796, d. 28 July, 1822, a. 26: m. 1820, Rhoda Howard, of Easton. They had one ch.
Leonard, who d. a. 4 years.
567. VII. Melinda Alden, Randolph, Mass, dau. of Silas, (287) b. 22 July, 1800; m. 19 Mar. 1822, Joshua Thayer of Randolph.

CHILDREN

1. George Henry, 30 Sept. 1824 2. Sarah Elizabeth, 8 Feb. 1829. 3. Augusta, 18 Oct. 1831. 4. Leonard Alden, 30 June, 1834. 5. Thomas H. Barton, 12 Apr. 1836, 6. Ednah Maria, 10 Mar. 1841. 7. Albert 16 Nov. 1843. Leonard and Thomas were both in 4 Mass. Reg. Mass. Vol. U. S. Army.
568. VII. Cynthia Alden, Randolph, Mass, dau. of Silas, (287) b. 1808; m. 14 Aug. 1843, Walter Cartwright, Randolph, Mass.
Ch. 1. Mary Thompson, 19 Dec. 1845. 2. Grace Anna, 15 July, 1849.
569. VII. Silence Alden, Randolph, Mass, dau. Silas, (287) b. 1810, m. 26 June, 1828, Edwin Howard, Randolph, Mass.
Ch. 1. Edwin Williams. 2. Alden.
570. VII. Hannah Alden, dau. of Solomon, (288) b. 10 Oct. 1793; m. 3 Sept. 1820, Joseph G. Goldthwait, of Boston, who was b. Apr.4, 1798.
Ch. 1. Joseph Lorraine, 30 May 1821: m. Lydia Ann Newcomb, has 3 ch. 2. Mary Brackett, 2 July, 1827 d. 2 Nov. 1828. 3. David Ezekiel, 29 Jan. 1830, m. Mary Gushing; has 2 ch. 4. Hannah Alden, 22 Aug., 1832: m. William R. Bowen of Bos-

ton: has 4 ch. 5. Mary Johnson, 26 Jan, 1835, d. 13 May, 1842. 6. Charles Wesley, 23 July 1836, d. 10 Aug, 1864. 7. George Fisher, 11 July, 1840, m. 1865, Anna Maria Emery Hayes.

571. VII. Betsey Alden, dau. of Solomon, (288) b. 25 May 1796, d. 5 Dec. 1832; m. Dr. Nathan Richardson, of Reading, Mass.

Ch. 1. Elizabeth R. 30 May, 1822. 2. Warren 1 Dec. 1823. 3. A. Bradford, 27 Sept. 1825. 4. I. Varnum, 30 July 1827. d. 5. I. Varnum, 11 June 1829. d. 6. Triphosa, 31 March, 1831. d. 7. Almira, 10 Nov. 1832, d.

572. VII. John Alden, Chelsea, Mass, merchant, son of Solomon, (288) b. 1796; m. Betsey Fernald.

CHILDREN

1. John Henry, 12 Feb. 1822, (862) 2. Elizabeth Jane, (863) 3. Charles Fernald: is d. 4. George Washington: k. at battle of Antietam. 5. William Fernald, (864).

573. VII. Joseph Alden, Memphis, Tenn., son of Solomon, (288) b. 1801; m. Mary Cheever, of Saugus, Mass, who d. He m. 2. in Kentucky; had two ch. Ellen and Theodore; perhaps others.

574. VII. Solomon Alden, son of Solomon, (288) was b. 1803, d. 10 Sept, 1834; m. Betsey Wiley of S. Reading, Mass. Had one ch. All d.

575. VII. Mary Alden, dau. Solomon, (288) was b. 1806; d. 3 Feb. 1837, a. 31; m. Adam Hawks, of South Reading, Mass.

Had 1. Ellen, who is m. 2. Leverett. d.

576. VII. David Alden, Boston, merchant, son of Solomon (288) b. 1808; m. 10 Sept. 1831, Lucinda, dau. of Samuel Kendall, b. April, 1807; d. 6 May, 1847. He m. 2. 19 Oct. 1847, Laura P. (Foster) Daggett, dau. of Jacob Foster, of Andover, Mass.

CHILDREN

1. Emily L. 12 May, 1833, d. 3 Feb. 1866. (865) 2. David A. 16 Apr. 1835. (866.) 3. Martha J. 10 Aug. 1837. (867) 4. Hattie E. 13 Feb. 1839; d. 17 Feb. 1863, a. 24. (868).

577. VII. William Alden, Boston, merchant, house of Atwood, Alden & Co. son of Solomon, (288) b. 30 Mar. 1810; m. 9 May, 1836, Eliza, dau. of C. C. Andrews of New York. b. 1821.

CHILDREN

1. Ellen Maria, 20 Aug. 1837 in Cleveland, O. She m. 18 June 1857, Frederick Curtis, and d. 29 June 1858. 2. William George, b. in Boston, 22 Apr. 1852.

578. (VII) John Adams, Alden, son of David, (250) had a family; left no ch.

579. VII. David Salmon Alden, son of David, (290) had a family; left no ch.

580. VII. Sally Alden, Randolph, Mass., dau. of Jonathan (291) b. 29 June, 1797: m. 29 May 1816, Thomas W. Tolman, merchant, Randolph, who d. 29 Mar. 1837 a. 44. She m. 2. Oct. 1839 Aminadab Thayer: and d. Apr. 15, 1849.

Ch. 1. Abigail, 2 Apr. 1817. who m. 8 Aug. 1837, Rev. Conant Sawyer, and d. 17 July 1841. 2. Sarah, 27 Sept. 1818, who d. 18 Feb 1839. 3. Adoniram Judson, 10 May, 1820, who d. 15 Oct. 1838. 4. Thomas, 20 Oct. 1822, who d. 14 Oct. 1840. 5. Royal Turner, 25 Jan. 1825, who d. 17 Mar. 1844. 6. Anna Weston, 31 Jan. 1827; m. 22 Oct. 1845, Frederick Howard, M. D. Randolph, Mass. Harv. Coll., 1839. who have 1 dau. Annie Tolman, b. 1851. 7. Gilbert Alden, 30 Sep. 1830, boot manufacturer, Randolph.

581. VII. Nancy Alden, dau. of Jonathan, (291) b. Newton; Mass., 30 Jan. 1799., m. Asahel Weston, Baltimore, merchant.

Ch. Jonathan Alden. 2. Florence, who m. Joseph Whitney, Baltimore. 3. Anna Maria, who m. Milton Whitney, m. 2, Royal T. Church, merchant, Baltimore, who was lost in the Lexington, 13 Jan. 1840. 4. Royal T. 5. Louiza Baldwin.

582. VII. Jonathan Alden, Philad'a, merchant, son of Jonathan (291) d. 15 Feb. 1849 a. 45, m. Eliza Arbuckle. She d. 4 Apr. 1864 a. 57, only sister of the late Rev. James Arbuckle. N. Y. Obs.

583. VII. John Tolman Alden, Cincinnati, O. merchant, son of Jonathan (291) b. 1806, m. 4 Mar. 1834, Elizabeth S. Tilton, Reading Pa. d. 14 Dec. 1850.

CHILDREN

1. Gilbert Tilton, 14 July, 18.35; d. 9 Aug 183-5. 2. William Tilton, 30 May, 1836; d. 13 June 1836. 3. Harriet Tilton, 7 Jan. 1838, who m. 1866 David Southworth. 4. John Tolman, 25 July, 1840; in army 4 years. 5. Edwin, 20 Aug. 1843, in army. 6. Walter, Apr. 1846, in army. 7. Frank Holt, 1 Sept. 1848; m. 2, 1853 Sarah, H. Tilton, b 1826. 8. Howard, 24 Mar. 1854. 9. Elizabeth Susan, 7 Feb. 1857. 10. Caroline Wood, 7 Aug 1860; d. 28 Dec. 1863. 11. Sidney Graves, 14 July, 1864, d. 28 Nov. 1864. 12. Willie, 14 Nov. 1865.

584. VII. David Packard Alden, Philad'a., teacher of Music: son of Jonathan, (291) d, 20 Feb. 1852; m. Rebecca Bipsham, b. 1808.

CHILDREN

1. Richard Coe, 24 Nov. 1834. 2. David Packard, 3. Jonathan; 15 Sep. 1837, m. at Albany. 4. Eliza Morse, 28 July, 1841. 5. Francis Buck, 11 July, 1843. 6. Mary Spalding, 23 Feb. 1848.

585. VII. Caroline Alden, dau. of Jonathan (291) was b. 23 Apr. 1813, d. at Wickliffe, Ill. 7 Aug. 1844 a. 31; m. 1836 Gustavus W. Southworth.

Had ch. 1. David Alden, 15 Feb. 1837. 2. Gordon Augustus, 11 Dec. 1839. 3. Rebecca Coe, 19 June, 1812.

586. VII. Susan Jane Alden, dau. of Jonathan, (291) of Baltimore, 3 Nov. 1819; d. Chicago, Ill. 30 Aug. 1854, a. 35: m. 1845 G. W. Southworth.

Ch. 1. William Steuben, 17 Nov. 1849. 2. Gilbert Weston, 15 Sept. 1852; d 2 Feb. 1855. In 1857 Mrs. S. was living in Kenosha, Wis., but is now (1866) dead.

587. 588. 589. VII. children of Isaac Alden, (292) of Walpole, Mass.; no account of their families has been received.

590. VII. Granville Alden, Salem, Mass., merchant: son of Lot, of Salem (293).

591. VII. Warren Alden, Salem, Mass., son of Lot of Salem, (293) d. in Lee, Ms.; m. Mary Dewey, had a dau. Julia Ann.

592. VII. Julia Ann Alden, dau. of Lot (293) m. Andrew Smith, of Salem, Mass.

593. VII. Miranda Alden, dau. of Lot, (292) m. 1847, John; Putnam, Salem, Mass., had two sons, and is d.

594. VII. Oliver Alden, Bridgewater, Mass., son of Caleb, (294) was b. 1792; m. 20 Oct. 1819, Melinck. dau. of Edward Mitchell.

CHILDREN

1. Caleb, Aug., 1820. 2. *Charles, 1822. 3. Edward, Feb. 1825.

595. VII. Sarah Alden, dau. of Caleb, (294) b. 1794;m. Sidney Howard, of Bridgewater, and went to Lancaster, Mass.

Had ch, Caleb, Charlotte, Parney, George, Sarah Ann, Sidney, Francena.

596. VII. Mehitabel Alden, dau. of Caleb, (294) b. 1796, m. John Thurston, Lancaster, Mass.

Had ch. Charles, John, Henry.

597. VII. Susan Alden, dau. of Caleb, (294) b. Apr. 22, 1798. She m. Samuel Sanger, son of Rev. Zedekiah Sanger, D.D.

598. VII. Cromwell Alden, Mid'o, Mass., son of Caleb, (294) b. 1800; m. 17 June, 1832, Mary, dau. of Joseph Hall, b. 4 Feb. 1811.

CHILDREN

1. Susan, 18 Dec. 1835. 3. John Franklin, 1836, d. 1839. 3. Sarah Hayward, 1839, d. 1839. 4. Priscilla Mullins, 1843, d. 1843.

599. VII. William Snell Alden, Bridgewater, Mass., son of Seth, (296) b. Aug. 1802; m. 1840, Sarah Horton, who d. in 1844.

CHILDREN

1. Eunice Gary, 26 July, 1841. 2. William Snell, 24 Dec. 1843.

Note.— Seth, No. 296, went to Winslow, Me. in Nov. 1801; his wife in August 1802. He returned to Bridgewater in Dec. 1841 — went West and was never heard from. It is supposed he was lost in going down the Mississippi river.

600. VII. Addison Alden, Wareham, Mass., son of Joseph (298) was b. 27 Sept, 1801: m. Deborah Leonard.

601. VII. Almira Alden, Bridgewater, Mass. dau. of Joseph, (298) b. 24 July, 1803, m. 5 July, 1842, Bela Hayward, who was b. 1779, d. 1847.

602. VII, Amos Alden, So. Abington, Mass., son of Joseph, (298) b. 24 June, 1808; m. Diantha Gurney, wid. of Gardner Powers, of So. Ab.

603. VII. Alexander Alden, South Abington, Mass. son of Joseph, (298) b. 4 Sept. 1814; m. 25 Nov. 1837, Maria D. dau. of Peter Conant, b. 1820; d. 1848; m. 2 1850, Louisa Clark of Hanover, Mass,

CHILDREN

Mary Josephine, 30 Aug. 1839. 2, Edward Cushing, 20 Jan. 1842; in 28 Reg. Mass. Vol. 3. John, 12 Apr. 1844; 4 Reg. Mass. Vol. 4. Lucy Mann, 28 Aug. 1846; d. 9 Sep. 1849. 5. Maria Louiza, 25 Nov. 1862. 6. Emily Augusta, 31 July, 1854. 7. George Eells, 26 Jan. 1857. 8. Seth, 30 Aug. 1859. 9. Frank Reed, 20 July, 1861.

604. VII. Daniel Alden, South Hadley, Mass, son of Daniel, (299) paper maker, b. 23 Feb. 1806; d. 14 Oct. 1855; m. 2 Nov, 1831, Lucy Keyes of Ludlow, b, 25 Sept, 1805; is d,

CHILDREN

1. Ach. 14 Nov. 1832; d. same day. 2. Lucy Amelia, 11 Aug. 1834. 3, Daniel Webster, 25 July, 1838; d. 20 July, 1839. 4. Sarah Elizabeth, 17 Feb. 1843. 5. *Eleanor Parker, Nov. 28, 1845; d. 10 June, 1865; was at school Mt, Holyoke Sem., d. of fever.

605. VII. Orlando Tillotson Alden, New Haven, Ct., New York, 1865; son of Daniel, (299) b. 29 Sept. 1808; m. 6 Aug. 1842, Sarah Elizabeth Bailey. She d. New Haven, Ct, 4 Dec. 1854.

CHILDREN

1. Mary Elizabeth. 2. William Croswell. 3. *Mary Joanna. All b. in Louisville, Ky. and d. under two years of ago.

606. VII. Freeman Alden, Belchertown, Mass., son of Daniel, (299) b. 21 Dec. 1809; m. 1846, Harriet, dau. of Eliha Root. She d. 1 May, 1850.

CHILDREN

1. Harriet Eliza, 8 Dec. 1847. 2. Maria Carver, 27 Oct. 1848.

607. VII. Joseph Alden, New York, merchant, son of Daniel, (299) b. 1813; unm. in 1866.

608. VII. Emily Alden, Belchertown, Mass., dau. of Daniel, (299) 16 June 1815; m. 17 June, 1849, Edward Holden of Roxbury, Mass., who was b. 4 Mar. 1816, son of Ezekiel Holden.

Ch. 1. Emily, 26 Apr. 1850. 2. Caroline Carver, 18 Apr. 1852. 3. Rose Standish, 9 Nov. 1856, d. 13 Feb. 1863.

609. VII. Thomas Alden, Belchertown, Mass, farmer, son of Daniel, (299) b. 21 June, 1817; m. Julia Ann Walker, b. 10 July 1816, dau. of Jason Walker.

CHILDREN

1. Julia Elizabeth, 27 Aug. 1851. 2. George Thomas, 12 Jan. 1853.

610. VII. Matilda Copeland Alden, Bridgewater, Ms., dau. of Thomas, (300) b. 18 Apr. 1818; m. 14 Apr. 1844; Joseph C. Norton, of Boston; b. 24 Aug. 1819.

Ch. 1. Joseph Chamberlain, 8 Jan. 1845. 2. Ellen Matilda, 24 Jan. 1847. 3. Edgar, 18 Nov. 1848. 4. *Agnes, 1855; d. 1859. 5. Frederic Bush, 1858; d. 1861. 6. Sarah Elizabeth, 4 June, 1861.

611. VII. Elizabeth Brown Alden, dau. of Thomas, (300) b. 4 Feb. 1820; m. 30 Aug. 1843, Simeon D. Wood, Bridgewater Mass., b. 13 Jan. 1817.
Ch. Mary Elizabeth, 16 Nov. 1844.
612. VII. Mary Jones Alden, dau. Cyrus, (301) b. 1814; m. George W. Little, of Va.
613. VII. Charles James Alden, son of Cyrus, (301) b. 1816; no particulars received.
614. VII. Caroline Perkins Alden, dau. Cyrus, (301) m. Edward Dodge, N. Y.
615. VII. Jane Frances Alden, dau. of Cyrus, (301) b. 1821; m. Walter C. Durfee, of Fall River.
616. VII. Eliza Wood Alden, dau. of Cyrus, (301) b. 1826 j m. Edward Chase "of St. Louis, Mo.
617. VII. Harriet Farquar Alden, dau. of Cyrus, (301) b. 1829; m. Joseph Pellet of Brooklyn, N. Y.
618. VII. John Carver Alden, S. Bridgewater, Mass., of the firm of Alden and Vose; Boston, son of Rev. Seth, (304) b. 29 July, 1823; m. 1851 Mary, dau. of Eleazer Carver; b. 1828.

CHILDREN

1. John Carver, 1852. 2. Henry Dyer, 1856. 3. Edward M. 19 Dec. 1882.
619. VII. Mary Denny Alden, Marlborough, Mass., dau. of Rev. Seth, (304) m. a Mr. Horton of New York City.
620. VII. Benjamin Franklin Rice Alden, son of Rev. Seth, (304) b. 1834; was in Mass. 6 Reg. Co. D. U. S. nine mo. service.
621. VII. Edward Winslow Alden, Worcester, Mass., merchant, son of Rev. Seth, (304) was b. 1840, and was in the sixth and 22 Mass. Reg. in the U. S. service.
622. VII. Adeline Augusta Alden, Marlboro', Mass., dau. of Rev. Seth, (304) b. 1842; m. 14 Jan. 1864, Capt. James W., Gird, of the 57 Mass. Reg., at Worcester, Mass.
623. VII. Solomon Alden, Bridgewater, Mass., son of Solomon, (307) was b. 25 June, 1787; d. 4 Jan. 1866; m. 1833, Betsey Leach.

CHILDREN

1. Harriet Lovinia, 11 Mar. 1834. 2. Emily Frances, 16 Feb. 1841. 3. Susan Elizabeth, 25 Sept. 1842, who m. 1865, Martin Van Buren Pratt, of N. Mid. and had a dau. Emily Alden, b. 4 Apr. 1866.

624. VII. Mary Alden, dau. of Solomon, (307) b. 1789; m. Caleb Alden. (628).

625. VII. Sarah Alden, dau. of Solomon, (307) was b. 1795; m.

626. VII. Lewis Thomas Alden, Bridgewater, Mass., farmer, son of Solomon, (307) was b. 1798; m. Abigail Howard, who d. 1849; had one ch. Lemira Eliza, who d. 4 Aug. 1842; a. 4 y. 1 m. 4 d. m. 2 Mar. 1865, Mary G. Stewart.

627. VII. Major Jesse Dunbar Alden, Westbrook, Me., son of Caleb, (314) b. 1 Aug. 1789; d. 26 May, 1835, a. 46; was a major of cavalry in the war of 1812; m. 8 May, 1819, Isabella B. Francis.

CHILDREN

1. Isabella, 1820; d, 1836. 2. Sarah R. 1822; m. George Merrill, Roxbury Mass. 3. Susan D. 1825; d. 1842. 4. Alpheus S, 1829. 5. John Quincy Adams, 1827; d. 1828. 6. Jesse F. 1835.

628. VII. Caleb Alden, N. Middleboro', Mass., carpenter, son of Caleb, (314) b. 30 Jan. 1790; m. Mary, dau. of Solomon Alden, (307) b. 6 July, 1789; d. 28 Nov. 1829; m. 2 Feb. 1831, Deborah, dau. of Thomas Thompson, b. 1799; d. 1836; m. 3 Mar. 1838; Mrs. Abigail Tinkham, dau. of Samuel Briggs.

CHILDREN

1. Jane. 4 Mar. 1820; d. 28 Dec. 1842. 2. Caleb C. 23 July, 1824; d. 27 May, 1832. 3. Mary King, 23 Nov. 1829. 4. Cyrus, 27 May, 1832; m. 29 Nov. 1856, Eliza A. Gilbert, o. Reuel Thompson, 30 Mar. 1834; m. 27 Mar. 1855, Isabella A. Warren.

629. VII. Ezra Alden, Lyme, N. H., farmer, son of Caleb, (314) b. 13 Jan. 1792: d. 2 Mar. 1835; m. Clarissa, dau. of James Beal. She was b. 20 Aug. 1795; d. 23 Jan. 1846, a. 51.

CHILDREN

1. *Clarissa, 29 Aug. 1817; d. 30 June, 1838. 2. Amos B. 13 Mar. 1819; m. Lydia H. Hall. 3. Jesse, 2 Mar. 1821; m. Mary E. Durkee. 4. Samuel; 21 Feb. 1823; m. Mary L. 5. S. Maria, 29 Jan. 1825: m. Geo L. Fogg, Natick. 6. Ezra Judson, 13 Jan. 1827; minister, (869) 7. Selah B. 18 May, 1833; resides in Natick, Mass.

630. VII. Betsey Alden, Lyme, N. H., dau. of Caleb, (314) m. Walter Bixby.

631. VII. Martha Alden, Lyme, N. H., dau. of Caleb, (314) m. Reuel Warren.

631. VII. David Alden, Lyme, N. H., son of Caleb, (314) and wife Lucy: had a son Alexander Mason, 18 July, 1840.

633. VII. Susan Alden, Lyme, N. H., dau of Caleb, (314) m. William Paine.

635. VII. Azubah Alden, Lyme, N. H., dau. of Caleb, (314) m. Cyrus Warren.

635. VII. Apollos Alden, Middleboro', son of Rufus, (315) no account.

636. VII. Darius Alden, Middleboro', Mass., son of Rufus, (315) b. 2 Oct. 1783; d. 29 Dec. 1808, a. 25; m. but had no children.

637. VII. Abigail Leonard Alden, dau. Rufus, (315) b. 1786: m. Benj. White.

638. VII. Chloe Alden, dau. Rufus, (315) b. 1792: m. Andrew Pratt.

639. VII. Rufus Alden, Middleboro', Mass., son of Rufus, (315) b. 1794: d. 3 Sept. 1841; m. 18 Mar. 1821, Betsey, dau. of Zechariah Weston, who d. 3 April, 1843, a. 44.

CHILDREN

1. Apollos Granville, 24 Mar. 1823, (870) 2. Zechariah Weston, 12 Dec. 1824. 3. Betsey Myrick, 15 Jan. 1827. 4. Caroline Frances, 24 Apr. 1829. 5. Damon Daronza, 31 Mar. 1831. 6. Martin Van Buren, 26 June, 1835. 7. Darius Greenleaf, 14 Jan. 1837. 8. Frederic Dasey, 1 Aug. 1839.

639a. VII. David Alden, Middleboro', Mass., farmer, son of David, (316) b. 10 Oct. 1789; m. Jan. 28, 1821, Sarah Weston, dau. of Daniel and Rebecca Weston, of Halifax, Mass. She was b. 23 Mar. 1800; d. 22 Apr. 1866, a. 66.

CHILDREN

1, Charles Henry, b. 8 June, 1822. (871) 2. John Thompson, 10 Nov. 1823 (872) 3. William Harrison, (873) 4. Sarah.

639b. VII. Oliver Hathaway Alden, Middleboro', Mass., son of David, (316) b. 22 Apr, 1795; m. 1816, Sally, dau. of Phinehas and Sally Pratt, of Middleboro'; m. 2. 1824, Lucinda, dau. of Ansel and Sally Cobb; b. 14 Jan. 1806.

CHILDREN

1. Betsey Hathaway, 23 May, 1817. (874) 2. Abner, 19 June, 1819. (875) 3. Henrietta, 22 Feb. 1825. (876) 4. Sarah Weston, 11 Jan. 1828. (877 5. Warner, 3 Feb. 1831, (878) 6. Lucinda. 21 Apr. 1835. (879) 7. Amelia Savery, 12 Feb. 1833. (880) 8. William Cobb, 11 Apr. 1841, who resides in Mid. 9. Gustavus Leonard, 17 Feb. 1845; d. 15 Dec. 1853. 10. Mary Franklin, 16 May, 1850.

640. VII. Jason Fobes Alden, Norton, Mass., son of Andrew, (317) b. 22 June, 1798; m. 25 Jan. 1821, Keziah E. dau. of John Shaw of Middleboro', Mass., b. 16 Dec. 1799.

CHILDREN

1. Selina A. F. 13 Mar. 1823, (881) 2. Adnah, 16 Jan. 1825; d. 10 Feb. 1825. 3. Emily E. 19 Sept. 1826; d. 4 Aug. 1861, (882) 4. William Henry, 18 July, 1823, (883) 5. Polly E. 1 Mar. 1831, (884) 6. Hannah W. 13 Sept. 1832.

641. VII. Philander Alden, Middleboro'; Mass., son of Andrew, (317) b. 10 Nov. d. 8 Mar. 1835, m. Polly S., dau., of Calvin Murdock.

CHILDREN

1. *Henry H. 2. George L. 3. Aug. 1822. (885) 3. Theodore Harris, 26 Aug. 1825. (886) 4. Thomas J. 3 Feb. 1831. (887) 5. Henry H. 1833. (888) 6. Philander M. Sycamore, Ill. 7. A dau. m. Samuel Alden.

642. VII. Andrew Leach Alden, Esq., North Middleboro', Mass., son of Andrew, (317) was b. 1804; m. 27 Nov. 1828, Olivia Murdock, dau. of Luther. She was b. 19 May, 1805.

CHILDREN

1. Leander Murdock, 3 Nov. 1829.(889) 2. Sidney Harris, 10 Nov. 1833, (890) 3. *Olivia Murdock, 5 Apr. 1841; d. 12 Not, 185G. 4. Asenath Ella, 8 Oct. 1849.

643. VII. Dea. Horatio Harris Alden, Bridgewater, (Titicut,) farmer, son of Andrew, (317) was b. 4 Nov. 1806; m. 1829, Abigail, dau. of John Clark, b. 1809; and d. 11 Aug. 1855.

CHILDREN

1. Horatio Williams, 11 Oct. 1830; d. 13 Oct. 1832. 2. Charles Edward, 9 Feb. 1832. 3. Horatio Williams, 20 Feb. 1834; d. 5 Jan. 1835. 4. John Clark, 4 Apr. 1836. 5. Andrew, 9 Sept. 1838. (891) 6. Sarah Abigail, 14 May, 1841; d. 19 June, 1842. 7. Marcus Morton, 9 Sept. 1843. 8. Ordney William, 21 Apr. 1848. 9; Sarah Bartlett, 21 Sept. 1850. 10. Franklin Pierce, 11 Jan. 1853; d. 19 Mar. 1858. He m. 2 1857, Abigail Keen Ripley. 11. Franklin Keen, 4 Jan. 1859.

644. VII. Josiah Vaughn Alden, Medford, Mass., carpenter, son of Andrew, (317) was b. 10 Jan. 1809; m. 16 May, 1836; Ann Bliss, dau. of Nathan T. West: was b. 28 Aug. 1816.

CHILDREN

1. Ann Malvina, 8 Sept. 1842. 2, Leah Fobes, 19 July, 1847; d. 4 Sept. 1849. 3. Ella Frances, 15 Sept. 1850.

645. VII. Peter Oliver Alden, Middleboro', Mass., son of Job, (320) b. May, 1801.

646. VII. Paraclete Alden, Middleboro', Mass., son of Job, (320).

647. VII. Zephaniah Shaw Alden, Middleboro', Mass., carpenter, son of Job, (320) b. 8 Dec. 1806; d. in Braintree, 8 Mar. 1849; m. 2 Feb. 1831, Myra, dau of Samuel Wales.

CHILDREN

1. Henry Augustus, 29 Oct. 1831; d, 3 Sept. 1853, a. 22. Grave stone in E., Randolph, Mass.

648. VII. Lois Alden, dau. of Job, (320) no account received.

649. VII. Lydia Alden, dau. of Job, (320)

650. VII. "Lucy Alden, dau, of Job, (320)

651. VII. Horatio Alden, Camden, Me., son of Ebenezer, (322) was b, 4 Feb. 1800; m. 1822, Sally, dau. of Capt. Nathaniel Bachelor: who was b. 12 Sept. 1802; and d. Feb. 1835; m. 2, 1835, Polly, sister of the former wife, b. 19 June. 1807.

652. VII. Louiza Alden, dau. of Ebenezer, (322) was b. 80 Jan. 1802; and d. at Thomaston, Me., 29 Sept. 1827; m. 1823; Phinchas Tyler.

Had ch. 1. William Parker, 30 Mar. 1824. 2. Edwin, 25 Oct, 1825.

653. VII. Silas Alden, Bangor, Me., son of Ebenezer, (322) b. 23 June, 1804; m. 27 Jan. 1828, Sarah, dau. of Capt. John W, Lindley.

654. VII. Lyman Alden, South Union, Me., son of Ebenezer, (322) m. 17 Sept. 1835: Sarah Elizabeth Williams of Orono, Me.

CHILDREN

1. Helen Louiza, 25 Aug, 1836. 2, Eugene Bartholomew, 6 July, 1839. 3. Lyman, 29 Sept. 1842. 4, Henry Ebenezer, 4 Apr, 1847.

655. VII. Melinda Alden, dau. of Ebenezer, (322) was b. 16 June, 1811; m. 6 May, 1837; George Abbott Esq., of Temple, Me., who d. in 1850.

Their ch. were 1. Lucy 6 June, 1839; 2, George Roscoe 6 Feb. 1842.

656. VII. Augustus Alden, Union, Me., son of Ebenezer, (322) was b, 3 July, 1814; occupies the homestead of his father; m. 10 Dec. 1840, Margaret Wiley, who was b. 24 Jan. 1815, dau. of Eleazer Bancroft Williams, of Gardner, Me.

CHILDREN

1. Patience Gillmor. 2 Mar. 1844*. 2, *Sarah Williams, 17 Apr. 1846; d. 1 Mar, 1847. 3. George Adelbert, 25 May, 1848.

657. VII. Ebenezer Alden, Thomaston, Me., son of Ebenezer (322) was b. 14 Dec. 1816; m. June 29 1845, Caroline Snow, of Thomaston.

CHILDREN

1. Frances Marion, 33 May, 1848.

658. VII. James Gillmor Alden, Janesville, Wis., merchant, son of Ebenezer, (322) b. 1 Mar. 1819, m. 24 Oct. 1842, Alvitia C. Miller, of Bangor, Me., dau. of Capt. John Miller, b. 7 Dec. 1821.

CHILDREN

1. James Francis, 20 Sept. 1843. 2. Louisa, 11 May, 1845. J. G. A.

659. VII. Dr. Edward Alden, son of Ebenezer, (322) b. 13 Dec. 1821. No particulars.

660—663. VII. Ch. of Spooner Alden, (323) near Bangor, Me. No particulars received.

664—670. VII. Ch. of Eliab Alden, Cairo, N. Y., (325). Amanda, Abna, Charles, who m. Elsie Casper, John, La Fayette, Henry, Oramel. No particulars received.

671. VII, James M. Alden, M. D., New York, son of Levi, (327) b. 24 April, 1818; studied medicine with Dr. Consider King, attending medical lectures at the Un. of Penn., where he received the degree of m. D. in 1838: settled after a brief residence in his native place in New York City: in June 1847 was appointed assistant physician at the Quarantine Hospital, Staten Island. In Feb. 1851 was appointed assistant physician to the Marine Hospital at Staten Is-

land, and on the 20 March, had an attack of ship fever, of which he died on the 26th. His remains were deposited in Greenwood Cemetery. "He lived an upright christian life, and died in the cause of humanity, administering to the relief and comfort of strangers, in sickness in a strange land, at the age of thirty-two years."

672. VII. Julius Tuttle Alden, Windham, N. Y. son of Levi, (327) b. 18 Feb. 1821; m. 18 Oct. 1853, Roxa A. Emmons, at Oneonta, Otsego Co., N. Y.

CHILDREN

1. Amanda Maria b. at Aldenhill, Wayne Co. Pa., 2 Aug. 1854. 2. Mary Emmons, b. Oneonta, N. Y, 24 May, 1858.

673. VII. Levi Hathaway Alden, Windham, N. Y. son of Levi, (327) b. 1 Jan. 1825; m. 27 May. 1857, Lois M. Strong.

CHILDREN

1. Lizzie A. 4 May, 1860. 2. James Strong, 1 Feb. 1863.

674. VII. Charles Henry Alden, M. D. Philadelphia, son of Rev. Charles Henry, (328) b, Philadelphia, 28 Apr. 1836: gr. Bro. U. 1856; M. D. U. Peun. 1858: entered U. S. regular medical staff, 1859; com. ass't, surg. 23 June, 1860; m. 25 Oct. 1864, Kate Russell Lincoln, dau. of E. Lincoln, Philadelphia.

675. VII. William Livingston Alden, Esq., N. Y., attorney at law, son of Rev. Joseph Alden, D. D. (330) gr. at Jefferson College, 1858; st. law with Wm. M. Everts, Esq.: m. 8 June, 1865, Agnes Margaret, dau. of Rev. Alexander W. McClure, D. D., has one son, William Livingston, Jr., b. 6 July, 1866.

676. VII. Ebenezer Alden, Fairhaven, Mass., farmer, son of John, (332) was b. 30 July 1794; m. 27 June 1822, Mary Pope, who was b. 1795, and d. 20 Jan. 1843. She was dau. of Jonathan Pope, of Claverick, N. Y.

CHILDREN

1. Lemuel Pope, 19 Aug. 1823; d. 27 Aug. 1824. 2. Mary Pope, 18 Not. 1828; d. 17 Aug. 1841. 3. William Newcomb, 30 Oct. 1830. 4. Amanda Malvina, 21 June, 1833. 5. Sarah Eunice, 12 Feb. 1837; d. 29 June, 1665. He m. 2. 30 Aug. 1844, Serena Thacher, b, 28 Jan. 1802; dau. of John and Deborah Thacher, of Dartmouth.

677. VII. Lois Alden, dau. of John, (332) b. 1 June 1803; d. 2 Dec. 1832, a. 29: m. Enos Pope, of Fairhaven, master mariner.

Had ch. 1. Nathaniel, 8 Sept. 1825, who m. Hannah Durfee. 2. Alden, 29 Oct. 1828, who d. 4 Aug. 1850; and m. 1849, Theresa Cummings of Edgartown. 3. Enos, 26 Oct. 1829; who m. Elizabeth Shaw, and resides in New Bedford.

678. VII. Ruth Alden, of Fairhaven, dau. of John, (332) b. 9 Nov. 1805; m. 14 Apr. 1825, Asaph Price Taber, master mariner, of Fairhaven, who was b. 21 July, 1803.

They had ch. 1. William Henry, 1827, seaman, d. 1857. 2. Elizabeth Alden, 24 Aug. 1829; d. 1857. 3. Asaph Rice, 14 July. 1831; seaman, d. St. Jago, 1859. 4.

Thankful Holt, 18 Feb. 1837; who m. Theodore E. Lawton, of Fairhaven. 6. Silas Alden, 8 Jan. 1840; seaman. 6. Emma Shiverick, Mar. 4 1842. 7. Benjamin Franklin, 29 Mar. 1845; d. 1847. 8. Benjamin Franklin, 10 Oct. 1847.

679. VII. John Alden, Fairhaven, master carpenter, son of John, (332) was b. 17 July 1807; living in 1832; d. soon after.

680. VII. Abigail Pope Aluen, Fairhaven, Mass., dau. of John, (332) b. 5 Apr. 1809; d. 7 Nov. 1845; m. 1832, Jacob Keith of Bridgewater, farmer, who was b. 1803, d. 1860.

They had ch. 1. Alexis Nelson, 1833; who d. 1840. 2. Jacob Augustus Fitzgerald," 1831. 3. Ellen Brace, 1836: who m. 18.59, Henry Alden Delano, of Fuirhaven. 4. Ruth Ann, 24 Jan. 1839; who m. 1864 William Newcomb Alden, miner, Waldo, Oregon, 5. Mary Abby. 22 July, 1841; who m. 1864, Welcome I. Lawton, of Fairhaven. 6. Franklin Alden, 20 Apr. 1845: d. 1846.

681. VII. William Pope Alden, Fairhaven, Mass., blacksmith, son of John, (332) b. 21 May, 1810; m. 8 Feb. 1835, Susan Lawrence, dau. of James and Mary Hudson, of Wareham.

CHILDREN

1. Mary Crowell, 22 June, 1836. 2. Samuel Pope, 16 Oct. 1838; d. 1 Aug. 1840. 3. William Frederic, 21 Dec. 1847.

682. VII. Silas Pope Alden, Fairhaven, Mass., master mariner, and farmer, son of John, (332) b. 5 Oct. 1812; m. 31 Jan. 1830, Mercy Pease Taber, b. 30 Oct. 1808, dau. of Elnathan and Mary Taber, of Fairhaven, now Ascushnet.

685. VII. Abner Alden, Fairview, Pa., farmer, was b. Middleboro', Mass., 1801: son of Earl, (335) m. 10 July, 1826, Elizabeth Westgate.

CHILDREN

1. Sarah. 23 Aug. 1827; d. 13 Mar. 1804, (892) 2. Lydia, 3 Sept. 1830; d. 23 Sept. 1851, (893) 3. Abby, 23 Feb. 1833; d. 15 May, 1862. (894) 4. Frederic, 23 Apr. 1836; d. 28 Jan. 1855. 5. Alanson, 11 Sept. 1841, (895) 6. Renardo, 23 Aug. 1843. 7. Eliza Jane, 30 Sept. 1846; d. 5 Apr. 1865.

686. VII. Charity Haskell Alden, dau. of Earl, (335) b. 1803; m. 12 Oct. 1828, Lorenzo Lincoln, of Taunton, Mass., paper maker.

Had ch. 1. Narcissa, 12 Aug. 1830, who m. 1864, Geo. Walker Jr. 2. Ann Eliza, 8 Nov. 1833, who m. 1859, Joseph Philbrick. 3. Mercy Emily, 2 Nov. 1837; m. 1862, Charles H. Paul. 4. Mary Wilson, 29 Jan. 1840. 5. *Willie, 2 Dec. 1841; d. 2 Oct. 1842.

687. VII. Mary Miller Alden, dau. of Earl, (335) was b. 1806; m. 12 Mar. 1845, John N. Pierce of Lowell, Mass., machinist.

Ch. 1. Edward Burgess, 27 May, 1847.

688. VII. Milton Alden, Middleboro', son of Earl, (335) was b. 14 Sept. 1807; Dep. Sheriff 10 yrs; m. 1830, Susan B. dau. of Aberdeen Keith.

CHILDREN

1. Mary Ann, 30 Mar. 1831, (896).

689. VII. Elbridge Gerry Alden, Boston and Cambridge, Lard Oil manufacturer, 181 Broad St., son of Earl, (335) was b. 1810; m.l831, Esther J. Stetson, d. 22 Feb. 1846.

Had ch. 1. Charles Henry, 1835; d. 15 Sep, 1835, a 2 m. 15 d. 2. James Crawford, 14 Sept. 1838. 3. Esther Jane, 16 Feb. 1846; m. 2. 12 Jan. 1847, Mrs. Sophia G. Gifford. Ch. 4. Emma Gerry, 3 Dec. 1847. 5. Charles Albert, 3 Dec, 1854.

690. VII. Anne Nelson Alden, dau. of Earl, (335) was b. 1812; m. 8 May, 1836, Charles Tisdale, who d. 2 Oct. 1850.

Had ch. 1. Anne Maria, 12 Feb. 1837. 2. Sarah Jane, 26 Jan. 1840. 3. Mary Elizabeth, 5 Jan. 1844. 4, Clara Nelson, 12 Mar. 1847. Sarah Jane m. 10 Aug. 1864, Daniel S. Pillsbury; had 18 Sept. 1865, Annie Sargeant.

691. VII. Samuel Nelson Alden, clerk, Boston, b. 1815; d. about 1847, a. about 32, m. Mary Crawford.

CHILDREN

1. Almina, who is m. 2. Thomas Earl.

692. VII. Sarah Rounseville Alden, dau. of Earl, (335) was b. 1820; m. 22 Apr. 1846, George Leonard, Jr., shoe manufacturer, Middleboro', Mass.

Had ch. 1. William Nelson, 29 Sept. 1847. 2, George Earl, 3 Dec. 1849. 3. Mary Richmond. 25 Aug. 1851. 4. Sarah Abby, 11 July, 1855. 5. *Ella Deborah, 23 Oct. 1857; d. 15 Nov. 1862.

693. VII. William Henry Alden, Wyoming, Iowa, a farmer, son of Elijah, (338) m. and had several ch.

694. VII. James Monroe Alden, Middleboro', farmer, son of Elijah, (338) m. 5 Feb. 1855, Mary. B. Clark.

CHILDREN

1. Charles H. who m. Annie Clifford, and have one ch., Charles Clifford. 2. Mary L. 3. Emma M. 4. Jennie B.

695. VII. John Francis Alden, Middleboro', Mass., son of Elijah, (338).

696. VII. Charles Frederic Alden, Middleboro', Mass., son of Elijah, (338) b, 1832; m. 17 May, 1860, Anna T. Clifford. Mid. Rec.

697. VII. Lucy Alden, dau. of Daniel, (339) b. 1824; m. Richard Howard.
Had one ch. Eliza Flora.

698. VII. Elizabeth M. Alden dau. of Daniel, (339) b. 1829; no account.

699. VII. Vienna Alden, dau. of Daniel, (339) was b. 1832; no account.

700. VII. Jacob F. Alden, Middleboro', Mass., Insurance agent, son of Daniel, (339) was b. 18 April, 1836; m. 13 Nov. 1852, Susie Pratt.
Had 1 ch. *Edith Foster.

701. VII. Henry Alden, Gorham, Me., farmer, son of Gardner, (347) b. 1823; lives on the old homestead; m. ____ Carroll, of Buxton, Me.

702. VII. Mary Alden, Duxbury, Mass., dau. of John, (349) b. 1811; m. Daniel Sampson, and had one son: m. 2. David Cushman, and had two ch. Mary and Walter.

703. VII. John Alden, Duxbury, Mass., seaman, b. 1813; had a wife and three or four ch.

704. VII. Henry Alden, Duxbury, Mass., son of John, (349) m. Sarah Woodward, and had ch.

705. VII. William James Alden, Duxbury, Mass., son of Briggs, (350) b. 1822; m. Lydia J. Woodward.

CHILDREN

1. William J. 19 Apr. 1845. 2. Briggs, 28 Apr. 1848; d. 1852.

706. VII. Judah Alden, Duxbury, Mass., son of Briggs, (350) was b. 1825; m. Julia Whitney.

707. VII. Samuel Alden, Duxbury, Mass., son of Briggs, (350) m. a Whiting: has gone to California.

708. VII. Amherst Alden, Boston, Clerk, P. Office, son of Briggs, (350) m. Georgianna, dau. of Peleg Cook.

CHILDREN

1. Carrie May, 4 Apr. 1853; d. 1862. 2. Jennie D. 4 Apr. 1856.

708a. VII. Ezra Hyde Alden, Bridgewater, Mass., son of Dr. Samuel, (353) was b. 16 Sept. 1830; m. 30 Apr. 1853, Mary E. dau. of Joseph Smith of Wayland, who was b. 7 Apr. 1829.

CHILDREN

1. Frank, Dec. 1853; 2. William Hyde 25, 'Slay, 1858. * 3. Maria, 10 May, 1860; d. 28 July, 1865. 4. Martha Williams, 23 May, 1862. 5. *Ezra Hyde, 26 Jan. 1866.

709. VII. Amherst Alden, Bangor, Me., farmer, son of Samuel, (354) b. 26 Apr. 1807; m. Abby Webster.

710. VII. Mary G. Alden, Duxbury, Mass., dau. of Samuel, (354) b. 2 Nov. 1817; m. Edmund Pratt, Jun.

711. VII. William Ripley Alden, Duxbury, Mass., son of Samuel, (354) was b. 7 Aug. 1819; m. Sarah Tooker: m. 2. Jane Pricher.

712. VII. Samuel G. Alden, Lewiston, Me., a tanner, son of Samuel, (354) b. 28 Oct. 1827: m. Sarah J. Blaisdell.

713. VII. Isaac Alden, Calais, Vt., son of William, (371) b. 19 Mar. 1789; d. in Essex, Lewis Co. N. Y. 17 Aug. 1860; a 71; m. 1813, Maria Stone, b. 1 Jan. 1792, d. Calais, Vt., 11 Feb. 1818.

CHILDREN

1. Edwin Augustus, 10 Mar. 1814, (897) 2. Joseph Judson, 9 Sept. 1815 (898) 3. Oliver Mann, 4 Aug. 1817 (899). He m. 2. 30 Aug. 1818. Hannah Snow, Montpel-

ier, Vt., b. 28 Oct. 1791. 4. Ruby Hammet, 8 Mar. 1821, (900) 6. Emily Doane, 15 Dec. 1824, (901) 6. Charles Lucas, 21 Aug. 1827, (902) 7. Avis Ellen, 28 Dec. 1830, (903) 8. Alonzo Isaac, 18 July, 1834.

714. VII. William Alden, West Newton, Mass., son of William, (371) b. 1797; d. 4 Aug. 1861; m. 1818, Ann Fuller, who d. 1822: m. 2, 1824, Elizabeth Bacon.

CHILDREN

1. Charles, 1819. 2. Curtis. 1825; d. 1827. 3. William, 1827. 4. Hiram, 1829; who resides in Natic. 5. Otis Bacon, 1846.

715. VII. Asa Alden, Calais, Vt., son of William, (371) b. 25 Sept. 1794; postmaster near 30 years: m. 29 Oct. 1822, Avis Hammet Snow.

CHILDREN

1. Lydia-Anna, 16 Sept. 1826. 2. Louisa Maria, 10 July, 1838.

716. VII. George Alden, Eden, Vt., son of William, (371) b. Needham, 1797; d. Eden, Vt., 27 Nov. 1846; m. 1826, Clarinda McIntyre, who was b. 13 Dec. 1803.

CHILDREN

1. William Edward, 1827. 2. George Elbert, 1832. 3. Mary Jane, 1834; d. 5 Apr. 1839. 4. *Male infant, 1839; d. 1839.

717. VII. Elizabeth Alden, dau. William, (371) b. 1802; m. Isaac Connor, Eden, Vt., had 5 ch.

718. VII. Hannah W. Alden, dau. William, (371) b. 1806; m. Washington Fisk, of Hyde Park Vt. had 3 ch.

719. VII. Reuben Alden, son of Moses, (372) m. Isabella Phillips: had 9 ch.

720. VII. Alvan Alden, Alstead, N. H., farmer, son of Moses, (372) b. 1791, in Needham, Mass; removed to Alstead, in 1832; m. Elizabeth Allen, of Surry, N. H., who was b. 1794; d. 23 March, 1866, a. 72.

CHILDREN

1. Warren, 2. William, twins, b. 1819, (904) William d. Dec. 1841, a. 22. 3.*Mary, (905) 4, Sarah, who d. May 1862. 5. Louisa.

721. VII. Betsey Alden, dau. Moses, (372) is dead: m. Rev. Warren Wilbur, and had one son and three daughters.

722. VII. Moses Alden, son of Moses, (372) m. and had

CHILDREN

Abigail, Sarah Ann, Mary Jane, Elizabeth, Hannah, of whom Joshua Gordon of Newton was appointed guardian 18 Mar. 1854.   Probate Rec.

723. VII. Sarah Alden, dau. Moses, (372) no account.

724. VII. Dexter Alden, Lowell, Mass., son of Moses, (372) d. in Lowell; m. Mary Ann Balcom, had one son and four daughters. Wid. Mary presented her

account as Adm. of her husband's estate, Dec. 2, 1845. Inventory $509. Prob. Rec.

725. VII. William Alden, son of Moses, (372); no account.

726. VII. Maria Alden, dau. Moses, (372) m. a Blanchard.

727. VII. Lucinda Alden, dau. Paul, (374) b. 1797; m. a Bonfils; "left four sons, of whom three are now (1866) living."

728. VII. Elizabeth Alden, dau. Paul, (374) b, 1798: m. Amasa Hewins; "left four sons and five daughters." S. A.

729. VII. Rebecca Newell Alden, Dedham; Mass., dau. of Paul, (374) b. 6 Apr. 1802; m. Moses Gragg, of Dedham; b. 20 Sept. 1791.

They have ch. 1. Elizabeth B, 11 Nov. 1820. 2. James H. 12 Jan. 1823. 3. Rebecca N. 18 Mar. 1825. 4. Moses H. 5 Dec. 1826; who m. Martha C. Veazie. 5. George T. 29 Apr. 1829. 6. Nancy A. 6 Sept. 1831, who m. Stephen S. Harris. 7. Ellen J. 14 July 1836, who m. Warren S. Davis. 8. Mary Frances, 30 June. 1839. 9. Isaac P. 1 Sept. 1842. 10. Caroline A. 1 Aug. 1845.   Mrs. Rebekah N. Gragg.

730. VII. Nancy Alden, dau. of Paul, (374) b. 4 Nov. 1804; d. 15 Mar. 1856; m. Capt. King L. Runnels, of Fall River, who is dead, had two daughters. S. A.

731. VII. Paul Alden, Esq. New York City, a successful merchant, son of Paul, (374) b, 18 July, 1807; d. in New York, 13 Oct. 1866, a. 59, and was buried at Mt. Auburn; first settled in Boston: m. Frances C. dau. of Henry Jones and wife who was dau. of Joshua Winship.

CHILDREN

1. Henry Jones, 3 March, 1836? d. 9 Jan. 1839. 2. Henry N. 6 Dec. 1840.

732. VII. Silas Alden, New Bedford, Mass., son of Paul, (374) b. 1809; m. Emily Howland, dau. of Frances and Emily (Parker) Howland. She was b. 11 Mar. 1810.

CHILDREN

1. Mary Howland. 8 Jan. 1842; d. 22 Sept. 1857. 2. George Newell, 10 July, 1845. 3. Ella, 27 Jan. 1847.

733. VII. Marshall Alden, Templeton, Mass., farmer, son of Silas, (375) b, 13 Mar. 1791; m. 23 July, 1816, Sylva, dau. of Capt. Asa Turner, b. 27 May, 1792.

CHILDREN

1. Addison, 22 May, 1818, (906) 2. Albert. 11 Sept. 1820, (907) 3. Marshall, 12 Nov. 1822; d. 1 Aug. 1825. 4. Abby Turner, 3 Mar. 1823. 5. Marshall, 2 Apr. 1829: d. 14 July, 1833.

734. VII. Col. Luther Alden, Templeton, Mass., farmer, son of Silas, (375) b: 20 Mar. 1793; m. 17 June, 1819, Sarah, dau. of Joseph Whitney, b. 1794; d. 10 Aug. 1820; m. 2. May 1825, Mary, dau. of Benjamin Edgell, who d. Jan. 1830; m. 3. June, 1831, Catherine M., dau. of Nathan Perry, who d. 29 Mar. 1854; m. 4. 24 Nov. 1859, Phebe M. dau. of William H. Skinner.

1. Sarah W. 10 Aug. 1820, 2. Luther P. 3 Aug. 1826, (908) 3. Silas B, 15 Apr. 1829, (909) 4. Charles P. 8 Sept. 1834, (910) 5. George H. 27 Sept. 1837 (911).

735. VII. Harvey Alden, Cambridge, Mass., connected with the R. Road, son of Silas, (375) b. 12 Jan. 1798: m. 1830, Abigail, dau. of Moses Wright, of Temple ton, Mass., b. 10 June, 1807.
They had one son, Frank, 16 Apr. 1835, who d. 1837.
736. VII. Francis Alden, Dedham, Mass., formerly innkeeper, son of Amasa, (376) b. 21 Jan. 1793; m. 7 June, 1818, Sarah S. dau. of Elisba Crehore.

CHILDREN

1. Emily, 12 Sept. 1819, who m. Reuben Farrington, Jun. 2. Abner, 29 Jan. 1821, who m. Maria Blodgett. 3. Clarissa, 18 Dec. 1823, who m. Sanford Carroll. 4. Maria, 22 Nov. 1825; m. Horace Bacon. 5. Francis, 1 Apr. 1827, who m. Carrie M. Smith. 6. Henry C. 1 Jan. 1830, who m. Emma F. Bailey. 7. Sarah J, 14 Mar. 1833; d. 29 Nov. 1861. 8. Adeline, 6 Mar. 1836: d. 4 Jan. 1844. 9. Elisha C. 1 Oct. 1838; d, 7 Sept. 1839. 10. Elisha C. 11 Sept. 1841. 11. Amasa, 16 Jan. 1849, F. A.

737. VII. Leonard Alden, Dedham, Mass., son of Amasa, (376) b. 1796; m. Adeline Swan.

CHILDREN

1. Samael Fales, 1821, who m. Sarah Fales, and had three ch. 2, Rebecca Swan, 1824, who m. Edward F. Sherman, of Lowell; no ch; 3. Martha Clark, b. 1832, who m. J. Fisher, of Dedham, and had two ch.

738. VII. George Alden, Dedham, Mass., son of Amasa, (376) m. Hannah Eaton.
739. VII. Amasa Alden, Rock Fish, near Fayetteville, N. C., son of Amasa, (376) b. 1812; m. Clarissa White.

CHILDREN

1. Adeline, 2. Frank.
740. VII. Simeon Alden, Milford, Mass., boot manufacturer, son of Samuel, (380) no particulars.
741. VII. Anna Richardson Alden, Stafford, Ct., dau. of Elisha; (382) m. Samuel Chapman; no further particulars.
742. VII. Clarissa Alden, Stafford, Ct., dau, of Elisha, (382) b. 12 Jan. 1800; m. Simeon Horton, Stafford, Ct.
743. VII. Austin Alden, Stafford Ct., son of Elisha, (382) b. 1 May, 1803; m. Nancy Oker; no further particulars.
744. VII. Augustus Alden, Stafford, Ct., son of Elisha, (3.82) was b. 23 July, 1804; m. Deborah Crowell.

745. VII, Alonzo Erskine Alden, of Stafford, Ct, machinist, son of Elisha, (382) was b. 8 Mar. 1812; m. 22 Nov. 1835, Eliza, dau. of James and Polly Orcutt of Coventry, Ct. She was b. 17 Oct. 1815.

CHILDREN

1. Albert Seymour, 14 Dec. 1837, (912) 2. Mary Henrietta, 17 Apr. 1839.

746. VII. William Chauncey Alden, Ogdensburg, St. Lawrence Co. N. Y. machinist, son of Elisha, (382) b. 1813; m. 1. Sophia Smith. 2. Hannah Ballard.

747. VII. Lydia Shephard Alden, dau. of Elisha, (382) b. 30 Sept. 1815; m. Henry Wilson. Ellington, Ct.

748. VII. Elisha Alden, Stafford, Ct., son of Elisha, (382) no particulars.

749. VII. Washington Alden, Ogdensburg, N. Y., machinist, son of Elisha, (382) has removed to the Oil regions in Pa., has a family.

750. VII. Noah Alden, Wilbraham, Mass., son of Nathan, (383) was b. 1 Dec. 1792; d. 14 July, 1845; m. Lovina Cooley, 4 Nov, 1813, who was b. 24 Jan. 1794; now (1866) living.

CHILDREN

1. Orville B. 2 July, 1813; (913.) 2. Mary Ann, 7 Sep. 1817; (914) 3. Nathan, (915.) 4. Lovina, (916.) 5. Emeline C. (917.) 6. Forinda B. (918.) 7. Clarissa A. (919.) After her husband's death she m. Elijah Alden a son of Dea. Noah 5 Noah 4 (68).

751. VII. Horace B. Alden, son of Nathan, (383) b, 1793; d. young.

752. VII. Sally Alden, dau. of Nathan, (383) b. 12 Jan. 1796; m. 3 Oct. 1816, Perley Converse of Stafford, Ct., who was b. 1792.

They had ch, 1. Judith Preston. 2. Orin, 3. Emeline, 4. Washington, 6. Laura Alden, 6. Phonema, 7. Louisa Augusta, 8. Amanda, 9. Minerva, 10. Jenet Dwight.

753. VII. Marcia Alden, dau. of Nathan, (383) son of Elisha, (158c) b. 8 Oct. 1798; m. Vashni Warner of N. Wilbraham, Mass.

They had ch.* Lyman, Sarah, Eunice, Alden, Vashni, Jatoes, Elam.

754. VII. Cyrus Alden, N. Wilbraham, Mass., son of Nathan (383) b. 21 July, 1799; d. 1835; m. 3 Dec. 1822, Lucy Warner, of N. Wilbraham, who was b. 10 June, 1804; d. 20 Aug. 1844.

CHILDREN

1. John R. 17 Oct 1825, (920) 2. Horace E. (921) 3. William J. b. 11 Oct 1831. (922) 4. Cyrus A. 28 Dec. 1833, (923).

755. VII. Nathan Alden, Wilbraham, Mass., son of Nathan, (383).

756—759, VII. left for ch. of Spencer Alden, (387) but no particulars have been received.

Eighth Generation

760. VIII. Henry Alden, Esq., East Bridgewater and Abington, Mass., farmer, son of Isaac, (404) b. 10 Apr. 1817; d. 4 Apr. 1858, a. 41. He removed from E. Br., to Ab., in 1852; was a magistrate, and much respected. He m. Charlotte, dau. of Salmon Dunbar. She d. Jan. 1848, leaving one child, William Henry, b. 14 Apr. 1842. He m. 2. Abby Cushing, dau. of Thomas Smith of Hanson, who was b. Sept. 1825, and had one son Isaac Cary, 20 Nov. 1851.

761. VIII. Bela Alden, S. Abington, Mass., son of Ezra, (407) was b. 11 Nov. 1813; m. 1834, Mehetabel, dau. of Joseph Dyer, of A.

CHILDREN

1. Joseph Henry, 29 Nov. 1836, (924) 2. Thomas Russell, 2 Nor. 1839, (925) 3. Bela, 6 Nov. 1844, (926) 4. *Winthrop Standish, 25 Sept. 1849; d. 17 Nov. 1851.

762. VIII. Mary Alden, S. Abington, dau. Ezra, (407) b. 14 Feb. 1817; m. 1834, Cyrus Bates, Hanover, Mass.

Ch. 1. Mary Breknell Hersey 3 Jan, 1836, 2. Cyrus Alden, 24 Aug, 1838. 3. Solon, 27 June, 1841, 4. Ezra Thomas, 29 Sept, 1843, 5, Julia Ann, 29 Jan. 1846; d, in infancy. 6. Abby Ann, 15 Mar. 1848. 7. Charles Oscar, 24 Mar. 1849. 8. Susan Ella, 3 May, 1851.

763. VIII. Jared Alden, Abington, Mass., son of Ezra, (407) b. 17 June, 1821; m. Hannah, dau. of Capt. William Reed, of Hanover, Mass.

CHILDREN

1. Amelia Gilbert, 7 May, 1844, 2. *Charles A. 9 June, 1846; d. in infancy. 3. Wealthy Lewis, 14 Feb. 1849, 4, * William Reed, 21 Dec. 1860; d. in infancy. 5. Jane Mehetabel, 24 April, 1853.

764. VIII. Susan Alden, S. Abington, Mass., dau. Ezra, (470) b. 17 March, 1826: m. 1845, Calvin W. Allen, Paxton, Mass, Shed. 26 Oct. 1848, leaving one ch., Charles Edward, b. T Dec, 1845,

765. VIII. Lucius Alden, E, Bridgewater, Mass., son of Thomas Russell Alden, (408) b. 1818 j d. 20 March, 1844, a. 26: m. Harriet, dau, of Dea. Charles Churchill, W. Br. She m. 2, Sidney Allen, and d. 20 Oct. 1848.

CHILDREN

1. Frank, 20 Oct. 1842: d. 26 Nov. 1843. 2. Lucius F., Aug. 20, 1844. L. F. Alden.

766. VIII. Russell Alden, Campello, (No. Br.,) son of Thomas Russell, (408) b. 1821: m. 18 Oct. 1843, Drusilla Vaughn, of Duxbury, Mass.: have one ch., Elmira Russell; b. 14 Nov. 1845.

766a. VIII. Allen Alden, son of Thomas Russell Alden, (408) was b. 1823; m. Elizabeth Vaughn, who is dead.

767. VIII. Mary Jane Alden, dau. of Thomas Russell Alden; (408) m. Matthias Burt, of Bridgewater.

768. VIII. Edward Alden, of Boston, son of Thomas Russell Alden, (408) b. 23 Feb. 1829; m. 1 Jan. 1851, Mary Elizabeth Phelps, of Boston; went to Davenport, Iowa; returned to Boston in 1859, and is engaged in mercantile pursuits.

769. VIII. James Elbridge Alden, Bridgewater, Mass., son of James Sullivan (409).

770. VIII. George Thomas Alden, Bridgewater, Mass., son of James Sullivan, (409) b. 1835.

771. VIII. Leonard Case Alden, Boston, son of William Vinton, (414) b. 22 Dec. 1839; d. at Hilton Head Hospital, S. C. 5 Oct. 1863. He gr. at Harv. Coll. 1861 with high honors; was immediately appointed a Proctor, and assistant to the professor in chemistry. He became interested in the plan of employing colored troops in the army; offered his services and received a Lieutenant's commission in the 55th Mass. Reg. He left with the Regiment for S. Carolina; but soon after his arrival fell a victim to the climate. He was a young man of uncommon promise. See Harvard Necrology 1864.

772. VIII. Phineas Allen Alden, St. Johnsbury, Vt., son of Ziba, (429) was b. 16 Mar. 1806; m. 18 Jan. 1830, Martha, dau. of Ebenezer Parkhurst.

CHILDREN

1. Charlotte Stone, 16 Oct. 1830: m. Walter N. Learned. 2. Horace Allen, 16 Feb. 1832: m. Lizzie M. Eaton. 3. Harriet Ingersoll, 18 April, 1833: d. 7 Aug. 1833. 4 Charles Parkhurst, 18 Aug. 1834: m. Martha J. Kendrick. 5. Henry Parkhurst, 18 Dec. 1837. 6. Delia Sibbel, 14 Feb. 1843.

Charles Parkhurst Alden, Springfield, Mass., druggist, firm of Alden and Brewster — son of Phinehas Allen Alden, (772) was b. at Lebanon, N. H., 8 Aug. 1834: m. 21 Nov. 1861, Martha Jane, dau. of Geo. S. Kendrick, Lebanon, N. H. She was b. 20 Mar. 1837.

CHILDREN

1. George Kendrick, 10 Feb. 1862: d. 22 March, 1862. 2. Ralph Parkhurst, 22 July, 1865.

773. VIII. Lydia Pinney Alden, Lebanon, N. H., dau. of Ziba, (429) m. B. A. Stevens, and has removed to Illinois.

774. VIII. Delia Allen Alden, Lebanon, N. H., dau. of Ziba, (429) m. James M. Smith, and removed to Princeton, Ill.

775. VIII. Adeline Eliza Alden, Hartford, Ct., dau. of Horatio, (436) b. 1816: d. 18 Dec. 1820.

Philena Deand Alden, sister of the above, was b. 9 Dec. 1818: m. Rev. Augustus A. Barton, of Andover, Mass., afterwards of Springfield, They had one daughter, Alice, in 1840, who d. a. 3 mos. She d. Dec. 1840, a. 22.

776. VIII. Jesse Deane Alden, Hartford, Ct., son of Horatio, (436) b. 12 Oct. 1820; m. Adeline S. dau. of William Bartlett, of Newbury port. He d. 16 Aug. 1860, a. 40; no ch.

777. VIII. William Cumming Alden, Hartford, Ct., son of Horatio, (436) b. 1826; m. 1848, a Daniels, of Medway, Mass. In 1854 no ch.

778. VIII. Isabella Graham Alden, Hartford, Ct., dau. of Horatio. (436) b. 1828; m. George H. Thomas, Norwich, Ct., who d. before 1854, when she was a wid. and res. with her father. They had a dau. Alice, b. 7 July, 1848.

779. VIII. Rev Edwin Hyde Alden, Tunbridge, Vt., son of Elam, (441) a congregational clergyman, gr. Dart. Coll. 1859, and at Bangor Th. Seminary 1862; has been settled in several places and has a family.

780. VIII. Joseph Wood Alden, Paris, Ill., farmer, son of Luther, (443) b. Lebanon, N. H., 9 Sept. 1826; m. 21 Aug. 1852, Jeannette Tucker of Northfield, Vt., b. 13 July, 1829.

CHILDREN

1. Charles Peck, 28 May, 1853. 2. Adelia Malvina, 30 Aug. 1855. 3. Alice Etella. 23 Apr. 1858. 4. William Tucker, 27 July ,1861.

781. VIII. Sarah Jane Wood Alden, Lebanon, N. H., dau. of Luther, (443) b. 3 Feb. 1828; m. 15 Jan. 1850, James Hubbard, Lebanon, N. H., b. 22 Feb. 1820.

Ch. 1. Ida Frances. 25 Oct. 1850. 2. Evangeline Maria, 1 Jan. 1854. 3 Lucy Arabella, 4 Jan. 1856. 4. Susan Catherine, 22 Mar, 1859. 5. James Frederic Burton, 3 July, 1861.

782. VIII. Rev, Ebenezer Alden, Marshfield, Mass., pastor of the First Congregational Church; son of Ebenezer, (444) b. 10 Aug. 1819: fitted for College at the Randolph Academy: gr. at Am. Coll. 1839; remained at home one year after graduation: in 1840 entered Andover Theological Seminary, where he continued three years. In the autumn of 1843 he went to Iowa, as a missionary; settled at Tipton, Cedar Co., where he continued until near the close of 1848, when, on account of the failing health of his wife, he returned to New England. During the remainder of that year, and part of 1850, he supplied various pulpits. Oct 30, 1850 he was installed pastor of the First Congregational Church in Marshfield, Mass., where (1866) he still continues.

He m. 4 April, 1848, Maria Louisa, dau. of Christopher Dyer, Esq., of South Abington, Mass., b. 9 April, 1821.

CHILDREN

1. Maria Louisa. 30 Apr. 1849. 2. Anna Porter, 10 Aug. 1851. 3. Ebenezer, 24 June, 1854; d. 15 Feb. 1857. 4. Edmund Kimball, 17 Feb, 1858. 5. Mary Kimball, 17 May, 1860; d. 12 Sept. 1860. 6. Alice Elizabeth, 22 May, 1863.

783. VIII. Rev. Edmund Kimball Alden, D. D., pastor of Phillips Congregational Church, South Boston, Mass., son of Ebenezer, (444) fitted for College at Randolph Academy; gr. at Amherst College in 1844; was a teacher in Williston Seminary the following year; entered the Theological Seminary, Andover, in 1845; gr. in 1848; became an Abbott resident; preached in various places, West Springfield, Worcester, Pine Street Church,. Boston, and others; was ordained pastor of the Congregational church in Yarmouth, Me., 2 Jan. 1850;

was dismissed by advice of council Feb. 1, 1854; installed pastor of the Congregational church in Lenox, Mass., Nov. 15, 1854, where he remained until Aug. 21, 1859, when he accepted a call from Phillips Church, So. Boston, and was installed pastor Sept. 21, 1859, and still (1866) continues in that office. He received the degree of D. D. at Amherst College in 1866. On the 25 Apr. 1850, he m. Maria, dau. of Dea. Gershom Hyde, of Bath, Me., b. 14 Apr. 1823.

784. VIII. Henry Augustus Alden, Randolph, Mass., engineer, son of Ebenezer, (444) was b. 8 Aug. 1826; received his preparatory education at Randolph Academy and Stetson High School, and was one term in the English department of Philips Academy, Andover. He was a good scholar and acquitted himself to the satisfaction of his instructors. Being disinclined to pursue a collegiate course, or to study a profession, he remained at home on the farm until he was nearly twenty two years of age. In May 1848 he went to Vermont and was employed on the Sullivan Rail Road until Feb. 1849, when he returned and soon after found employment in Boston and the vicinity, under the instruction of Mr. Eaton. In September of that year he had a severe attack of pneumonia, from which he slowly, but never fully recovered. The following winter he was in Boston, and in the spring, went to Illinois, where during the remainder of that year and the early part of the succeeding one he was employed on the Northern Cross Rail Road, leading from Quincy towards Chicago. In May 1851 he returned home, where he lingered a few weeks, and died of pulmonary consumption, June 9, 1852. On his tombstone the following words are inscribed; "My purposes are broken off!"

785. VIII. Isaac S. Alden, Warren, Pa., son of Richard, (462) b. 1830; m. 1857, Kate King.

786. VIII. Augustus E. Alden, Chickopee Falls, Mass., son of Rev. John, (466) b. 1837; m. Ella Blake, dau. of E. Blake Esq.; have a dau.

787. VIII. Samuel Ezra Alden, son of Samuel, (469) b. 15 Dec. 1819; m. Cynthia Russell.

788. VIII. James Milton Alden, Greenwich, Mass. son of Samuel, (469) b. 15 Dec. 1819; m. Mary James, b. July, 1819.

CHILDREN

1. Edward M. 21 June. 1845; d. 16 Aug. in Balfour Hospital, Portsmout Va., in the army. 2. Frank O. 14 June 1847. 3. Jane E. 22 Jan. 1860.

789. VIII. Fanny Eveline Alden, dau. of Samuel, (469) b. 27 Sept. 1823; m. 6 Sept. 1843, R. Hamblin, b. 26 Aug. 1820.

They had Flora, 15 Feb. 1853.

790. VIII. Franklin Alden, of Springfield, Mass., carpenter, son of Samuel, (469) b. 28 Nov. 1825: m. 30 Dec. 1849, Harriet Cecilia Canterberry, b. 25 Jan. 1831.

CHILDREN

1. Frank Merritt, 5 Sept. 1854. 2. Hattie Charlotte, 26 May, 1853.

791. VIII. Emma Charlotte Alden, dau. of Samuel, (469) m. John L. Parsons.

792. VIII. Alma Jane Alden, dau. of Samuel, (469) b. 25 Dec. 1831: m. Geo. H. Peck.

793. VIII. Ursula Maria Alden, dau. of Abel, Esq., of Greenwich, Ms., (471) b. 1823: m. 26 May, 1846, Jabez B. Root, who was b. 22 Jan. 1822, son of Capt. John Root, of Greenwich.

Had ch. 1. Lucy Eveline, 4 Nov. 1848. 2. Amelia Maria, 29 Mar. 1850, 3. Charles Edwin, 21 Oct. 1851. 4. Elliot Harvey. 20 Dec. 1853. 5. Julietta Frances, 15 Oct. 1855. 6. *Mary Schauffler, 20 Sept. 1857: d. 6 June, 1863. 7. Harriet Iola, 26 Mar. 1859: d. 7 June, 1863.

794. VIII. Frances Eveline Alden, Greenwich, Mass., dau. of Abel, (471) m. 9 Sept. 1851, Joseph P. Root, M. D. b. 23 Apr. 1826, ch.

1. Clarissa Melville. 1 Aug. 1852; d. 4 May, 1857. 2. Frank Orlando, Sept. 1859. 3. Joseph P. Mar. 1862.

795. VIII. William Thompson Alden, Greenwich, Mass., son of Abel, (471) b. 15 Jan. 1830; m. Oct. 1851, Florilla, dau. of Josiah Sanderson, Greenwich.

CHILDREN

1. Emma Florilla. 2. Charles William.

795a. VIII. Harriet Hadassa Alden, Greenwich, Mass., dau. of Abel, (471) b. 14 Nov. 1835; m. 2 Jan. 1866, B. Spencer, New Hartford, Ct.

795b. VIII. Augustus Dewey Alden, Greenwich, Mass., son of Abel, (471) m. 17 Aug. 1862, Mary H. Thomas, of Belchertown, Mass.; ch. had Harry L., b. 7 July, 1866.

796. VIII. Addison Alden, Greenwich, Mass., son of Emery, (472) b. 9 Dec. 1824; m. 10 May, 1851, Marie Davis.

797. VIII. Caroline Cordelia Alden, Greenwich, Mass., dau. Emery, (472) b. 27 Jan, 1829; m. 28 July, 1856, Charles Field; ch. 1. Charles Addison, 18 Mar. 1857, Cambridge.

798. VIII. Julius E. Alden, Greenwich, Mass., son of Emery, (472) b. 12 May, 1832; m. 31 Dec. 1850, Louisa Maria Pike.

CHILDREN

1. Fannie Louisa, 23 Apr. 1854; b. Southbridge. 2. Caroline Alice, 16 July, 1857; b. do.

799. VIII. Angelina Alden, Hardwick, Mass., dau. of Fesus, (473) b. 29 Nov. 1832; m. 28 Nov. 1850, Lathrop Spicer, rho d. 1857; m. 2, 4 July, 1861, William Mason.

They had ch. 1. Mary L. 20 May, 1862. 2. A son, 15 Jan. 1866.

799a. VIII. Theodore L. Alden, Hardwick, Mass., son of Festus, (473) b. 17 May, 1841; m. 30 Apr. 1863, Emilie Legrow.

799b. VIII. Sarah E. Alden, Greenwich, Mass., dau. of James Milton, (474) m. 6 Dec. 1865, George P. Parmelee.

799c. VIII. James M. Alden, Greenwich, Mass., son of James Milton, (474) b. 1839; m. 16 Nov. 1860, Hannah Richardson, who was b. in London, Eng., 19 Feb. 1826.

799d. VIII. Mary E. Alden, dau. of James Milton, (474) b. 14 Mar. 1844; m. 23 Sept. 1861, Cyrus Preston.

799e. VIII. Timothy C. W. Farrelly Alden, Pittsburg, Pa., son of Timothy J. Fox Alden, (479) m. 10 July, 1862, Anna R. Jones, Reading, Pa., no eh.

799f. VIII. Josephine Willis Alden, dau. of Timothy J. Fox Alden, (479) m. 8 July, 1845, Franklin H. Eaton, formerly of Framingham, Ms., now of Pittsburg, Pa.

Ch. 1. Josie Alden, 5 Mar. 1847. 2. Mary Brewer, 16 Jan. 1849. 3. Howard, 8Feb. 1851. 4. Willis, 9 Dec. 1852. 5. Alice Dilworth, 25 Oct. 1854. 6. Lizzie Parker, 10 Dec. 1856. 7. Alden, 24 Mar. 1859. 8. Charles Stone, 24 Apr. 1861.

799g. VIII. Harriet S. Alden, dau T. J. Pox, (479) m. 4 Sept. Robert Arthur, of Pittsburg, Pa.

Ch. 1. Robert Alden, 19 May, 1852. 2. Mary, 27 May, 1864.

800. VIII. Harriet Alden, North Bridgewater, dau. of Otis, (492) was b. in Jay, Me., 4 Mar. 1812; m. 24 July, 1836, Alexander Thayer, of North Bridge-water, b. 9 Sept. 1794; d. 4 Apr. 1862, a. 68; no ch.

801. VIII. Otis Gary Alden, Randolph, Mass., shoemaker, son of Otis, (492) b. 4 July, 1814; d. 14 Oct. 1862, a. 48; m. 27 May, 1841, Susan Maria, dau. of Samuel Thayer. They had Harriet Maria, b. 12 Sept. 1844.

802. VIII. Albert Alden, Middleboro', Mass., proprietor of the Bay State Straw Works, son of Otis, (492) b. 1827.

803. VIII. Olive Alden, Randolph, Mass., dau. of Daniel, (493) b. 5 Nov. 1820; m. 1844, Edward Packard, of North Bridgewater, who removed to Urbana, Ill., where he d. Sept. 1858, leaving two sons;

1. Edward Alden, b. Apr. 1815. 2. Walter Oscar, b. 1847. She m. 2. 18 July, 1863, Dr. Abel W. Kingman. See (516).

804. VIII. Ann Judson Alden, Randolph, Mass., dau. of Daniel, (493) was b. 25 Feb. 1822; m. 11 Dec. 1844, Samuel French of North Bridgewater, Mass., d. 3 Aug. 1848, leaving one son Charles.

805. VIII. Lucia Ware Alden, Randolph, Mass., dau. of Daniel, (493) b. 13 Apr. 1825; m. Lucius French, of N. Bridgewater, and removed to Chicago, Ill.

They have had four ch. 3 of whom d. in infancy. George is living.

806. VIII. Abigail Amanda Alden, of Randolph, Mass., dau. of Daniel, (493) was b. 2 Sept. 1829; m. Samuel French, of Campello, Mass.: have had five ch. of whom two d. young.

807. VIII. Mart Marsh Alden, Randolph, Mass., dau. of Daniel, (493) was b. 27 Nov. 1830: m. 1858, John Hills: d. 1859, leaving no ch.

808. VIII. Francis Wayland Alden, Randolph, Mass., son of Daniel, (493) b. 23 Sept. 1834; m. 3 June, 1856, Caroline F. dau of Silas Dyer: had, 2 Sept. 1857, a dau. Caroline Dyer.

809. VIII. Lucas Wales Alden, No. Bridgewater, Mass., marketman, son of Daniel, (493) b. 1836; m. Mary Ann, dau. of Nathaniel M. Davenport, of E. Br., who was b. 4 July, 1842; ch. 1. Mary Marsh, 1865.

810. VIII. Addison Tucker Alden, No. Bridgewater, Mass., son of Alpheus, (495) m. Jane Tirrell.

811. VIII. Sarah Ann Alden, dau. of Alpheus, (495) m. H. M. Bearse.

812. VIII. Montgomery Morrison Alden, Randolph, Mass., carpenter, son of Silas, (498) b. 15 Dec. 1833; no family.

813. VIII. Columbus Alden, Winthrop, Me., son of Silas, (498).

814. VIII. Emily Alden, Winthrop, Me., dau. of Silas, (498)

815. VIII. Ellen Alden, Winthrop, Me., dau. of Silas, (498).

816. VIII. Harriet Ann Alden, Winthrop, Me., dau. of Williams, (500) m. — Perley, of Winthrop, Me.

817. VIII. Rutilus Alden, Winthrop, Me.

818. VIII. Sanford Otis Alden, North Bridgewater, bootmaker, son of Sanford, (510) was b. 23 Aug. 1829; m. 19 Apr 1849, Dorothy Augusta Foss.

CHILDREN

1. Agnes, 16 July, 1850. 2. Carrie Eliza, 10 Oct. 1853. 3. Charles Henry, 13 July, 1855. 4. Abby Frances, 17 July, 1S57. 5. Lizzie Augusta, 4 Aug. 1859. 6. Marianna, 20 Nov. 1865.

819. VIII. Samuel Ford Alden, N. Bridgewater, Mass., son of Sanford, (510) was b. 23 Aug. 1829,m. 11 Nov. 1849, Lucinda F. Fames, b. Dec. 18, 1830; d. 2 Feb. 1856; m. 2, Laura P. Foss, 29 Apr. 1858, who was b. 1837, and d. 4 Nov. 1865; m. 3, 15 Feb. 1866, Lizzie Foster, who was b. 28 Mar. 1847.

CHILDREN

1, *Abby Frances, 24 June, 1851; d. 12 Dec. 1856. 2. Lizzie Forest, 17 Apr. 1853; d. 12 Sept. 1853. 3. Frederic Williams, 1 Oct. 1860; d. 28 Oct. 1862. 4. Abby Lucinda, 8 Oct. 1861. 5. Annie Laura, 2 Oct. 1865.

820. VIII. Sarah Alden, dau. of Sanford, (510) of N. Bridgewater, m. at Braintree, by Rev. Jonas Perkins, 15 Sept. 1858, Howard P. Keith, of North Bridgewater. — Braintree Records.

821. VIII. Hannah Copeland Alden, N. Bridgewater, dau. of Sanford, (510).

822. VIII. Mary Ann Alden, East Stoughton, Mass., dau. of Lysander, (519) m. Joseph Stickney, Turner, Me.; had four ch. of whom two d. in infancy.

823. VIII. Samuel Bingley Alden, of S. Randolph, Mass. son of Lysander, (519) was b. 12 May, 1830; m. 20 Jan. 1853^ Mary Jane Leonard, dau. of John, b. 14 June, 1838.

CHILDREN

1. Hiram Bingley, 25 Jan. 1854. 2. Charles Ellis, 16 Apr. 1863.

824. VIII. Betsey Jane Alden, of East Stoughton, Mass., dau. of Lysander, (519) was b. 29 Oct. 1835; m. Merrill Goodwin, Turner, Me. He is d.: had 2 ch. John and Mellen.

825. VIII. Ellen Augusta Alden, E. Stoughton, Mass., dau. of Lysander, (519) m. John Watson; shed. 1859; had one dau. Emma Frances.

826. VIII. Susan Maria Alden, E. Stoughton, Mass., dau. of Lysander, (519) m. George Ingraham Young, who was k. in the army.

Had ch, George and Charles; m. 2, David Penniman, have one ch.

827. VIII. Ann Amelia Alden, East Stoughton, Mass., dau. of Lysander, (519) m. John Penniman, S. Randolph, Mass.

828. VIII. Sarah Sophia Alden, Ludlow, Mass., dau. of Azel, (537) b. 1822; m. 18 Dec, 1845, Zina Whitney, of Ludlow; farmer; had one ch. Charles Merrick, b. 20 Dec. 1851.

829. VIII. John Brown Alden, Springfield, Mass., son of Azel, (537) b. 11 Feb. 1825; m. 1833, Delia, dau. of Ezekiel Foudelot; b. 1834; no ch.

830. VIII. Charles Wesley Alden, Ludlow, Mass., farmer, son of Charles, (542) b. 1832; "He has in his possession a hammer which John Alden brought over in the May Flower.' He m. 14 Apr. 1858, Lura Savilla, dau. of Rev. Daniel Levi Chapin.

CHILDREN

1. Flora Delia, 17 July, 1861. 2. Charles Ely, 2 Oct. 1863.

831. VIII. Elizabeth Jane Alden, Ludlow, Mass., dau. of Charles, (542) b. 1834; m. 2 Sept. 1852, Jefferson Stewart of Ludlow, Mass., now resident in Millbury, Mass.

They had ch. 1. Alice Idora, 11 Aug. 1853. 2. Charles Edward, Mar. 1855; d. 18 June, 1861. 3. Ralph Edward, 26 July, 1865.

832. VIII. Fletcher Clark Alden, Ludlow, Mass., son of Charles, (542) b. 1836; d. 18 Aug. 1856. "He was a young man of fine talents, who, while pre-paring for college, was prostrated by disease which terminated in death."

833. VIII. Lucius D. Alden, Springfield, Mass., son of David, (550) b. 15 Dec. 1835; m. 17 Feb. 1859, Sarah Jane Holkiss, b. 15 June, 1842.

CHILDREN

1, Jennie, 31 Aug. 1860. 2. George Henry, 6 Sept. 1862.

834. VIII. Mary B. Alden, of Randolph, Mass., dau. of Horatio Bingley, (554) b. 25 Jan. 1816; d. 5 Aug. 1845; m. 15 Jan. 1840, Benjamin P. Spaulding; they had 1 ch. who d. in infancy.

835. VIII. Horatio B. Alden, Jun. Randolph. Mass., boot manufacturer, son of Horatio B. (554) was b. 8 Apr. 1820; gr. Yale College 1842; m. 28 Feb. 1852, Clara, dau. of Hiram Wales, b. 1830.

CHILDREN

1. Weston Pendexter, 19 Dec. 1852. 2. Horatio Bingley, 31 Oct. 1854. 3. Mary Hannah, 1 Nov. 1857. 4 Arthur Wales, 4 Apr. 1860. 5. Clara Wales. 31 Dec. 1862. 6. Margaret Albree, 20 Jan. 1866.

836. VIII. Mary Alden, Randolph, Mass., dau. of Hosea, (555) m. 10 July, 1828, Holmes Cain, and had three dau.; m. 2, Richard H. Cox, who d. in the army 22 Sept. 1862; had one ch.

837. VIII. Rachel Alden, Randolph, Mass., dau. of Hosea, (555) d. 7 Oct. 1859; m. Seth Pratt of Bridgewater, Mass.; had 2 children.

838. VIII. Henry Averill Alden, Randolph, Mass., boot maker, son of Hosea, (555) b, 10 Nov. 1813: was in the army three years. He m. 19 Apr. 1835, Ellen Maria, dau. of Charles Tileston, b. 25 Aug. 1812.

CHILDREN

1. Ellen Frances, 6 Feb 1836. 2. Frederic Henry, 28 Nov. 1838. 3. Theodore Storer, 2 Apr. 1843. 4. George Averill, 24 Feb. 1851. 5. Emma Maria, 21 Jan. 1856.

Ellen Francis, dau. of Henry A. Alden, (838) m. 9 Aug. 1855, John Franklin Poole, of Randolph, Mass; b. 9 Mar. 1834. He was 2d Lieut, in the U. S. service, and was killed in the battle of Winchester, Va., 19 Sept. 1864, while leading his company into action; his captain and first lieutenant being detailed for other duty. They had ch. Ellen Vesta, 15 July, 1856; d. 6 Feb. 1868. Ellen Louisa, 15 Oct. 1858. Emma Frances, 14 Dec. 1860.

Frederic Henry Alden, Quincy Mass., boot maker, son of Henry Averill, (838) m. Elmira Ann Bicknell, who d. 29 Apr. 1859; m. 2. Laura Ann Soule, of Quincy; ch. 1. Elmira Ann, 21 Mar. 1856. 2. Frank Averill. 3. Lauretta. 4. Frederic Elmer.

839. VIII. Jane Alden, Randolph, Mass., dau. of Hosea, (555) m. 1840, Henry Tileston; now in Mexico; is a machinist.

Had ch. 1. Mary. 2. Charles. 3. Justin Webster, who was in the army and k. at the battle of Winchester, Va.

840. VIII. Emily Howard Alden, Randolph, Mass., dau. of Hosea, (555) m. 7 Apr. 1845, Charles Amerigo, who is d.; m. 2, a Jones of Boston. No ch.

841. VIII. Martin Alden, Randolph, Mass. boot maker, son of Hosea, (555) was four years in the army; m. Sally Hayden, who d. 19 Mar. 1845, a. 19; had one ch.; m. 2, and had one ch.; m. 3, 31 Dec, 1853, Sarah Jane Hutchinson, of Bristol, N. H. b. 28. Mar. 1835.

Have ch. George Francis, b. 23 Apr. 1856; Charles Addison, 15 Jan. 1861.

842. VIII. Eliza Ann Alden, Randolph, Mass., dau. of Hosea, (555) m. William Gardner, who is d.; had three ch.

843. VIII. Martha Alden, dau. of Hosea, (555) d. 1866; m. George W. Richards of Sharon, Mass.

Had 3 ch. Elsie A. 16 June, 1856. George B. 12 June, 1859; and one other

844. VIII. Albert Alden, Quincy, Mass., boot maker, son of Hosea, (555) m. 29 Oct. 1854, a dau. of William Thayer.

845. VIII. Julia Ann Alden, Randolph, Mass., dau. of Hiram, (559) b. 1825: m. Allen W. Belcher. No ch.

846. VIII. Capt. Hiram Carroll Alden, Randolph, Mass., son of Hiram, (559) b. 1826; is Town Clerk and Treasurer; was Capt. in Co. D, Mass., Vol. com. 1 Sept. 1862; discharged 28 Aug. 1863: m. 17 June, 1848, Julia Caroline, dau. of John King, Esq.; had one dau. Sarah King, b. 13 Aug. 1849.

847. VIII. Charlotte Augusta Alden, Randolph, Mass., dau. of Hiram, (556) was b. in 1831: m. John Berry Thayer; had one son, Carroll Alden, b. 10 Apr, 1851.

848. VIII. Margaret Alden, Randolph, Mass., dau. of Hiram, (559) was b. in 1833; m. J. Warren Belcher, of Randolph, boot manufacturer; no ch.

849. VIII. William Hart Alden, Randolph, Mass., son of Hiram, (559) served three mo. in Co. D. 4. Mass. Reg. as sergeant and was detailed and acted as ordinance sergeant while in the service: was b. 1839; has no family.

850. VIII. Charles Alden, Newburg, N. Y., merchant, son of Silas, (562) b. 28 Feb. 1810; m. Aug. 1828 Mary Ann, dau. of Shadrach Thayer; who d. 2 May, 1864.

CHILDREN

George Frederic, 1 Oct. 1829. *Simeon, 20 Aug. 1831; d. 20 Sept. 1831. *Eliza Ann, 28 Sept. 1832; d. 2 Feb. 1833

IX. George Frederic Alden, Esq., New York, attorney at law, son of Charles, (850) -was b. Randolph, Mass., 1 Oct. 1829, d. at Grenada, 26 Apr. 1856. He was a young man of great promise. Leaving his native town with his parents at the age of twelve years, he went to New York, where he pursued his preparatory studies, and then commenced the study of the law in the office of Hon, Daniel E. Sickles, with whom he continued until admitted to the Bar. At the age of twenty-three years he was elected a member of the Legislature of New York, and served two terms. He was then appointed Clerk of the Supreme Court of the city of New York, and served about three years, when his health failing he was advised to seek a more genial climate. In Jan. 1856, he left N. Y. intending to travel in Central America. He went to Nicaraugua, where his health was somewhat improved. In April, after some exposure he took cold which was succeeded by fever, which terminated his life. He was much beloved, and his death was lamented by a wide circle of friends.

851. VIII. George Alden, Cambden, S. C., merchant, son of Silas, (562) b. 8 May, 1812; m. Mary Ann, dau. of Samuel Johnson, of Baltimore, Md.

852. VIII, Clementina L. Alden, Randolph, Mass., dau. of Silas, (562) b. 1816; d. 1840; m. 28 Mar. 1839, Charles Fuller, of Randolph, Mass.; had Walter, 27 Dec. 1839.

853. VIII. Julia Ann Alden, Randolph, Mass., dau. of Silas, (562) b. 1820; is dead; m. 7 Apr. 1847, Henry W. Smith; had Henry E. 11 Mar. 1848.

854. VIII. Helen Augusta Alden, Randolph, Mass., dau. of Silas, (562) b. 1825; m. 2 July, 1854, Peletiah Gould of New Bedford Mass., who is d.; had one dau. Hattie.

855. VIII. Calvin Alden, Randolph Mass., bootmaker, son of Calvin, (563) was b. 5 Aug. 1808: d. 4 Dec. 1843, a. 35; m. 5 June, 1831, Susan, dau. of Joseph Wales of Dorchester, Mass. b. 5 Oct. 1813.

CHILDREN

1. Susan Wales, 20 Aug. 1832; d. 31 Aug. 1841. 2. Martha Theyer, 26 Mar. 1834; m. 22 Oct. 1801, William II. Paine, of E. Randolph, Mass., and has two ch. Louisa and Mary Ellen. 3. Ellen Frances. 8 Sept. 1838; m. 25 Dec. 1856, Lyman E. Tribou, N. Br. She had one ch. who d. soon, and she d. 10 July, 1858.

856. VIII. Martha Hayden Alden, Randolph, Mass., dau. of Calvin, (563) b. 1811: d. 4 Apr. 1833; m. 2 Apr. 1829, Charles Thayer, of Randolph, b. 26 June, 1801; had one son, Charles Frederic, who d. 30 Nov. 1833, a 1 V. and 7 mo.

857. VIII. Mary French Alden, dau. of Calvin, (563) b. 1813, d. 1864, a. 51; m. 10 May, 1835, Warren Belcher, Randolph. Ms,

Ch. 1. Mary Eliza, 1836. 2. Warren Alden, 1839. 3. Adrianna, 1841. 4. Frederic Lewis, 1846. 5. Edmund.

858. VIII. Lewis Alden, Randolph, Mass., boot maker, son of Calvin, (563) b. 1815; d. Sept. 1848: m. Abigail Nash, dau. of Thomas Belcher, She m. 2, Ludo Wild.

CHILDREN

1. *Leonard, d. young. 2. Abby Maria. 12 Dec. 1842. 3. Lewis, Apr. 1847.

859. VIII. Lucy Ann Alden, Randolph, Mass., dau. of Calvin, (563) b. 1819; m. John R. Doggett.

Had ch. 1. Henry Trask. 2. John Codman. 3. Martha Hayden. 4. Georgianna. 5. William.

860. VIII. Adoniram Alden, Randolph, Mass., teacher, son of Calvin, (563) b. 1824: d. 21 Aug. 1859; a. 35; m. 30 Mar. 1851, Mary Elizabeth, dau. of Wales Wentworth; had one son John Codman, b. 9 May, 1856.

861. VIII. Charles James Alden, Randolph, Mass., shoemaker, son of Samuel, (564) was b. in New Orleans, La., 1815; and d. in Randolph, Mass., 9 Nov. 1854, a. 40; m. 3 Nov. 1833, Catherine P. Worcester.

CHILDREN

1. Catherine Virginia. 2. Mary Isabel, twins, b. 15 July, 1836. 3. Susan Worcester, 1838. 4. William Purvis, 1843, d. 1848. 5. Silas, 28 June, 1845. 6. Anna Maria, 22 Mar. 1847.

Catherine V. m. Zaavan Jordan, and had six ch. Virginia Maria, 12 Sept. 1851; William Z. who d. in 1854; Lydia Theresa, 11 May 1855; Ardell, 16 June, 1858; Emily Lucinda, 11 Aug. 1860; Silas Zaavan, 27 Nov. 1861; Susan Worcester, who is dead; John Thayer, 21 Dec. 1864. Mary Isabel, m. John H. Jordan, 27 Feb. 1851, and have had ch. John Alden, Anna, Abby, Rodney, Thomas, d. Sarah Allen. Susan Worcester, m. 8 Apr. 1853, Newton Townsend; have 4 ch. Henry Newton, Charles Alden, William Byron, Susan Lenora.

Silas, resides in Randolph; enlisted in the army 4 Dec. 1863, in Co. m. 2 Mass. Heavy Artillery; was discharged 11 Aug. 1865; was a prisoner in Richmond, Va., nine months. Anna Maria. m. in 1865, Levi W. Hollis, of N. Br; has one ch.

862. VIII. John Henry Alden, Boston, clerk, son of John, (572) has a family.

863. VIII. Elizabeth Jane Alden, dau. of John, (572).

864. VIII. William Fernald Alden, Boston, son of John, (572).

865. VIII. Emily L. Alden, dau. of David, (576) b. 1833; d. 1866: m. Addison Davis, Lynn, Mass.; had two ch. one is d.

866. VIII. David A. Alden, Boston, son of David, (576). m. Almira Peavy, b. 1833. She d. 1863, a. 30; had 4 ch. 2 d.

867. VIII. Martha J. Alden, Boston, dau. of David, (576). was b. 1837; m. T. J. Beers, Boston.

868. VIII. Hattie E. Alden, dau. of David, (576) b. 1839; d. 1863; m. 20 Mar. 1861, Lorenzo D. Gates, Boston, had 1 ch.

868a. VIII. Susan Elizabeth Alden, N. Mid. Mass., dau. of Solomon, (623) b. 21 Sept. 1842; m. 1865, Martin Van Buren Pratt, N. Mid'o. They have one ch. Emily Alden, b. 4 April, 1866.

868b. VIII. Cyrus Alden, N. Mid'o, Mass., son of Caleb, (628) was b. 27 Aug. 1832; m. 29 Nov. 1856, Eliza Gilbert.

868c. VIII. Ruel I. Alden, N. Mid'o, Mass., son of Caleb, (628) b. 30 March, 1834; m. 27 March, 1855, Isabella A. Warren.

869. VIII. Rev. Ezra Judson Alden, Napiersville, Ill., son of Ezra, (629) b. 13 Jan. 1827: gr. Dart. Coll., 1852: Th. Sem. Andover, 1856: Congregational minister; was in Richmond, Me., in 1856-7: in Mittineague, Mass. in 1860: in 1861 in Boston, or 1862: in 1863 — 1865, Sycamore, Ill.; has a family.

870. VIII. Apollos Granville Alden. Middleboro', Mass., merchant, son of Rufiis, (639) b. 24 Mar. 1823: m. 1857, Hannah, dau. of Joseph Macomber, of M. She d. 16 Feb. 1858; m. 2, Dec. 1865, Mrs. Anna C. Macy. He had a son, Alton Cushman, in 1858, who d. in 1862.

871. VIII. Charles Henry Alden, Providence, R. I., son of David, (139a) b. 8 June, 1822: m. 23 Aug. 1843, Mrs. Mary King, dau. of William and Polly Pratt, of Bridgewater.

CHILDREN

1. Charles Thompson, 7 Aug. 1844. 2. Martha Jane, at Foxboro, Mass., 26 Mar. 1847. 3. Sara Weston, at Foxboro, 25 June, 1851; d Providence, R, I. 5 Apr. 1863. 4. Alice, at Foxboro, b. 17 Oct. 1858.

872. VIII. John Thompson Alden, merchant, Foxboro, Mass., son of David VII, (639a) was b. 1828; killed on the Boston and Providence Rail Road, 22 Apr. 1802; m. Apr. 22 1845, Almira Carpenter, dau. of Daniel and Abigail Carpenter of Foxboro; had one eh. Erastus Carpenter, b. 17 Nov. 1845.

873. VIII. Rev. William Harrison Alden, Albany, N. Y. clergyman, son of David, (639a) b. 14 Apr. 1825: m. 23 May, 1865, Mrs. Susan Almira C. Alden, wid. of John T. Alden, (872). He gr. at Brown Un. 1845; and at Newton Th. Sem. in 1852; was ord. pastor of the 1st Bap. chh. North Attleboro', Mass., 1 Sept. 1852; inst. pastor of the 1st. Bapt. chh. Lowell, Mass., 10 June, 1857; and of the Tabernacle Bapt. chh. Albany, N.Y., 17 Apr. 1864.

874. VIII. Betsey Hathaway Alden, dau. of Oliver Hathaway, (639b) m. 1833, William Swift, son of William Swift of Wareham, Mass.

875. VIII. Abner Alden, son of Oliver Hathaway, (639b) m. 1843, Anna Powers, of the State of Indiana.

CHILDREN

1. Charles Henry, 1844. 2. Martha Jane, 1846. 3. Henrietta, 1851. 4. Sarah Pratt, 1853. 5. Caroline Josephine, 1855. 6. Isabella, 1857. 7. Susanna, 1859. 8. Clarence Warner, 1862. 9. Oliver, 1855.

876. VIII. Henrietta Alden, dau. of Oliver Hathaway, (639b) was b. 1825; m. 1846, Solomon Washburn, of Middleboro', Mass.

877. VIII. Sarah Weston Alden, dau. of Oliver Hathaway, (629b) was b. 1829; m. 1845, Elihu Wood of Halifax Mass.

878. VIII. Warner Alden, Taunton, Mass., mason, son of Oliver Hathaway, (639b) b. 1832; has a family,

879. VIII. Lucinda Alden, dau. of Oliver Hathaway, (639b) b. 1835; m. 1854, Thomas Bessie, Middleboro', Mass.

880. VIII. Amelia Alden, dau. of Oliver Hathaway, (639b) b. 1833; m. Sept, 1859, Joseph Cobb, of Carver.

881. VIII. Selina A. F. Alden, Norton, Mass., dau. of Jason Fobes, (640) b. 13 Mar. 1823; m. Austin Messinger.

882. VIII. Emily E. Alden, Norton, Mass., dau. of Jason Fobes, (640) b. 19 Sept. 1826; d. 4 Aug. 1861; m. William Wetherell.

883. VIII. William Henry Alden, Norton, Mass., son of Jason Fobes, (640) b. 18 July, 1828; m. Angelina M. Clapp.

884. VIII. Polly E. Alden, Norton, Mass., dau. of Jason Fobes, (640) b. 1 Mar. 1831; m. Oliver H. Lane.

885. VIII. George L. Alden, Middleboro,' Mass.. son of Philander, (641) was b. in Mid. Mass., 3 Aug. 1822; m. 5 Oct. 1845, Marietta, dau. of Joseph Bump, b. 15 Mar. 1827.

CHILDREN

1. Marietta P. 14 Jan. 1847. 2. Phebe A. 4 Jan. 1850. 3. George I. 20 Sept. 1853; d. 12 Apr. 1854. 4. Charles Carroll, 18 Aug. 1855. 5. George W. 14 Jan. 1859.

886. VIII. Theodore H. Alden, Middleboro', Mass., son of Philander, (641) m. 30 Dec. 1849, Mary E. Murdock, of Mid. dau. of William; b. 8 Nov. 1824; no ch.

887. VIII. Thomas J. Alden, Middleboro', Mass., son of Philander, (641) b. 3 Feb. 1831; m. 26 Oct. 1850, Julia Weston of Mid.; b. 10 Dec. 1832.

CHILDREN

1. Philander, L. 21 June, 1853; d. 10 Aug. 1853. 2. Thomas J. 30 Aug. 1856; d. 27 Sept. 1856. 3. Mary L. 13 Sept. 1857. 4. Lizzie Frances, 15 Aug. 1859,

888. VIII. Capt. Henry H. Alden, New York city, son of Philander H. (641), b. in Middleboro', Mass., 1833, settled in New York. He was shot on the field of battle at the head of his company, 21 Oct. 1861, at Ball's Bluff, Va. He belonged to the 42d N. Y. Reg.; known as the Tammany Regiment; Gen. Stone commanding that Division.

889. VIII. Leander Murdock Alden, N. Middleboro', son of Andrew Leach Alden, (642) was b. 3 Nov. 1829. He enlisted in the 18 Mass. Reg. of Volunteers, and served three years and one month until his regiment was mustered out, as armorer of the first Brigade, fifth Corps of the Army of the Potomac. He m. 30 Mar. 1858, Susan Miller, dau. of Obadiah Sampson, b. 28 Sept. 1837; have one son, Josiah Edwards, b, 23 Aug. 1866.

890. VIII. Sidney Harris Alden, Middleboro', Mass., son of Andrew Leach Alden (642) b. 10 Nov. 1833; m. 23 Nov. 1860, Mary Ann, dau. of Ora Wood; b, Upton Mass., 30 Jan. 1831. They have one dau. Fannie Wood, b. 7 Nov. 1861.

A. L. A.

891. VIII. Andrew Alden, of Middleboro', Mass., son of Horatio Harris, (643) was b. 9 Sept. 1838; m. 17 Jan. 1857, Abby W. Thompson.

892. VIII. Sarah Alden, dau. of Abner, (685) b. 1827; d. 10 Mar. 1854; m. 2 Nov. 1844, Norman Hilldam.

Ch, 1. James. 2. *Lydia Jane, d. young. 3. Emma Nettie. 4. Ida Ann.

893. VIII. Lydia Alden, Fairview, Pa., dau. of Abner, (685) b. 1830; d. 23 Sept. 1851; m. 23 Sept. 1849, John M. Cully; had a son James Monroe, who d. young; 2. Charles.

894. VIII. Abby Alden, dau. of Abner 7, (685) b. 1833: d. 1862; m. 4 July 1853, to John Jewett.

Ch. 1. Mary. 2. William. 3. *Frederic, d. young. 4. Frank. 5. Sarah. 6. Abby.

895. VIII. Alanson Alden, son of Abner, of Fairview, Pa., (685) was b. 1841; m. 15 Sept. 1864, to Emma Hawkins.

896. VIII. Mary Ann Alden, dau. of Milton Alden, (688) of Middleboro', was b. 1831; m. 26 May, 1852, Charles T. Thatcher, of Mid. now (1866) in business with E. G. Alden, Boston; have one ch. Charles Milton, b. 19 Dec. 1856.

897—903. VIII. See supplement.

904. VIII. Warren Alden, Alstead, N. H., farmer, son of Alvan, (720) b, 1819; m. Lucy, dau. of Col. Jesse Slader; had four ch. Walter and Willie, twins; Mary and Lizzie L. Willie d. 19 July, 1864.

905. VIII. Mary E. Alden, Alstead, N. H. dau. of Alvan, (720) m. Cyrus H. Vilas, s. of Dea. Nathaniel Vilas. She d. 26 Oct. 1842; left no ch.

906. VIII. Addison Alden, son of Marshall, (733).

907. VIII. Albert Alden, Springfield, Mass., painter, son of Marshall, (733) b. 11 Sept. 1820; m. 1846, Phebe Whitaker, b. 1821.

CHILDREN

1. George Albert, 9 Dec. 1847. 2. Warren Edgar, 1849; d. 19 July, 1854, 3. Ella Maria, 28 Apr. 1851. 4. William, 1857; d. 1859.

908—912. VIII. No further particulars.

913. VIII. Orville Alden, son of Noah, (750) b. 1813; m. and had three dau; one of whom is dead.

914. VIII. Mary Ann Alden, dau. of Noah, (750) b. 7 Sept. 1817; m. 1 Jan. 1840, Sylvester Crane, who was b. 4 Nov. 1813. They had ch. Sylvester, 1842; Marietta, 1846: d. 1847; Elsie A. 1848; Henry, 1851; Mary E. 1856; Ellen J.

915. VIII. Nathan Alden, son of Noah, (750) b. 14 Feb. 1820; m. Electa E. Burpee, b. 19 Feb. 1825; had ch. Nathan, 10 Nov. 1851; Mary E. 28 Sept. 1854; d. 4 Sept. 1855; Sarah, 1 Oct. 1857; Jessie A. 4 Mar. 1862.

916. VIII. Lovina Alden, dau. of Noah, (750) b. 27 Aug. 1822; m. 1845 a Clark; had three ch.

917. VIII. Emeline C. Alden, dau. of Noah, (750) b. 26 Aug. 1825; m. 12 Mar. 1845; d. 23 Aug. 1845.

918. VIII. Forinda Alden, dau. of Noah, (750) is living; has a family: no particulars.

919. VIII. Clarissa A. Alden, dau. of Noah, (750) has a family.

920. VIII. John R. Alden, No. Wilbraham, Mass., son of Cyrus, (754) b. 1825; m. 25 Jan. 1845, Mary Ann Prouty, of Amherst, Mass., b. 5 Sep. 1823. They had ch. Emma L. 1 Aug. 1847; d. 27 Aug. 1848. Ellen M. 9 Oct. 1849. Charles H. 17 Mar. 1852; d. 27 Aug. 1855. John A. 20 Aug. 1857. Edward R. 14 Aug. 1862.

921. VIII. Horace E. Alden, son of Cyrus, (754) b. 1 Feb. 1829; m. Julia King; have five ch.

922. VIII. William J. Alden, son of Cyrus, (754) b. 11 Oct. 1831; d. 30 July, 1849.

923. VIII. Cyrus A. Alden, son of Cyrus, (754) b. 28 Dec. 1833; no further particulars.

Supplement - Additions and Corrections

4. II. Elizabeth Alden, (4) m. 26 Dec. 1644, to William Paybody.   Dux. Rec.

9. II. David Alden, (9) had a dau. Sarah it is supposed b. about 1681; m. about 1700, to Thomas Southworth, son of Edward. See Hist. of Dux. p. 315. She d. about 1739. Her grave stone is in Duxbury. C. Southworth.

58. IV. David Alden, Mid., and wife Judith had a dau. Hannah, b. 18 Jan. 1736. His son Silas, (132) d. 23 Mar. 1764; a, 25.

65. IV. Joseph Alden, Middleboro', d. 26 Jan. 1787, a. 70, 4. 4. His wife Hannah, d. 1 July, 1766, a, 48. Their ch. Ebenezer, b. 4 Feb. 1743-4; Joseph, 11 Feb. 1745-6; Mercy, 23 July, 1747; Phebe, 25 Apr. 1749; Hannah. 24 Aug. 1750.

66. IV. John Alden, Mid. His first wife, Lydia Lazell, d. 6 Apr 1749, a. 27. His second wife, Rebecca Weston, d. 16 June, 1807, a. 73.

68. IV. Rev. Noah Alden. His dau. Lucy, d. about 1830, in Long Meadow, Mass. The name of her first husband was Markham, not Marshall. She m. 2, an Allen.

75. IV. Seth Alden, was a mariner. In March 1759, was master, or commander of the sloop Mermaid, and in October following of the schooner Sally, which cleared from the Custom House in New Loudon, 12 Oct. 1759.

Dr. Seth Alden, Caldwell, N. Y., son of Seth, (75) was b. probably at Shaftsbury, Vt., in 1749; d. at Caldwell, 30 July, 1809. We have no account of his early life, but that he was a man of some note in his profession is evident from the fact, that in 1783 he was requested by Col. Ethan Allen to visit his dau. in consultation with Dr. Hutton, his family physician, at the distance of some forty miles. From Shaftsbury he removed to Caldwell, N. Y., where he continued until his death.

He m. Priscilla Cole, who d. 20 Nov. 1798, a. 44; 2, Keziah Beach, 1 Mar. 1800, who d. 10 Oct. 1810, a. 51.

CHILDREN

1. Parthenia, 1777, who d. in 1800, a. 23. She m. John A. Ferris, and had a dau. Rachel, who d. 17 Mar. 1801, a. 11 mos. 2. Hannah, 15 May, 1779, who d. 5 Nov. 1865, a. 86. She m. 21 Oct. 1801, at Kingsley, N. Y., John A. Ferris of Glens Falls, his second wife. Their ch. were, 1. Emily, 1802, who d. 10 Sep. 1808. 2. Henry, 3, Henrietta, twins b. 16 Apr. 1807. Henry d. 12 Jan. 1832: Henrietta d. 17 Apr. 1866. 4. Abigail T. 16 Feb. 1809; who m. N. Edson Sheldon at Glens Falls, 3 Oct. 1842, and had a son John Alden, b. 15 Aug. 1844. 5. John Alden, 16 Aug. 1811. 6. Orange, 26 Nov. 1814, who m. 22 June, 1852, Amelia Martin, who d. 7 Sept. 1854, leaving a dau. Amelia H. b. 15 May, 1854. He m. 2, Cornelia W. Carpenter 22 May 1860, and they have a son, Louis Duane, b. 6 June, 1864. 3. Felix, 1781, d, 1849, a. 68. 4. Dorastus, 1782, d. 1837. 5. David, 1784; residence Caldwell, N.Y., tanner and currier, d. 26 Nov. 1822, a. 38; m. Sarah McCullough of Kingsbury, N. Y. They had ch. 1. Edmund, who d. in 1837; 2. Jane, who d. 1840; 3. Henry, 10 May, 1815, who settled at Menasha, Winnebago Co., Wis., as a merchant: m. Eliza A. Decker, b. 14 Mar. 1818. 4. Sidney, 12 Aug. 1817; manufacturer, Cohoes, N.Y. House of Alden, Frink & Weston. He m. 26 Aug. 1848, Harriet, dau. of Southwick Weston, of Caldwell, N. Y., and they have ch. 1. Charles S. b. 2 May, 1850; 2. John F. 19 Mar. 1852; 3. Harriet N. 12 July, 1856, who d.-14 Jan. 1857. 5. Anna Maria, 1819, who m. 22 May, 1844, Samuel Galentine, M. D., of Mt. Morris, N. Y. They have ch. Lucius Bingham, 1 Sept. 1845; d. 2 Nov. 1849. Alice Sarah, 5 Nov. 1848; L. S. 21 Feb. 1853. 6. Sarah R. 1821; d. 1844.

83. IV. David Alden, had ten children, 1. Hannah, 1 Dec. 1752. 2. Elizabeth, 17 Oct. 1754, who m. 1782, L. Dyer. 3. Bursheba, 22 Aug. 1759 who m. 1793, John Henderson. 4. Rebecca, 17 Sept. 1762, who m. a Pendleton, about 1781, and d. at Northport, Me., 5 Mar 1864, a 101. Her faculties, with the exception of hearing, were preserved to the day of her death. When nearly a hundred years old she walked two miles and back on the same day, to attend the funeral of her daughter, about eighty years old. 5. David, 30 Oct. 1764. 6. Mary, 9 May, 1766. 7. Benjamin, 23 Aug. 1768. 8. John, 8 June, 1771. 9. James, 3 July, 1775. 10. Abigail, 25 Dec. 1777.

[Gen. Reg. 18. 299.

100. V. Ezra Alden, d. 5 Nov. 1767.

Dea. J. Cary's Journal.

101. V. Isaac Alden, Jun. d. 10 May, 1758. Do.

103. V. John Alden. His dau. Beriah, b. 7 Mar. 1781, d. at Claremont, N. H., 1865, a. 84.

She was a lady of more than ordinary intelligence and piety, and took quite a lively interest in the genealogy of the Alden Family. Upon one of the fly leaves of her old Bible, which has for years been the companion of her life, we find carefully pinned the following paragraph cut from a newspaper:

Family Meeting. A meeting of the descendants of the late Holland Weeks, of Salisbury, Vt., was held the 22 Sept. 1860. Eighty of the family attended who were all descendants of John Alden, whose feet first touched Plymouth Rock. These meetings, have been held occasionally for more than a century. One of its objects is to keep the Genealogy perfect from the landing of the Pilgrims in New England to the latest posterity. The list is soon to be published and already amounts to more than four thousand names."

It was the privilege of the author of this memorial to be present by invitation at that meeting, which was a very pleasant one, and was adjourned for five years. Holland Weeks m. Hannah Moseley, dau. of Nathaniel Moseley, and wife Sarah Capen; dau. of Christopher Capen, and his wife Abigail Thayer: dau. of Joseph Thayer, son of Ephraim Thayer, and his wife Sarah Bass; dau. of John Bass, and his wife Ruth Alden; dau. of Hon. John Alden, and his wife Priscilla, of blessed memory.

108. V. Abigail Alden Whitman, d. 1814, a. 92. Her son, Eleazer, d. 1846, a. 91.

109. V. Zephaniah Alden, was received into the church in E. Br. Mass., 13 June, 1762.

111. V. Barnabas Alden, Ashfield, Mass., son of Daniel (51)

VI. Barnabas, son of (111) b. 16 Dec. 1759; d. 1 Apr. 1830, a. 71; m. 27 Nov. 1782, Mehetabel Gould, b. 16 May, 1765; d. 23 Sept. 1847, a. 82. They had ch. 1. a son 1 Feb. 1784; d. same day. 2. Jonathan, 24 Apr. 1785; 3. Elizabeth, 7 Feb. 1787; 4. Paschal, 25 Aug. 1788, d. 22 June, 1790; 5. a son 5 June, 1790, d. 6 June 1790; 6. a dau. 7 Apr. 1791, d. Apr. 17; 7. Martha, 13 June. 1792, d. Oct. 1852; 8. 9. twins, 29 Mar. 1794, d. 1794; 10. Mehetabel, 25 Oct. 1795, d. 13 Mar. 1829; 11. Roxana, 6 Apr. 1797, d. 14 Jan. 1861; 12. Mary, 14 Feb. 1799, d. 19 July, 1801; 13. Lydia, 18 Oct. 1800, d. 1854; 14. Mandana, 5 Mar. 1803, d. 22 May, 1824; 15. Barnabas G. 21 Nov. 1804. 16. Mary G. 15 July, 1806; 17. a son 15 Dec. 1808, d. same day.

VII. Jonathan Alden, son of Barnabas, VI. above named m. Lucy Bryant, and had ch. Paschal, Zephaniah, William, Mehetabel Abigail, Barnabas, Gilbert and Mary, twins, Jonathan and Leonard. The last two d. young. He m. 2, Orpa White, of Hawley, Mass., and had ch. Philander and Philetus, twins. Lucy, Rufus, Gustavus, and Malvina.

VIII. Abigail Alden above named m. Ira H. True, and had a son Russell, 17 Apr. 1821.

VIII. Barnabas Gilbert Alden, of Louis Co. Va., b. 17 Apr. 1821; m. 1845, Betsey True, and they have ch. 1. Alice Elvira, b. 8 Sept. 1845. 2. Warren Alonzo, b. 25 Aug. 1847.

VII. Mary Gould Alden, dau. of Barnabas, VI. above named was b. 15 July, 1806; m. 4 May, 1843, Josiah Parsons, of Northampton, Mass., his 2d wife, son of Josiah Parsons and Sarah, dau. of John Strong. They had ch. 1. Ellen

Calyeta, 8 Mar, 1844. 2. Sarah Pomeroy, 31 Mar. 1845. 3. Anna Alden, 26 Dec. 1848. 4. Harriet Gould, 20 Apr. 1850.

B. G. Alden.

123. V. Simeon Alden, d. in Roxbury of small pox, and was there buried in that part of the town called Canterberry.

H. B. Alden.

128 V. Dea. David Alden, Middleboro', d. 16 Jan. 1814, a. 83 V. 11 m. 21 d. His wife Rhoda d. 5 July 1814, a. 78.

130. V. Huldah Alden, m. 20 Feb. 1783, Israel Butler, of Bridgewater.   Mid. Rec.

131. V. Job Alden, was b. 1737, and m. Lucy Spooner, 1764.   Mid. Rec.

135. Ebenezer Alden, son of Joseph (65) b. 4 Feb. IT43; d. 6 Jan. 1773; unm.

Wood.

140. V. Joseph Alden, Middleboro'; was b. 11 Feb. 1746; m. 3 Sept. 1767, Deborah Williamson of Mid.

144. V. Abner Alden, son of Joseph, (65) d. 1820, a. 56.

146. V. John Alden, New Bedford, Mass. Will proved 28 Mar, 1817; names wife Lois, son Nathan; gr. sons Francis LeBaron and Gideon Augustus; also children John, Seth, Nathan, Mary Tompkins, Sally Johnson, Lydia Church.

Gideon Southworth Alden, VI. son of John, (146) of New Bedford, merchant. Will dated 10 Apr, 1809. Wife Priscilla, and son John named executors.

148. V. Nathan Alden, Middleboro', m. 16 Oct 1766; d. 9 Dec. 1820, a. 77. His wife Priscilla, 19 Sept. 1807, a. 62.

151. V. Elijah Alden, Middleboro', d. 26 June, 1826, a. 72.

154. V. Ruth Alden, dau. of John, (66) m. 1793, Walter Howard of Br.; had ch. Alden, 1798. Louisa, 1801. Franklin, 1802. Thomas Jefferson, 1804. Walter, 1808. He d. 1808.

188. V. John Alden, 10 Caroline, b. 11 July, 1813, m. Clinton Walworth; went to Michigan and there died.

213. VI. Samuel Greene Alden, had a son Samuel Greene Alden, b. 1809; m. 20 May, 1840, Harriet, dau. of Lewis Keith and had children, 1. Ellen Greene. 2 Nov. 1841. 2. Frances Maria, 19 Nov. 1843. 3. Addison Cushman, 21 Apr. 1846. 4. Morton, 6 Aug. 1848, d. 6 Apr. 1853. 5. Samuel, 24 Jan, 1851. 6. Harriet, 12 June, 1852. 7. Rhoda Richards, 4 Aug, 1854. 8. Azuba Churchill, 11 Nov. 1858. 9. Alice Slater, 22 Mar. 1857, d. 2 Oct. 1857. 10. Alice Stetson, 22 Mar. 1857, twins. 11. Samuel, 10 July, 1858.

Note. Frances Maria, m. 22 June, 1864, Otis Lewis of East Boston. Ellen m. Francis M. Kingman, 1859; d. 1861.

VII. Benjamin Alden, East Turner, Me., farmer, son of Benjamin, (228) I suppose who resided in Greene, Me., was b. 7 Aug. 1791; m. 17 May, 1812, Mary, dau. of David Hood, who was b. 3 June, 1790. Ch, 1. Vesta, 11 Feb. 1814, d. 15 Feb. 1841. 1. Lebbeus, 9 Apr. 1816. 3. Lewis, 21 July, 1818. 4. Columbus, 23 July, 1820. 5. Eliza, 22 Feb. 1824. 6. Olivia, 15 Aug. 1827. 7. Mary, 1 Aug. 1832. Lebbeus Alden.

231. VI. Sarah Alden, m. Noah Davis, Stafford, Ct. b. 28 Apr. 1741; d. 30 Oct. 1828, a. 87 years and 6 mo. Their dau. Asenath, b, 9 May, 1774, d. 20 July, 1863. She m. Asa Patten, 16 May, 1797, and had ch. Asa, 1798, who m. Mary R. Cady. 2. Asenath, 1799. 3. Eben, 1801; merchant; d. 1840. 4. Noah, 1804. 5. Sally, 1808. 6. Celinda, 1810. 7. Esther, 1812, who m. David Davis. Asenath with her seven ch. and seven gr. ch. were members of the church. Asa Patten.

233. VI. Abigail Alden, d. 30 May, 1815, in the 68th year of her age. Aaron Eaton, her 2d husband d. 25 May, 1815, a. 79. Their son Luther, is dead. Joshua Wells, who held the office of deacon more than thirty-six years, d. 16 Mar. 1865, a. 73. He was thrice m.; had seven ch. all with one exception members of the church. Luther Eaton had three ch. all chh. mem.   Asa Patten.

239. VI. Col. Amos had a son Seth Alden, who m. Plana, dau. of Dennis Bement of Enfield, Ct., and had six ch. 1. Seth, b. 20 Aug. 1805; d. Thompsonville, Ct., 7 Apr. 1866. He m. in Tolland, Ct., 17 Nov. 1836, Mary Ann Grover, b. 28 Jan. 1807. They had ch. Seth, 8 Oct 1837; Roselle, 27 Feb. 1839, who d. 19 Aug. 1840; Mary R. 18 Oct. 1840. 2. Edmund B. res. in Thompsonville, Ct. 3. Hannah B. who m. Lester H. Grover, Somers, Ct. 4. Diantha M. who m. Harlow Dunham, Pontiac, Ill., d. 12 Feb. 1866. 5. Anpha H. who m. Charles Kilham, Enfield, Ct. 6. Louisa, who m. Sylvender Ellis, New Britain, Ct.

240. Jonathan Alden, farmer, Philo, Champaign Co., Ill., perhaps son or gr. son of Jonathan, (240) was b. 20 Oct. 1823; was in the army in the 22 Reg. of Ohio Vol. during the war; in many battles, yet escaped with only a slight injury from a spent ball. In Oct. 1865, he removed from Lower Salem, Wash. Co. O., to his present residence. He m. 6 Apr. 1845, Lucy, dau. of Harvey C. Hovey. b, 2 Apr. 1827; had ch. 1. Esther, Angelina, 27 Feb. 1846. 2. Clara Lucina, 18 Dec. 1847, d. 25 Oct. 1863. 3. Dennis Bryant, 14 Jan. 1849. 4. Julius Franklin, 17 July, 1850. 5. Edward Augustine, 4 Jan. 1853. 6, Ellen Sophia, 4 Oct. 1854. 7. Lucy Mehetable, 12 Aug. 1861.   Mrs. L. H. Alden.

247. VI. Abigail Alden, dau. of Eleazer, (213) m. 2, David Howard, his 3d wife, and d. in Tamworth, N. H.   Mitchell.

274. VI. Hannah Alden, dau. of Samuel, (121) b. about 1775 or 1776: d. before 1803; m. 1798, James Gary of North Bridgewater: had a dau. Lydia, 21 Dec. 1800, who m. Ephraim Howard, of N. B.

303. VI. Bethiah Alden, Bridgewater, Mass., dau. of Joseph, (126) m. Apr. 1813, Alfred Arnold, of Enfield, Mass.
Their ch. were 1. William Frederick, Sept. 1815. 2. Eunice Alden, Oct. 1810; m. Albert Warren, of Enfield, Mass., now of Lawrence; d. July, 1861, 3. Eliza Ann, Apr. 1819, who m. Freeman Pepper, of Ware, Mass., and 2, Albert Warren, of Lawrence, Mass. 4. Frances Maria, Jan. 1822. 5. Sarah Jane, Sept. 1826. 6. Mary Miles, Nov. 1830, who m. Warren Shepherd of Warren, Mass.

308. VI. Noah. Alden. Elizabeth, wid. of Noah Alden, d. 12 June, 1790.
                                                            Grave Stone.
Mrs. Voadicea Alden, wife of Noah Alden, d. Sept. 1827, a. 61. Grave Stone.

310. VII. Sarah Alden, of Middleboro', Ms., dau. of Amasa, (310) m. Oct. 1836, Rev, Darius Dunbar, of Edgartown, Mass., now of N. Middleboro'.

315. VI. Rufus Alden, Middleboro', b. 1757: d. 19 Aug. 1825, a. 68. His wife Sally d. 10 Apr. 1813, a. 54.

317. VI. Andrew Alden, was b. 1766: d. 26 Mar. 1836. The name of his wife was Salina Fobes.

320. VI. Job Alden, Middleboro', d. 1 Mar. 1825, a. 87 had a son, Peter Oliver, b. May, 1801.

321. VI. Peter Oliver Alden. Children of Peter Oliver and Lydia Alden, Melina Foster, 13 Feb. 1826; d. 4 Apr. 1830. Mid. Rec. Isaac Keith, 16 Apr. 1828. Gustavus Oliver, 2 Sept. 1830. Louisa Melina, 7 Feb. 1833; m. 2, Nancy F. Otis, of Barnstable; no ch. by her.

Note. Hon. Peter Oliver Alden, was a lawyer; resided for a time in Brunswick, Me.

356. VI. Robert Tate Alden, d. 22 Apr. 1853, a. 48.

364. VI. Isaiah Alden, Esq., Scituate, Mass., m. 1819, Mercy W. Vinal, b. 27 Jan. 1799. They had ch. 1. Isaiah. 2. Mercy, who m. in 1847, Samuel W. Blake of Boston, and d. 8 Dec. 1850: they had one s. Frank Thomas, b. 7 Feb. 1849; d. 27 Aug. 1854. 3. Thomas, b. 17 Aug. 1827; m. 6 Mar. 1851, Elizabeth W. Peterson of Duxbury, Mass., b. 21 Jan. 1831; they have ch. 1. Mercy, b. 10 Apr. 1852. 2. Alice Thomas, 31 July, 1857. 3. Benjamin, 25 May, 1860. 4. Annie, 12 Aug. 1862.

367. VII. Peleg J. Alden, Chelsea, Mass., son of James, (367) b. 1835; m. Sarah E. dau. of Dea. Jonas Dodge, of Blue Hill, Me.

CHILDREN

1. Hannah, M. 18 July, 1855. 2. Lizzie E. 14 Mar. 1857. 3. Mary W. 25 Nov. 1858. 4. Frank, 21 June, 1661; d. 12 Sept. 1861. 5. Hattie, 18 Mar. 1863; d. 27 June, 1863.

375. VII. George Ide Alden, Templeton, Mass., is gr. son of Silas (375); has no family.

383. VII. Laura Alden, dau. of Nathan, m. Dea. Harvey Foster, Springfield, Mass. She d. a few years since, left 8 sons.

384. VII. Simeon Alden, d. Aug. 1847; m. Polly Bester, of Stafford, Ct, who d, 22 Oct. 1820.

CHILDREN

They had fourteen ch. 1. Horace, 27 Jan. 1797; d. 20 Oct. 1811. 2. Polly, 3 Jan. 1799, who m. 1825, Henry Hurd, and had ch. Henry, George, Lester, Amanda, Nancy, Hannah. 3. Simeon, 18 July, 1800, who m. Mary Campbell, at Annsville, N. Y., and removed to Downer's Grove, Du Page Co. 111. 4. Harriet, 6 Dec. 1801, who m. 1, a Woodworth, 2, a Gliddon; is d. left no ch. 5. Lester, 3 Sept. 1803; res. Vienna, Oneida Co. N. Y. He m. Lois White, of Trenton. 6. Sophronia, 4 Feb. 1815; res. at Wilbraham, Mass. 7. Lucinda 13 Oct. 1806; m. Walter Buckland, Springfield, Mass.. and had three ch. who d. young; m. 2, Dennis Dale, of Lyme, Huron Co. O. 8. Benjamin F. 21 Jan. 1808. 9. Lucetta, 10 Sept. 1809. 10. Lorinda, 26 Mar. 1811. 11, Welthea, 24 Aug. 1816; m. Willis Sage, of Greenfield, Mass; rem. to Big

Springs, Adam's Co., Wis., and is d. 12. Amanda, 25 Jan, 1818; m. Solon C. Markham, E. Long Meadow, Mass; had 5 ch. 13. Rosette, 5 Jan. 1819. 14. Hotace, 17 Oct. 1820; d. Oct. 20. — He m. 2, 1823, Mrs. Miriam Hurd: had a dau. who d. in infancy.

386. VII. Darius Alden. had six ch. Solomon, Ogden, Matilda, Emily, Elsie, Mary Ann; have all gone to California. Ogden, m. dau. of Thurlow Weed Esq., Albany, N. Y.

410. VIII. Libbeus Alden, East Turner, Me., shoe manufacturer, son of Benjamin, (410)? perhaps; b. 9 Apr. 1816; m. Mar. 1840, Abigail Harris, dau. of Matthew Reed, of Abington, Mass., whose mother Thirza Harris, was grand dau. of Samuel, (55); had ch. 1. Marcia Harris, 27 Jan. 1841. 2. William E. 15 Jan. 1843. 3. Eugene F. 3 June, 1846. 4. Thirza A. 10 Mar. 1850; d. 25 Apr. 1852. 5. Edgar Harris, 14 Apr. 1853. L. Alden.

441. VII. Jane Blodgett Alden, dau. of Elam, (441) b. 1825; m. Bernard Wyman, of Cornish, N. H. no ch. in 1865.

VIII. Ellen Maria Alden, dau of Elam, (441) m. Elijah Hurlburt, of Hanover, N. H.: has three ch.

469. VII. Samuel Alden, d. 17 Jan. 1854; his wife Fanny, b. 8 Feb. 1791; they had a dau. Achsah Ursula, b. 29 July, 1818; d. 28 Jan. 1819.

500. VII. William Alden, d. 27 Sept. 1866, a. 59.

898. VIII. Joseph Jackson Alden, Sand Lake, N. Y., manufacturer, son of Isaac, (713) b. at Newton, Mass., 19 Sept. 1815: m. 27 July, 1842, at Troy. N.Y., Sarah Waterman, dau. of Capt. Benjamin Marshall, b, 4 Oct 1824.

CHILDREN

1. Maria Stone, 29 May, 1844, who m. 1 June, 1864, Jonathan Alden, son of David Alden, (584) now,' 1866, Brooklyn, N. Y. They had a son Marshall, b. 29 Mar. 1865. 2. Marshall Benjamin, 27 Nov. 1846; d. 8 Aug. 1847. 3. Harry Marshall, 2 Aug. 1848. 4. Emma Hepsabeth, 11 Mar. 1854. 5. Mary Newcomb, 26 Nov. 1856. 6. Edward Marshall, 21 Mar. 1860.

899. VIII. Olive Maria Alden, dau. of Isaac, (713) b. 4 Aug. 1817, at Calais, Vt.; m. 2 Feb. 1840, in Lewis, N. Y, John James Knox; b. 26 Oct. 1815.

Ch. 1. Charles Lucius, 1 Sept. 1841. 2. Ruby Eveline, 1 June, 1846. 3. Elizabeth Viola, 23 Mar. 1852. 4. Eliza Cornelia, 27 Feb. 1854.

900. VIII. Ruby Hammet Alden, dau. of Isaac, (713) b. 18 Mar. 1821; m. 20 Aug. 1845 in Lewis, N. Y., David Swan Sykes, farmer, Delaware, Wis.

Ch. 1. Maria Jane, 1846. 2. David, 1848. 3. Horatio, 1854.

901. VIII. Emily Doane Alden, dau. of Isaac, (713) b. 18 Dec. 1824, in Essex, N. Y., m. 29 Dec. 1841, Shubal Moses Call, farmer, b. 20 Jan. 1821, in Westport, N. H.

Ch. 1. Sarah Marshall, 30 Nov. 1842. 2. Mary Elizabeth, 11 Feb. 1845. 3. Francis Herbert, 23 Dec. 1846. 4. Isaac Levi, 20 Feb. 1852.

902. VIII. Avis Ellen Alden, dau. of Isaac, (713) b. S Dec. 1830; m. 23 Sept. 1848, George Palmer Prescott.

Ch. Richard, 28 Oct. 1859. Anna Maria, 26 Nov. 1851. Alice, 15 Jan. 1854; d. in infancy.

903. VIII. Charles Lucius Alden, Esq. Troy, N. Y., attorney at law, son of Isaac (713), associated in business with John B. Gale Esq., has no family. He was b. in Essex, Vt., 18 July, 1834; gr. at Williams College in 1851. To him I am under special obligations for facts relating to his relatives.

903a. VIII. Alonzo Alden, Esq. Attorney at Law, son of Isaac, (713) gr. at Williams College, 1859; was admitted to the Bar in the state of New York, before he went into the army. He was a Brigadier General and was discharged in August, 1865. He m. 5 Apr. 1866, Charlotte, dau. of Edward Nathan Dauchy, of Summit, Albany Co., N. Y., who was b. 20 Feb. 1845.

-----

266. VI. Oliver Alden, son of Rev. Timothy, (116) at the age of twenty left the parental home and went to Charleston, S. C. where he spent ten years, and then returned to his native State. He m. 11 May, 1809, Lucy dau. of David Alden of Williamstown, Mass., and was engaged in mercantile pursuits in Yarmouth, Mass. for many years. His father, Rev. Timothy Alden, resided with him until his death, 13 Nov. 1828, at the age of 92.

In 1829 he removed to Pennsylvania; and in 1834 to Ohio, where he d. in Barton, Granger Co. 20 Aug., 1849, a. 73 years, 5 mos. He was a man whom "None knew but to love." His address was pleasing: his attachments ardent, and he had many friends. Although subjected to many reverses and trials, he was always hopeful and cheerful; never murmuring, or complaining. He exemplified the power of the religion he had long professed, in his daily life, and its close was not only peaceful, but triumphant.

Three weeks after his death his widow removed to Oshkosh, Wis. where she d. suddenly Nov. 4, 1849, a. 63.

486a. VII. Nancy Ward Alden, dau. of Oliver, (266) was b. Yarmouth, Mass. 23 Mar. 1810: d. in Lind, Waupacca Co. Wis. 13 Dec, 1865; m. at Aldenia, Crawford, Co., Pa. James Webb, farmer, who d. at Vineland, Wis. 7 May, 1856.

They had ch. 1. Henry Alden b. in Madison, Granger Co., O. 25 Apr. 1833, who m. 1858, Lauretta Jane Enos of Edwardsburg, Mich. res. at Neenah, Wis. have one ch. Martha L. b. 29 Dec. 1863.

486b. VII. Julia Ann Alden, dau. of Oliver, (266) b. Dartmouth, Mass. 3 Oct. 1812, m. Samuel Lawrence Brooks, of Oshkosh, Wis. 17 May, 1845: his 2d wife. 'His first wife was Lucy Alden, dau. of Dr. Enoch Alden of Redfield, N. Y., and had one son, Samuel Alden, b. 31 Dec. 1847; enlisted in the 21st Wis. Vol. and d. 1862.

They had ch. Lucy Minty b. 31 Dec. 1847, Frederic Duane Alden 10 Nov. 1852.

487. VII. David Chandler Alden, son of Oliver, (266) b. Barnstable, Mass, 10 Aug., 1817, tailor, d. Morris 111. 23 Oct. 1853.

488. VII. Oliver Noble Alden, son of Oliver, (266) carpenter, m. 2 Sept. 1841, Theodocia Norton of Southington, Trumbull Co. O.

Ch. 1. Oliver Norton, b. 1842 d. Vincland 1853. 2. Charles Fox Osmyn, 1843, who enlisted in the 21 Regt. Wis. Vol. and d. Louisville Ky., 10 Dec. 1862 a 19y. 1

m. 20d. 3. Clinton Howard, 1847. 4. Martha Elizabeth, 1852. 5. Violet Minerva 1854. 6. Oliver Newton, 1856.

489. VII. Henry Williams Alden son of Oliver, (266) was b. Athens, N. Y. 27 Oct. 1819, merchant, New York City, m. 18 June 1851, Frances E. Schofield of N. Y. City, had two ch. Florence and Francis Henry: both d. in infancy.

He was connected with his cousin, Timothy Alden in inventing the type setting machine.

490. VII. Charles Fox Alden, son of Oliver, (266) was b. Yarmouth, Mass. 24 March 1822 and d. in Cleveland O. 17 May, 1842.

490a. VII. Lucy Thomas Alden, dau. of Oliver, (266) was b. in Yarmouth, Mass., 1 April 1824; m. 1 Mar., 1854, John Calvin Enos, his 2d wife, res. Neenah, Winnebago Co. Wis. jeweller.

Ch. 1. Florence Laurinda 16 July 1859. 2. Lillian Francelia 23 Dec. 1862.

491. VII. Clinton Alden, New York, N. Y. son of Oliver, (266) b. in Yarmouth, Mass., 4 Mar. 1827, silver plater.

-----

897. VIII. Edwin Augustus Alden, son of Isaac, (713) b. Newton, Mass., 10 March 1814, m. Mary Elizabeth, dau. of Dr. Ira Hayward, Clintonville, N. Y. 18 Sept. 1848. She was b. 10 Feb. 1828: d. 12 Nov. 1856.

CHILDREN

1. Helen Maria, 26 Sept. 1850. 2. George Hayward, 3 Oct. 1852. 3. Kate 26 Nov. 1854.

Additions - Received Too Late For Insertion in Their Proper Place

924. VII. Jonathan Alden, Salem, Washington Co. O., son of Barnabas, (111 Sup.) b. 24 Apr. 1785; is living (Jan. 1867) but very infirm; m. 28 Sept. 1809 Lucy, dau. of Zebulon Bryant; b. 1783: d. 1826: m. 2, 9 May, 1827, Mrs. Orpha (Rice) White dau. of Jonas Rice of Hawley, Mass. She was b. 24 Feb. 1796: d. 4 Mar. 1865.

CHILDREN

1. Paschal 18 May, 1810, (925.) 2. Zephaniah 11 June, 1812. (926.) 3. William 14 July, 1811, d. 3 Sept. 1831. 4. Mehetabel 4 Dec, 1816. (927.) 5. Abigail. 6. Gilbert 11 Apr 1821. 7. Mary 11 Apr. 1821; twins. (928.) 8. Jonathan. 9. Lemuel 29 Jan. 1826 d, in infancy. 10. Lucy 8 June 1828 (929) 11. Philander 14 May 1830. (930.) 12. Philetus 14 May 1830: twins: (931.) 13. Lucinda 24 Feb. 1832, d. 6 Feb., 1848. 14. Rufus Gustavas 23 May, 1834. (932.) 15. Malvina Charlotte 3 Oct., 1831. (933).

925. VIII. Paschal Alden, s. of Jonathan Alden, (924) b. 1810: m. 1835, Asenath Newland, who d. Feb. 1864.

CHILDREN

1. Lucy b. in Ind., 1836. 2. Mary. 1838. 3. John Williams, b. Wash. Co. O., 1842: was three years in the Army.

926. VIII. Zephaniah Alden, son of Jonathan (924) b. 11 June 1812; d. 4 Oct. 1850; m. 8 May, 1837, Damaris, dau. of Rev. Samuel Thompson of Maine.

CHILDREN

1. Caroline 1838: d. in infancy. 2. Philena, 5 Jan., 1840, who m. 25 Dec. 1860, A. John Kerry. 3. Sarah Cornelia, 18 Aug., 1841, who m. 13 Sept., 1866, Lt. Abraham Hoft. Lydia Thompson 16 Jan., 1845. 5. John Kerry 2 Mar., 1847. 6. William b. Henry Co., O., 10 July, 1849, d. 6 Nov. 1860.

927. VIII. Mehetabel Alden, dau. of Jonathan (924) b. 1816, m. 20 Nov. 1836, Moses True, farmer, Wash. Co., O. son of Ephraim True of N. H. an officer in the Rev. War.

They had ch. 1. Melvin Clark, 1835, who served through the war of the rebellion; was in twelve battles and eighteen skirmishes: had both hands wounded. 2. Wilbur Lorain, 29. Nov., 1842: was in the army fifteen months: discharged on account of injuries received. 3. Hiram True 26 Nov., 1844. 4. Abby Louisa 18 Nov., 1851. 5. Lucy Bryant, 19 Oct., 1858. 6. Julia Lucretia 11 June 1862.

928. VIII. Mary Alden, dau. of Jonathan, (924) b. 1821, m. Sept. 1841, Eli S. Robinson, farmer. They had ch. 1. Ancil Sylvester, 1842: k. accidently, Nov., 1860. 2. Lucius Lorain, June, 1846. 3. Charles Eli 1848. Lucius and Charles served in the Army, each two years.

929. VIII. Lucy Alden, dau. of Jonathan, (924) and wife Orpha, b. 8 June, 1828: m. Oct. 1848, Josephus Rhodes.

They had ch. 1. Orpha Mandana. May, 1850: d. 1856. 2. Eunice Abigail, Nov., 1851, d. 1866. 3. Ira True, July, 1853: d. March 1854.

930. VIII. Philander Alden, Lower Salem. O., s. of Jonathan, (924) b. 1830: m. 15 Mar. 1853, Mary Elizabeth, dau. of Benjamin Gould, of Charlemont, Mass., b. 21 Ap., 1832.

They have a son Edward Melancthon, b. 13 Oct., 1854.

931. VIII. Philetus Alden, s. of Jonathan, (924) farmer, b. 1830: m. Hannah, dau. of Joel Tuttle.

They have ch. 1. Frank Russel, b. Aug., 1859: 2. Henry Tuttle b. June 23, 1866.

932. VIII. Rufus Gustavus Alden, s. of Jonathan, (924) farmer, m. 24 May. 1851, Sophia Eliza, dau. of John Stacy.

They had ch. 1. Clark Stacy. 1858: drowned in the Ohio River, 24 May, 1866. 2. Charles Rice, July. 1859. 3. Russel True, Sept., 1861. 4. Orpha Sophia, Aug., 1866, in Wash. Co., O.

933. VIII. Malvina Charlotte Alden, dau. of Jonathan, (924) b. 3. Oct., 1837: m. 9 Oct., 1853, Caleb Oliver Robinson, b. 1830, d. 1858: m. 2, 26 Aug., 1860, John Septimus Clark, who was in the army two years.

Ch. 1. Francis Dudley Robinson, 1854, d. 1860. 2. Addie Elenora Robinson, 6 Mar., 1856. 3. Ethel May Clark, b. Belmont, Ohio, 28 Apr., 1864.

-----

229. VI. Rev. Abishai Alden, gr. at Dartmouth College; studied divinity under the direction of Rev. John Willard, D. D. of Stafford, Ct.; was first settled in Willington, where he continued more than eleven years; then in Montville, Ct, where he continued twenty-three years. He d. in Dover, N. H., 11 Oct., 1833, a 68.

He m. 16 Aug., 1792, Elizabeth Parker, who was b. 14 Nov., 1767: d. 14 July, 1852, a. 85.

CHILDREN

1. Almira, b. July 1793. (984) 2. Dolly Coffin, 22 Feb., 1795, d. 29 Jan., 1796. 3. Augustus, 26 Nov. 1796. (935) 4. Sophronia, 8 Sept. 1799, d. 1 Apr., 1888. (936) 5. Elizabeth Parker, 1 Apr., 1802 d. 1 Feb., 1833. (927) 6. Edward Parker, 17 Apr., 1805, d. 12 Aug., 1833. (938) William Hillhouse, 21 Nov., 1809. (939).

934. VII. Almira Alden, dau. of Rev. Abishai, (229) m. Rev. David Root, now, 1867, res. in New Haven, Ct., had ch. Claudius Buchanan, Elizabeth, Almira, Caroline, Alden, all deceased.

935. VII. Augustus Alden, s. of Abishai (229) gr. Yale Coll., settled in Georgia as a teacher: supposed to be living: m. Ann, dau. of Gov. Joseph Lumpkin.

Had ch. Ann Elizabeth, Marcellus, d. Lucy, Maria, Joseph Lumpkin, Almira, Oscar, Florence.

936. VII. Sophronia Alden, dau. of Rev. Abishai, (229) m. Alvah Wilson, Attorney at Law, Madison, Ga.: had ch. Lucilla, who m. a Yates, and Edward.

937. VII. Elizabeth Parker Alden, dau. of Rev. Abishai, (229) m. O. B. Blackely, merchant, Cincinnati, O.; left two ch:

Elizabeth Parker who m. Edward P. Beach, New York City, and Mary who m. J. T. Collis, merchant, N. Y. City.

938. VII. Edward Parker Alden, s. of (229) gr. at Dart. Coll.: st. law; d. in Mississippi.

939. VII. William Hillhouse Alden, merchant, Westville, Ct., son of (229). m. 1837, Harriet B. Riley.

CHILDREN

1. Elizabeth; Ann, who m. Dec, 1860, Geo. M. Beard, M. D., N. Y. City. 2. John Abishai 3. William Henry. 4. Mary Blackley. 5. Edward Augustus. 6. Darius Root. 7. David Root. 8. Harriet Riley. 9. Oliver Blackley.

Alden Graduates from N. E. Colleges

AMHERST.

1831 *John.*
1839 *Ebenezer, Mr.*
1844 *Edmund Kimball*, 1866 D. D.

BOWDOIN.

1847 Walter B.

BROWN.

1787 Abner, Mr.   *1820
1792 Peter O. Mr.
1806 Nathan Mr.
1807 Cyrus, Mr.   *1855
1814 *Seth, Mr.*   *1853
1821 *Lucius, Mr.*
1825 *Charles H.Mr.**1866
1838 David,   *1864
1849 *William Harrison, Mr.*
1856 Charles H. Mr.

DARTMOUTH.

1787 Abishai, Mr.   *1833
1795 Samuel, Mr.   *1842
1802 Augustus,   *1850
1811 Ebenezer, M. B.
       Harv. 1808.
1825 Samuel, M. D.
       Harv. 1821.
1826 Edward P.   *1833
1852 *Ezra Judson.*
1859 *Edwin Hyde.*

HARVARD.

1692 Zechariah,   *1709
1762 *Timothy, Mr.* *1828
1794 *Timothy, Mr.* *1839
1799 Isaiah,   *1843
1799 *Martin,*   *1838
1808 Ebenezer,Mr.
       M. B. Dart'h
       1811, M. D.
       Penn. 1812.

HARVARD.

1812 Henry Bass,Mr.*1851
1821 Samuel, Mr.
       M.D,Dart.1825.
1861 Leonard Case, *1863

WILLIAMS.

1837 *Joseph,D.D.*Un.1828
1851 Charles L., Mr.
1859 Alonzo, Mr.

YALE.

1773 Roger, Mr.   *1836
1817 Augustus,
1821 Robert, W.
       All.   *1821
1821 Timothy, F.
       All.   *1821
1842 Horatio B. Mr.

www.ingramcontent.com/pod-product-compliance
Lightning Source LLC
Chambersburg PA
CBHW051834040426
42447CB00006B/519